P9-DEE-520

FOOL'S ERRANDS

FOOL'S ERRANDS

AMERICA'S RECENT ENCOUNTERS WITH NATION BUILDING

Gary T. Dempsey
with Roger W. Fontaine

Washington, D.C.

Library of Congress Cataloging-in-Publication Data

Dempsey, Gary T.
Fool's errands: America's recent encounters with nation building / by Gary T. Dempsey with Roger W. Fontaine.
p. cm.
Includes bibliographical references and index.
ISBN 1-930865-06-6—ISBN 1-930865-07-4
1. United States—Foreign relations—1993-2001—Case studies. 2. Intervention (International law)—History—20th century—Case studies. 3. United States—Foreign relations—Developing countries—Case studies. 4. Developing countries—Foreign relations—United States—Case studies.– I. Fontaine, Roger W. II. Cato Institute. III. Title.
E885.D46 2001
327.730172'4—dc21 2001028833

Cover design by Elise Rivera.

Printed in the United States of America.

CATO INSTITUTE
1000 Massachusetts Ave., N.W.
Washington, D.C. 20001

For
Joaquin Andrade Fuentes
Hijo de California
1914–2001

Contents

Acknowledgments

We owe a debt of gratitude to several people who helped make this book possible: Edward H. Crane and William A. Niskanen, president and chairman of the Cato Institute, respectively, for their tireless support of Cato's foreign policy work; Cato's executive vice president, David Boaz, and Cato's vice president for defense foreign policy studies, Ted Galen Carpenter, for their advice and encouragement; and David Lampo, the Institute's publications director, for keeping us on schedule.

1. Introduction: Fool's Errands?

After NATO's 78-day bombing campaign against Yugoslavia came to a close in June 1999, U.S. Secretary of State Madeleine K. Albright toured the Stenkovic refugee camp in northern Macedonia, where 25,000 ethnic Albanians from Kosovo lived in temporary shelters. To great cheers, Albright announced to the refugees, "All the world knows about your suffering" and now "the Serbs have lost control over Kosovo."[1] Albright then paid a visit to thousands of U.S. troops preparing to move into Kosovo as peacekeepers. "The country you will be freeing has gone through some dreadful times," she declared. "I know this is not easy on you. We are deeply honored to have you do this."[2] The task at hand would be appropriate, added Albright. "This is what America is good at: helping people."[3]

Several days later, U.S. President William J. "Bill" Clinton toured the same refugee camp that Albright had. Ethnic Albanians chanting "USA, USA" and "Clinton, Clinton" greeted him. With his wife and daughter at his side, the president walked through the muddy camp making family-to-family visits. Stopping to chat with one family, Clinton placed a young boy on his lap and said to the child's parents, "We hope with each passing day you will become less afraid. You have a beautiful boy." "He is still very much afraid," said the boy's mother. "He has suffered very much. He has seen people killed and wounded." Surrounded by reporters, Clinton replied, "There are some things children should never see."[4]

Before leaving the camp, Clinton thanked the refugees for "sharing their lives" with him and his family and declared, "You have suffered enough. . . . I don't want any child hurt. I don't want anyone else to lose a leg or an arm or a child."[5] He then delivered a short speech in which he echoed Secretary of State Albright's belief that "helping people" is a U.S. foreign policy priority that America is "good" at doing: "We are proud of what we did. We think it's what America stands for. . . . We are committed not only to making

Kosovo safe, but to helping people rebuild their lives, rebuild their communities."[6]

But is what Clinton and Albright both claimed while touring the Balkans correct? Is the U.S. government really any good at "helping people" in troubled places? America's recent encounters with nation building suggest the contrary. Indeed, Washington said it would bring order to Somalia, but left chaos; it went to Haiti to restore democracy, but produced tyranny; it intervened in Bosnia to reverse the effects of a civil war, but now oversees a peace that is not self-sustaining; and it occupied Kosovo to build a multiethnic democracy, but has instead observed widespread ethnic cleansing. That all these attempts at nation building have not actually solved the problems they set out to address seems not to have bothered the proponents of nation building. But before the reasons behind Washington's pattern of failure can be explained in more explicit detail, it is first necessary to define the term "nation building" and its place within America's post-Cold War foreign policy, especially as it developed during eight years of the Clinton presidency.

Nation Building

Nation building is perhaps the most intrusive form of foreign intervention. It is the massive foreign regulation of the policymaking of another country. The process usually entails the replacement or, in the case of a country in a state of anarchy, the creation of governmental institutions and a domestic political leadership that are more to the liking of the power or powers conducting the intervention. Because such profound interference tends to elicit resistance, the nation-building process typically requires a substantial military presence to impose the nation-building plan on the target country.

The United States is not new to nation building. It concluded the 19th century with a war to "liberate" Cuba from Spanish "tyranny." For the next quarter century, U.S. Marines tried to teach various countries in the Western Hemisphere to "elect good men," as President Woodrow Wilson put it. During the 1920 presidential campaign, candidate Warren Harding criticized the Wilson administration's nation-building policies after Wilson's vice presidential running mate, Franklin Delano Roosevelt, boasted that he had written Haiti's constitution while he was serving as assistant secretary of the Navy. Harding replied that he "would not empower an assistant secretary of the Navy to draft a constitution for helpless neighbors in the West Indies and jam it down their throats at the point of bayonets borne by U.S. Marines."[7] When the U.S. government departed Haiti in 1934, according to one Haitian historian, it left "some good roads and a few schools, but little democracy."[8] It also left a U.S.-trained paramilitary that brutalized the Haitian people and dominated Haitian politics for several decades to come.

After World War II, the United States mobilized extraordinary resources to transform America's wartime enemies, Nazi Germany and Imperial Japan, into liberal democracies. During the Cold War, the United States undertook nation-building efforts in South Korea, Vietnam, Lebanon, and El Salvador. Since the end of the Cold War, nation-building experiments have been tried in Somalia, Haiti, Bosnia, and Kosovo.

The concept of nation building became a topic of analysis among political scientists during the 1960s, and it was closely linked with the idea of postcolonial modernization.[9] Much of the analysis, however, focused on cultivating a sense of national identity in the newly independent colonies, rather than on the formation of the countries themselves. That focus had much to do with the fact that the territorial boundaries and governmental institutions of most of the former colonies were those left behind by the withdrawing colonial powers, so those two elements were often presumed. Still, some analysts questioned the very premise of "building" new nations. In 1963, for example, Harvard University professor Carl Friedrich pointedly asked, "Are nations really built? Or, rather, do they grow?"[10] To be sure, there is one view—epitomized by Machiavelli—that holds that nations are built by "superior men of heroic stature," but according to Friedrich, the question of "reason of state" must also enter the picture; that is, what are the concrete historical "reasons which require rulers and others" to take action in the first place?[11] Or, to put it somewhat differently: Are nations really built, or do they result because a collective imperative is believed to exist?

Gunpoint Democracy

By the time President Clinton entered office in January 1993, foreign policy thinking in Washington had shifted away from focusing on the geopolitical containment of the Soviet Union toward redefining U.S. foreign policy for the post-Cold War world. One theme that proved popular with the foreign policy establishment—and which coincidentally required maintaining Cold War-era levels of global activism and defense spending—was "promoting democracy." An exhaustive review of the literature employing that theme is beyond the scope of this book, but a few examples are in order. In an influential article in the summer 1993 issue of *Foreign Policy*, Morton H. Halperin urged the United States to "take the lead in promoting the trend toward democracy," adding that "when a people attempts to hold free elections and establish a constitutional democracy, the United States and the international community should not only assist but should guarantee the result."[12] Halperin was subsequently appointed head of the Clinton State Department's policy-planning staff. Other voices also joined in the promoting democracy chorus. Tufts University professor Tony Smith, for example, asserted that the "promotion of democracy worldwide" should be put at the center of America's post-Cold War national security strategy, and Harvard University professor Stanley Hoffmann suggested that a "world steering committee" be set up to bring order and democracy to regions in chaos.[13]

Using the promotion of democracy as a pretext for continued global activism was not an idea limited to scholars and pundits on the political left. In 1991, American Enterprise Institute scholar Joshua Muravchik argued that the "promotion of democracy" should be made "the centerpiece of [post-Cold War] American foreign policy."[14] Echoing that view in 1996, Michael A. Ledeen, also with AEI, recommended that America "embrace the Democratic Revolution and make it the centerpiece of [its] international strategy."[15]

For its part, the Clinton administration used the promotion of democracy, or what it called "democratic enlargement," as its clarion call to justify eight years of interventionist foreign policy.[16] The administration's first outright use of the democratic enlargement theme was in September 1993, when President Clinton and his foreign policy team delivered a series of coordinated foreign policy speeches. In Clinton's speech, delivered before the UN General Assembly, the president proclaimed, "Our overriding purpose must be to expand and strengthen the world's community of market-based democracies. During the Cold War, we fought to contain a threat to the survival of free institutions. Now we seek to enlarge the circle of nations that live under those free institutions."[17]

Madeleine Albright, who was the U.S. representative to the United Nations at the time, hit upon the same themes in her speech, and Clinton's national security adviser, Anthony Lake, summarized the administration's new foreign policy agenda in a speech he titled "From Containment to Enlargement."[18] "Throughout the Cold War we contained a global threat to market democracies," Lake asserted, and

> now we should seek to enlarge their reach. . . . We should strengthen the community of major market democracies. . . . We should help foster and consolidate new democracies and market economies, where possible, especially in states of special significance and opportunity. . . . We must counter aggression—and support liberalization—of states hostile to democracy and markets. . . . We need to pursue our humanitarian agenda not only by providing aid but also by working to help democracy and market economies take root in regions of greatest humanitarian concern.[19]

Democratic enlargement, Lake added, would not only serve America's moral mission in the world, but also serve its national interest.

> The addition of new democracies makes us more secure, because democracies tend not to wage war on each other or sponsor terrorism. . . . These dynamics lay at the heart of Woodrow Wilson's most profound insights; . . . . He understood that our own security is shaped by the character of foreign regimes. Indeed, most presidents who followed, Republicans and Democrats alike, understood we must promote democracy and market economics in the world—because it protects our interests and security and because it reflects values that are both American and universal.[20]

Using the theme of democratic enlargement to justify maintaining high levels of foreign policy activism, however, was implicit in Clinton's foreign policy even before he was elected president. Indeed, during the 1992 presidential campaign, he called for more vigorous efforts to restore democracy in Haiti, arguing that President George Bush's policy "must not stand."[21] Moreover, in an October 1992 campaign-trail speech on foreign policy, he charged that Bush was not aggressive enough in promoting the spread of democracy in the Balkans.

> President Bush seems too often to prefer a foreign policy that embraces stability at the expense of freedom; a foreign policy built more on personal relationships with foreign leaders than on consideration of how those leaders acquired and maintained their power. . . . He sent his secretary of state to Belgrade, where in the name of stability, he urged the members of the dying Yugoslav federation to resist dissolution. This would have required the peoples of Bosnia, Croatia, and Slovenia to knuckle under to Europe's last Communist strongman.[22]

Time and again, candidate Clinton criticized Bush for his pragmatism and his realpolitik approach to foreign policy. In fact, a month before the national election, Clinton derided Bush for his "ambivalence about supporting democracy," "his eagerness to befriend potentates and dictators," and his not being "at home in the mainstream pro-democracy tradition of American foreign policy."[23]

After he defeated Bush at the polls, Clinton began selecting his chief foreign policy aides. Ensuing news reports made it even clearer that Clinton would use the theme of democratic enlargement to justify his foreign policy activism. A *New York Times* profile of Anthony Lake, for example, noted that the Clinton choice for national security adviser believed that with the end of the Cold War,

> The new foreign-policy debate . . . is between those who, like President Bush, see the world through a classic balance-of-power prism and those who, like Mr. Clinton and himself, take a more "neo-Wilsonian" view in which the United States uses its military and economic power to intervene in promoting democracy.[24]

Within months of assuming the White House, Clinton and his foreign policy team began putting their words into practice. That move was not surprising given that Clinton raised that very prospect during his January 1993 inaugural address, in which he declared, "Our hopes, our hearts, our hands are with those on every continent who are building democracy and freedom. Their cause is America's cause."[25] Nor was it surprising given Clinton's stated convictions that America should help "create a just, peaceful and ever more democratic world," and that Americans have an obligation "to give back to a contentious world some of the lessons we learned during our own democratic voyage."[26]

By June 1993, Secretary of State Warren Christopher had announced in a cable to the U.S. diplomatic corps that the Clinton administration's priority in Somalia would be to transform that nation into a stable democratic member of the world community. "For the first time," explained Christopher, "there will be a sturdy American role to help the United Nations rebuild a viable nation state."[27] Clinton's special coordinator for Somalia, David Shinn, said the mission would be aimed at nothing less than "re-creating a country," and on August 27, 1993, Secretary of Defense Les Aspin told a gathering at Washington's Center for Strategic and International Studies that American troops would stay in Somalia until calm was returned to its capital, Mogadishu; "real progress" was made in "taking the heavy weapons out of the hands of the warlords"; and "credible police forces [were in place] in at least the major population centers."[28] But when 18 U.S. soldiers were killed and 76 were wounded in a Mogadishu firefight several weeks later, Clinton quickly began to distance himself from the nation-building experiment in Somalia. Indeed, he announced that it was not America's responsibility to rebuild Somalia and that Washington had obligations elsewhere.[29]

Although the term "nation building" was exorcised from the Clinton administration's vocabulary after the Somalia debacle, it continued to engage in the practice of nation building elsewhere. On September 19, 1994, for example, Clinton dispatched 20,000 U.S. troops to Haiti as part of Operation Uphold Democracy. The mission's objectives, explained the president, were to

> provide a secure environment for the restoration of President [Jean-Bertrand] Aristide and democracy [in Haiti], to begin the work of retraining the police and the military in a professional manner and to facilitate a quick hand-off to the [U.S.-led] United Nations mission so that the work of restoring democracy can be continued, the developmental aid can begin to flow, Haiti can be rebuilt and, in 1995, another free and fair election for president can be held.[30]

In similar fashion, Clinton announced on December 18, 1997, that U.S. troops would not be leaving Bosnia until there were

> joint institutions strong enough to be self-sustaining . . . [the] political parties [had] really given up the so-called state-run media . . . the civilian police [force was] large enough, well-trained enough, [and] well-managed enough to do the job it has to do . . . [and] we have confidence that the military is under democratic rule.[31]

Repeatedly tasked with those sorts of missions, defense analysts began to differentiate between "traditional warfighting" and what they had come to dub "military operations other than war."[32] U.S. soldiers and Marines thereafter found that time they formerly used to spend practicing how to execute combat missions was instead dedicated to learning the importance of "indigenous conflict resolution techniques" and how to "work with the [disputing] parties to identify common ground on which to build meaningful dialogue"—which were just two of the many subjects covered in the Pentagon's 1997 *Joint Task Force Commander's Handbook for Peace Operations.*[33]

Virtuous Power

Another promise Clinton made early in his presidency was to focus more on human rights than did the Bush administration. Clinton officials claimed that their devotion to democratic enlargement was part of that new commitment. Indeed, according to the administration's reasoning, basic human rights—such as freedom of expression, freedom of association, freedom of movement, and equality under the law—were the defining elements of a democratic society; thus a policy aimed at promoting democracy would by extension promote those human rights. As Secretary of State Christopher summarized the administration's thinking,

> The great new focus of our agenda for freedom is this: expanding, consolidating, and defending democratic progress around the world. It is democracy that establishes the civil institutions that replace the power of oppressive regimes. Democracy is the best means not just to gain—but to guarantee—human rights.[34]

In other words, the Clinton administration regarded its democratic enlargement agenda as a means to another goal: the goal of creating an idealistic new world free of widespread inhumanity. President Woodrow Wilson tried to do that more than 80 years ago and failed.[35]

But during the 1990s, the Clinton administration insisted that things were different. Indeed, its view was that Washington faced a special moment in history when the United States and its allies had the military, economic, and political strength to be able to run a foreign policy designed not only to defend American citizens' human rights, but also the human rights of other countries' citizens. As David J. Scheffer, Clinton's ambassador at large for war crimes issues, put it in 1992,

> Concern about the plight of oppressed people can now be expressed without the shackles of the Cold War preventing action on their behalf. . . . [and] if one considers how far the world community has journeyed since 1989, it might be possible that . . . the senseless abuse of people within borders will be a strictly historical phenomenon.[36]

Similarly, Clinton's assistant secretary of state for human rights and humanitarian affairs, John Shattuck, stated in August 1993,

> With the passing of the Cold War, all of [its negative impact] has changed. The basic principles of human rights and democracy must no longer be debased with impunity. Nor should they be blinked at for the sake of some larger geostrategic goal. Rather, they must be restored to their rightful primary place in the relationship among nations.[37]

For his part, Clinton claimed during the 1992 presidential campaign, "Now that we don't have to worry about Moscow, we can finally give content to our saying that human rights is central. We can help in all kinds of humanitarian ways where we couldn't before because we feared war with the Soviets."[38] During his January 21, 1993, inaugural address, Clinton even promised to use the U.S. military not only when American vital interests are at stake, but also when "the will and the conscience of the international community is defied."[39] Madeleine Albright was even more direct, declaring at her swearing-in as U.S. ambassador to the United Nations that "if there is one overriding principle that will guide me in this job, it will be the inescapable responsibility . . . to build a peaceful world and to terminate the abominable injustices and conditions that still plague civilization."[40]

Thereafter, the Clinton administration fashioned what might be called a doctrine of "virtuous power": the policy view that in a properly ordered world, human rights are at the center, and just as legislation—backed by the coercive power of the state—must be enlisted to enforce this vision at home, international norms—backed by U.S. military force—must be applied abroad. The logic behind the administration's thinking was that human rights violations could be greatly reduced, if not eliminated entirely, by creating a just world order in which human rights were elevated to a military priority and a preeminent foreign policy value. After that happens, explained one proponent of the view, the "higher, grander goal that has eluded humanity for centuries—the ideal of justice backed by power"—could become a global reality.[41]

Defining Away Sovereignty

In June 1999, shortly after NATO ended its bombing campaign against Yugoslavia, CNN reporter Wolf Blitzer asked President Clinton if the Kosovo war amounted to a new U.S. foreign policy doctrine. Clinton responded affirmatively. "Whether within or beyond the borders of a country, if the world community has the power to stop it, we ought to stop genocide and ethnic cleansing," he said.[42] Despite initially backing away from the policy implications of that statement, Clinton later reiterated his view, saying that universal human rights is "an important principle . . . that I hope will be applied in the future . . . whether within or beyond the borders of a country."[43] An influential Clinton adviser added that the Kosovo war was designed to show that men like Slobodan Milosevic "cannot hide behind a border."[44]

Whatever the merits of the moral reasoning behind NATO's bombing campaign against Yugoslavia, Washington and the West did cross an important threshold in international politics: the United States and its allies ignored the "great powers" consensus required by the UN Charter and deliberately violated the sovereignty of a country. But that move was not as surprising as it would have been a decade ago. Since the end of the Cold War, an increasing trend has been to try to elevate human rights to the chief organizing principle of the global system. Former UN secretary-general Javier Pérez de Cuellar identified that policy trend early on, noting in 1991, "We are clearly witnessing what is probably an irresistible shift in public attitudes toward the belief that the defense of the oppressed in the name of morality should prevail over frontiers and legal documents."[45] More recent examples of the trend include the high-profile attempt by a Spanish magistrate to extradite former Chilean dictator Gen. Augusto Pinochet from Britain to stand trial for torture and other crimes committed during his regime, and the ongoing treaty initiative to create a standing international criminal court to prosecute war crimes, crimes against humanity, genocide, and aggression.

Whether or not the trend is irresistible is debatable. Yet it is certainly a popular refrain among advocates of the standard precursor of nation building, the "humanitarian intervention," or more precisely, the use of U.S. military force for the purpose of protecting the citizens of other countries from widespread deprivations of human rights.[46]

According to proponents of humanitarian intervention, such as the UN's special representative for displaced persons, Francis Deng, sovereignty has been "reinterpreted as a concept of responsibility to protect one's own citizens. . . . The sovereign has to become responsible or forfeit sovereignty."[47] Similarly, Thomas G. Weiss, executive director of the Academic Council on the United Nations System, says that over "the past 10 years, the concept of sovereignty has become infused with the notion that governments must act responsibly toward [their] citizens or lose the rights of sovereignty."[48]

Outside UN circles, a similar view has been expressed by a variety of other proponents of humanitarian intervention. Jan Nederveen Pieterse, a professor with the Institute for Social Studies in the Netherlands, notes that "statehood could be interpreted as being conditional upon respecting the rights of people. It is not so much that sovereignty is becoming an 'archaic' notion, as some assert, but that it is increasingly being viewed as conditional in relation to human rights."[49] University of Arizona Law School professor Fernando Tesón goes even further, arguing that there is a "right" to humanitarian intervention. Tesón's argument is based on the premise that only individuals have rights, not states, and the legitimacy of a state can be justified only if it promotes the rights of all its citizens. If a state fails to perform that task, his argument continues, the state loses its legitimacy and the legal protection conferred by the principle of nonintervention. Under those circumstances, concludes Tesón, other states are perfectly entitled to intervene in order to end the human rights abuses; that is, international law should permit "transboundary help, including forcible help, provided by governments to individuals in another state who are being denied basic human rights."[50]

Clinton administration officials made similar arguments in their attempt to define away state sovereignty as an obstacle to their "virtuous power" doctrine. Indeed, when Washington first threatened military action against Yugoslavia in October 1998, a reporter asked Secretary of State Albright, "In the eyes of the United States has [Yugoslav] President [Slobodan] Milosevic forfeited sovereignty over his country?" Albright answered,

> I think that that is an international legal question that I think I don't want to answer in a specific form. . . . [But] I think that it's very important that he understand that as the leader—an elected leader—of a sovereign nation, he has responsibilities not only to his own people but to the international community for trying to pursue civilized behavior.[51]

Later, in a letter to Senate Majority Leader Trent Lott (R-Miss.), National Security Adviser Samuel R. "Sandy" Berger justified violating Yugoslavia's sovereignty on the grounds that Milosevic

> initiated an aggressive war against the independent nation of Croatia in 1991; against the independent nation of Bosnia-Herzegovina in 1992; and is currently engaged in widespread repression of Kosovo, whose constitutional guarantees of autonomy he unilaterally abrogated in 1989. . . . Arguments based on Serbian "sovereignty" are undercut by this history.[52]

By January 2000, Deputy Secretary of State Strobe Talbott announced that the United States had "accepted the principle that the way a government treats its own people is not just an 'internal matter.' It's the business of the international community."[53]

American officials were not the only ones who were advancing that kind of view. Prime Minister Tony Blair of Great Britain, for instance, declared during the Kosovo war, "We are fighting not for territory but for values, for a new internationalism where the brutal repression of whole ethnic groups will no longer be tolerated."[54] After the war, Blair recommended embarking on a "new moral crusade," explaining that the West can now build a "new doctrine of international community" that transcends sovereignty and allows military intervention in defense of human rights.[55] Similarly, Canada's foreign minister, Lloyd Axworthy, was an advocate of what he called the "human security" agenda, which he said would put the "safety and well-being of people" above traditional conceptions of state sovereignty.[56] And in Germany, Foreign Minister Joschka Fischer had become a proponent of what has been called "NATO's new military humanism"—the notion that the defense of human rights is itself an alliance mission.[57]

It would be a mistake, however, to conclude from these examples that those who favor redefining sovereignty reside only on the political left. As with promoting democracy, there are adherents on the right too. For example, William Kristol and other editors at the neoconservative *Weekly Standard* have recommended that sovereignty be made secondary to a U.S. "benevolent global hegemony" that aims to universalize Western values.[58] Indeed, during NATO's air war against Yugoslavia they editorialized,

> The struggle in Kosovo today is about more than human suffering. It is about more even than European stability and NATO's credibility. At stake is the single overriding question of our time: Will the United States and its allies have the will to shape the world in conformance with our interests and our principles, challenging as that task may be?[59]

Norman Podhoretz, longtime editor of *Commentary*, noted "I . . . do agree . . . that we violated the sovereignty of Yugoslavia when we intervened in Kosovo. Still . . . I find it hard to quarrel with the emerging idea that the principle of sovereignty should no longer embrace the right of political leaders to butcher their own people."[60] Norman Naimark of the Hoover Institution went even further, arguing that Slobodan Milosevic's "wanton aggression in the [Balkan] area" meant that Yugoslavia should not only have forfeited its sovereignty to NATO, but also that the separation of Kosovo from Yugoslavia was "legitimated." Naimark added that the U.S. military should be used to effectuate that separation and to "help liberate [Kosovo] from chaos, violence, poverty, and maladministration"—a recipe for nation building if there ever was one.[61]

The Nation Builders

Today's nation builders are brimming with advice on how to build nations, recommending everything from "forging a more equitable distribution of wealth"[62] and "rehabilitating the health [care] sector in postconflict situations"[63] to encouraging "psychosocial healing"[64] and "enfranchisement-based collective identity."[65] The World Bank recommends reconstructing the "enabling conditions" of peacetime society and suggests seven distinct nation-building activities.[66] A report by the Overseas Development Council identifies no fewer than 10 activities that should receive the "early attention" of the nation builder. These include providing a sufficient level of internal security to enable economic recovery; persuading the foreign business community to invest; strengthening the government's capacity to carry out key activities; assisting the return of refugees and internally displaced persons; supporting the rejuvenation of household economies; assisting the recovery of communities; rehabilitating crucial economic infrastructure, such as major roads, bridges, marketplaces, and power-generation facilities; giving priority to the basic needs of social groups and geographic areas most affected by the conflict; removing land mines from critical sites; stabilizing the national currency and rehabilitating financial institutions; and promoting national reconciliation.[67]

Besides the U.S. military, one of the Clinton administration's chief nation-building organs was the U.S. Agency for International Development, which, according to the agency's self-description, "has taken a leading role in promoting and consolidating democracy worldwide."[68] After Clinton took office, USAID came to be dominated by a variety of new nation-building priorities. "One of our main goals is to have concern about gender issues be a part of all of our programs," explained one USAID official in 1994.[69] By Clinton's second term, USAID officials said they planned to "launch an effort to advance compliance with labor codes, particularly with regard to the rights of union organizing, collective bargaining, elimination of child labor, and adherence to work-place health and safety standards." They also said they would seek to develop "human capacity," "stabilize the world population," and protect the global environment for "sustainable development."[70]

The Clinton administration also utilized the National Endowment for Democracy, a little-known foreign-aid program intended to promote democracy abroad. The NED is nominally a private organization, but all of its funds come from the federal treasury.[71] It says its programs are aimed at encouraging "democratic political development."[72] In practice, however, the NED under the Clinton administration took advantage of its quasi-private status to influence foreign elections in ways that would be illegal if a foreign group tried to conduct the same activity in the United States.[73] The NED also supported myriad nation-building programs. In Bosnia, for example, it has been financing an array of human rights and civic organizations that provide "training to local citizens in the areas of conflict prevention and dispute mediation, responsible journalism, micro-enterprise development, and local public administration."[74]

Another of the Clinton administration's nation-building organs was the United States Institute of Peace, a federally funded institution that was created during the Reagan era to "strengthen the nation's capacity to promote the peaceful resolution of international conflict."[75] However, with its board of directors appointed by the president of the United States, the USIP under the Clinton administration became a cheerleading section for nation building.[76] Indeed, from Somalia to Kosovo, USIP publications advocated nation-building programs ranging from enhancing "computer connectivity" in the legal information infrastructure of Bosnia to improving preschool children's "self-esteem" in postwar societies.[77]

Of course, any description of the Clinton administration's nation-building organs would be incomplete without addressing the specific kind of nations they were repeatedly tasked with creating—namely, nations that embodied American-style pluralism. From Somalia to Haiti to Bosnia to Kosovo, that was the assigned goal. Indeed, the Clinton administration's efforts were all basically aimed at getting large numbers of people to get along with each other, without regard to whether their differences were based on clan, class, religion, or ethnicity. As Clinton's deputy secretary of state Strobe Talbott summarized Washington's view with respect to the Bosnian conflict,

> If there is to be a post-Cold War peace in Europe . . . it must be based on the principle of multiethnic democracy. The United States is one of the first and one of the greatest examples of that principle. What's more, the civic behavior and constitutional structures associated with pluralism are conducive to regional peace and international trade. Hence, it is in our interest that multiethnic democracy ultimately prevails in Europe and elsewhere.[78]

The Clinton administration's enthusiasm for the pluralistic ideal should have been evident from its early emphasis on "multilateralism" and "international community" and its willingness to abandon the longstanding tradition of American troops serving only under the American flag. The administration's pluralistic pretensions, however, became most evident with NATO's bombing campaign against Yugoslavia. On the eve of the first night of air strikes, for example, President Clinton implored, "I want us to live in a world where we get along with each other, with all of our differences."[79] Several weeks later, Clinton explicitly linked his Kosovo policy with his support for domestic hate crimes legislation. "We first have to set an example, as best we can—standing against hate crimes against racial minorities or gays; standing for respect, for diversity." "Second," he said, "we have to act responsibly, recognizing this . . . fleeting position the United States now enjoys of remarkable military, political and economic influence. We have to do what we can to protect the circle of humanity against those who would divide it by dehumanizing the other."[80]

With the end of NATO's bombing campaign, Clinton continued to place the pluralistic ideal at the center of his rhetoric, telling a unit of the Illinois Air National Guard in Chicago,

> You have people of Serbian and Albanian descent flying together, proving that we do find strength in our diversity and we come together for the common good. . . . We want people who live in the Balkans to be able to work together the way the people in this unit who come from the Balkans work together.[81]

In practice, explained Vice President Al Gore, that meant Washington's starting point in Kosovo was that "there must be a genuine recognition of and respect for difference . . . [and] then . . . a transcendence of difference."[82]

Making Excuses

From early on, realist critics correctly identified such thinking for what it was, global do-goodism masquerading as foreign policy. Johns Hopkins professor Michael Mandelbaum, for example, attacked what he called Clinton's "Mother Teresa" foreign policy, which he said aimed to turn America's national security pursuit "into social work."[83] Similarly, Robert Manning of the Council on

Foreign Relations and Patrick Clawson of the Washington Institute for Near East Policy suggested that Clinton's nation-building operations all were "instances of social engineering passing as foreign policy."[84] Despite those criticisms, however, the empirical question is left unanswered: Does nation building even work?

Today's advocates of nation building will usually concede that Washington's recent attempts have either failed or are in the process of failing. Yet that has not dampened their enthusiasm for the practice of nation building. They tend to dismiss the failures by arguing that nation building hasn't really failed, it just hasn't been tried hard enough. Typical of that kind of excuse is an October 28, 1999, report by the Washington and Brussels-based International Crisis Group. That report first admits that the Dayton Agreement—Washington's blueprint for nation building in Bosnia—is failing. After years of NATO occupation, the report explains, Bosnia

> has three de facto mono-ethnic entities, three separate armies, three separate police forces, and a national government that exists mostly on paper and operates at the mercy of the entities. . . . In addition, two out of the three ethnic groups actively oppose Dayton, and are prepared to wait until such a time as the international community withdraws and the agreement can be laid to rest.[85]

But the report then goes on to assert that Dayton's nation building "can succeed if implemented properly," if only the "NATO-led international force" in Bosnia were to work "more robustly" to "act as an implementing agent."[86]

In a similar vein, *World Policy* deputy editor David Rieff admits that "what rules in Bosnia is not peace, but an absence of war," and "almost nobody, either in Bosnia or abroad," believes the peace there "would last for a week if . . . [NATO's] soldiers were withdrawn." But he then adds,

> The reason for this is simple. Neither the major powers nor the forces they deployed in Bosnia after the peace accord paid enough attention to the return of the refugees. . . . Had NATO chosen to turn Bosnia into a protectorate, as even some Bosnians demanded at the time of the Dayton agreement, things might very well have turned out differently.[87]

Jakob Finci, head of the Open Society Fund in Bosnia, agrees. In his view, nation building would be succeeding in Bosnia if the

West had created a "full protectorate without even a small part of local self-rule lasting as long as the situation is not normal."[88] "We made a mistake," likewise claims an American official in Bosnia. "This is only a half dictatorship. We should have made it a full dictatorship."[89]

In the case of Somalia, the excuse is much the same; that nation building would have succeeded if only it had been pursued more vigorously. The commander in charge of the United Nations pullout, for example, told a news conference,

> We didn't have enough forces or resources to disarm the country. That's why Operation Hope can't fulfill all its goals. . . . The international body and contributing nations must be committed enough to accept the violence and loss of life associated with war, and then stay the course.[90]

In a similar fashion, former Brookings Institution scholar Richard Haass acknowledges that the Somalia operation had a "tragic and failed ending," but he then adds that it is

> at least plausible and perhaps likely that alternatives would have met with greater success. . . . The principal alternative . . . was to embark from the outset on a policy of concerted peacemaking and nation building. This would have required disarming the local factions and arresting those who resisted, setting up a transnational political authority, and creating a professional police force and military. It would have meant a greater willingness to accept [human and financial] costs at the beginning of the intervention. . . . The advantage of this approach is that after an initial period of peacemaking by U.S. forces, the conditions might have existed for UN forces to carry out peacekeeping and nation building activities.[91]

A nearly identical excuse is given in the case of Haiti. Hugh Byrne and Rachel Neild of the Washington Office on Latin America, for example, concede in a 1997 *Christian Science Monitor* op-ed piece, "The truth is that three years after the intervention, U.S. and international policy in Haiti has been no great success." The aim of America's Haitian policy, they point out, has failed to restore democracy or jump-start the economy.

> Some $2.8 billion in aid—sent or pledged—held out the promise of building infrastructure, modernizing the state,

> restoring economic growth, and alleviating poverty. There are precious few signs of any of this. Instead, there are rutted roads, a weak and ineffective state, stagnant growth, and poverty. Politically, the picture is no better. A dynamic grass-roots movement that helped topple the [Jean Claude "Baby Doc"] Duvalier dictatorship and elect Mr. Aristide has been sidelined and largely demobilized. Political ambition and opportunism are the order of the day.

But then Byrne and Neild go on to argue that a more vigorous nation-building effort is the answer:

> Now is the time to begin crafting a new, long-term international approach. International donors should commit for the long haul. . . . But greater emphasis should be placed on development in the rural sector, where some two-thirds of Haitians live, and on long-term strategies to create jobs and alleviate the country's crippling burden of poverty.[92]

Lastly, in the case of Kosovo, some analysts are already explaining away the unfolding nation-building failure there by arguing that it would be working if only the United States and NATO had been more assertive in imposing their will in the pursuit of a nation-building agenda. Typical of those holding this view is columnist Georgie Anne Geyer, who blames many of the problems in Kosovo on U.S.-NATO peacekeepers not doing enough: "NATO is bogged down by contortions of excessive protocol, hapless collective decision-making in the European defense establishments and the refusal of Washington to lead and make judgments."[93] Her solution: "A no-nonsense military occupation in the style of Gen. Douglas MacArthur . . . with the military and the civil power combined."[94]

Such arguments, however, are dubious. Because all nation-building missions could theoretically be started earlier or pursued more vigorously, no way exists to directly refute someone who makes such excuses. Moreover, such excuses are self-reinforcing; that is, they employ success, failure, and everything in between as evidence in favor of the nation-building agenda. Research indicates, however, that there is more to building democratic nations than bold dominion over a geographical area and the people who live there. Indeed, the authors of two different multivolume studies argue that the successful democratization of a country is by and large the product of domestic factors.[95] Furthermore, a recent analytical survey suggests that no significant relationship exists between more intrusive or proactive forms of foreign intervention and success in preventing the recurrence of conflict in strife-torn areas.[96] Several historical retrospectives on America's Vietnam experience also clearly demonstrate that nation building can fail, even when it is vigorously pursued.[97]

False Comparisons

Other advocates of nation building prefer to argue that it succeeded in post-World War II Germany and Japan, so the practice must work if done right. Then-Sen. Paul Simon (D-Ill.), for example, endorsed nation building in Somalia in 1993, claiming, "We didn't do too badly in Germany and Japan."[98] Writing in *Commentary*, AEI's Joshua Muravchik similarly claimed,

> Nor should it be doubted that America is capable of using force effectively on behalf of democracy. When the U.S. invaded Grenada in 1983, Sen. Daniel Patrick Moynihan exclaimed: "I don't know that you restore democracy at the point of a bayonet." But that in fact is what we did . . . in Japan [and] Germany . . . after World War II.[99]

The *New Republic* has defended nation building, asserting, "Somalia has given nation building a bum rap. The United States helped build pretty good nations in Japan [and] West Germany."[100] Krishna Kumar of USAID says,

> the cessation of civil wars presents an unprecedented opportunity for . . . countries to rebuild their societies, polities and economies and to embrace reforms that have been elusive in the past. There are many successful examples of this: The war-shattered countries of Europe rebuilt themselves into powerful democracies. Japan emerged from the ashes of war as a leading economic power.[101]

But postwar Germany and Japan cannot justifiably be compared with places like Somalia, Haiti, Bosnia, or Kosovo. First of all, it is an abuse of history to imply that Somalia, Haiti, Bosnia, or Kosovo comes anywhere close to warranting the same military concern (and commitment of resources) as postwar Germany or Japan. Those four places—even combined—could not build a military-industrial capacity that could threaten the United States and its allies as Germany and Japan both once did. Moreover, the security payoff of rebuilding Germany and Japan—in terms of shoring up Europe and Asia against communist expansion—and the economic payoff—in terms of foreign trade—were critical to the United States. The same cannot be said for Somalia, Haiti, Bosnia, or Kosovo.[102]

Second, the postwar political situations in Germany and Japan were historically unique. Unlike America's recent encounters with nation building, Germany and Japan were totally defeated in war and their leaders thoroughly discredited. In fact, University of Illinois political scientist Richard Merritt explains that the "failure of Nazism and the confusion of potential leaders" in the wake of Germany's unconditional surrender "made the German people receptive to discourse on governance . . . [and] imposed social change."[103] The same cannot be said of Somalia, Haiti, Bosnia, or Kosovo, where the troubling politics and politicians remained constant if not popular. Moreover, says Merritt, even before the war's end, Germans had become amenable to the policy prescriptions Washington and its allies wanted to impose.

> We must consider first the extent to which Germans were predisposed, even before the war's end, to accept the programs that AMG [the American Military Government] and other Tripartite Allies might propose. The data show that substantial numbers of German respondents were disgusted by what the Nazis had done and increasingly realized that Nazi actions were not accidental but were consistent with and even prefigured by Nazi ideology. . . . To some measure, then, AMG enjoyed a ready market for its product.[104]

By the end of the war in the Pacific, the Japanese, too, had become receptive to profound political change in ways not replicated in Somalia, Haiti, Bosnia, and Kosovo. Indeed, according to renowned historian John Dower, the U.S. occupying force "encountered a populace sick of war, contemptuous of the militarists who had led them to disaster, and all but overwhelmed by the difficulties of their present circumstances in a ruined land." The Japanese, moreover, embraced their defeat not as an end, but as a beginning to make a better future. As a result, explains Dower, "the ideals of peace and democracy took root in Japan—not as a borrowed ideology of imposed vision, but as a lived experience and a seized opportunity. . . . It was an extraordinary, and extraordinarily fluid, moment—never seen before in history and, as it turned out, never to be repeated."[105]

Third, with regard to Bosnia and Kosovo specifically, the inhabitants there fought a war *with each other*. The inhabitants of Germany and Japan did not participate in such communal bloodletting. Perhaps if a third party had tried to force the French to live with the Germans, or the Koreans to live with the Japanese under a single government after the war, then a comparison could be made with Bosnia or Kosovo today. Otherwise, the postwar political situations are radically different.

Fourth, the high level of education and industrial know-how in postwar Germany and Japan facilitated an economic recovery inconceivable in Somalia, Haiti, Bosnia, or Kosovo. Germany also had a strong tradition of the rule of law, property rights, and free trade before the Nazi era.[106] Japan's elite embraced an honorific culture that respected and obeyed the wishes of the victor in battle.[107] Somalia, Haiti, Bosnia, and Kosovo, in contrast, have little in the way of either liberal traditions or cultural attitudes that are agreeable to massive foreign interference.

Despite all the sharp historical differences, the Clinton administration nevertheless spent tens of billions of dollars and huge amounts of diplomatic capital trying to nation build. In one sense, its efforts mirrored those of Britain and France in the late 19th century. Those two powers expended their limited resources and diplomatic energy in areas of secondary importance when their attention should have been devoted to their chief security problem—the rise of Germany. Britain and France may have gained some peripheral security, but they lost their core security. For eight years, the Clinton administration repeated the same mistake, devoting America's limited resources and diplomatic energy to the periphery in Somalia, Haiti, Bosnia, and Kosovo, while ignoring the security concerns that should actually demand a superpower's attention—Russia and China.

Fool's Errands

Putting the excuses and false comparisons aside, this book will demonstrate that several important lessons can be learned from America's recent encounters with nation building. One lesson is that nation building is a fool's errand when the American people are unprepared to sacrifice the blood and treasure of their countrymen in a place they consider strategically unimportant; that is, nation building totally unattached from national self-interest is not sustainable if there are casualties. A second lesson is that nation building is a fool's errand if the country in question is not "ripe" for the effort. That is, favorable historical conditions must be in place for nation building to succeed. Or to put it another way, an ambitious nation-building program is not a sufficient condition to transform a country into a self-sustaining, democratic member of the family of nations; other conditions must be present as well. A third lesson is that nation building is a fool's errand when it perpetuates a "security dilemma" between formerly opposing sides in a bloody dispute; that is, when it preserves an environment in which each side's efforts to increase its own security decreases, or appears to decrease, the security of the other side.[108] A fourth lesson is that nation building is a fool's errand when one of the factions in a place targeted for the effort has not given up its wartime objective; that is, when they are not yet so worn out that they cease believing there is still more to gain by continuing to agitate, provoke, and fight.

Each of the cases examined in this book will emphasize one of those four lessons. What will become apparent along the way, however, is that today's nation builders seem oblivious to the evidence before them. They seem to have chronic trouble distinguishing between what they aspire to attain through their policies and the real world. Hans Morgenthau warned of this tendency more than 50 years ago in *Politics among Nations*, wherein he noted that the true study of politics must take account of "what is" and not focus just on "what should be."[109] The latter is what the nation builders do regularly. Indeed, in their exuberance to solve the world's problems, they often overlook how the world actually works, particularly when it will expose the contradictory patterns and unintended consequences of their actions, such as the way nation building tends to breed dependency and corruption where it is attempted.

Conducting foreign policy on the basis of "what should be," moreover, may be more than just flawed. It could prove unwise as it may end up producing side effects that are detrimental to the security of the United States and its citizens. Indeed, if Washington continues to make a habit of intervening in and remaking other countries, it risks enlarging the substantive number of international matters over which the United States and other nations can disagree, which significantly increases the potential for dispute, armed confrontation, and even war. Such a policy also encourages larger countries to form countervailing military alliances to prevent unchecked U.S. meddling in their backyard, and gives an incentive to smaller and insecure countries to acquire weapons of mass destruction as an insurance policy against Washington's would-be nation builders.[110] Lastly, such a policy risks putting inessential strains on the U.S. military's readiness and its ability to recruit and retain members.[111] In short, the potential costs associated with nation building are far greater than today's nation builders have grasped.

2. Somalia: "If You Liked Beirut, You'll Love Mogadishu"

On March 26, 1993, roughly nine weeks after taking office, President Bill Clinton had his newly appointed ambassador to the United Nations, Madeleine Albright, cast Washington's vote in favor of UN Security Council Resolution 814. Described as "the mother of all resolutions" by a senior UN official, the six-page document formally commenced America's first post-Cold War attempt at nation building.[1] The main objectives laid out in the resolution included the "economic rehabilitation of Somalia"; the "reestablishment of national and regional institutions and civil administration in the entire country"; the "reestablishment of the Somali police, as appropriate at the local, regional or national level"; "political reconciliation, through broad participation by all sectors of Somali society"; and the creation of "conditions under which Somali civil society may have a role, at every level, in the process of political reconciliation and in the formulation and realization of rehabilitation and reconstruction programs."[2] The resolution, Albright summarized approvingly, "aimed at nothing less than the restoration of an entire country."[3]

Just over six months later, the Clinton administration was saying precisely the opposite. "It is not our job to rebuild Somalia's society," announced the president in an October 11, 1993, speech.[4] A few days later, the White House dispatched a letter to the U.S. Congress that boldly declared, "The U.S. military mission [in Somalia] is not now nor was it ever one of 'nation building.'"[5] Despite such claims, however, two things were abundantly clear: the U.S. government had spent $2.3 billion doing much more than just delivering food aid to starving Somalis, and more than 200 American soldiers were wounded or killed in the process.[6] By April 1994, U.S. troops were no longer in Somalia.

The standard explanation for the nation-building failure in Somalia is that it was conducted incorrectly, and that had it been conducted "correctly," it would have worked. Martin Ganzglass, a former U.S. State Department adviser in Somalia, for example, argues that if the United States had attempted to rebuild Somalia's police force sooner after intervening—a fanciful recommendation with no political traction at the time—civil society could have been restored.[7] Kenneth Allard, a senior military fellow at the National Defense University, says the failure was the result of an inadequate integration of the "diplomatic, military, and humanitarian" components of the operation.[8] But the reason the mission failed was not because Somali police were too few or because the world's nation builders were inefficient. Failure resulted because Washington pursued policies that paved its way into the vortex of Somali politics, and because it overestimated public and congressional support for a mission that was divorced from national self-interest.

Trouble on the Horizon

The country of Somalia was granted independence in July 1960 when the colonies of British Somaliland and Italian Somaliland were officially joined together. Although the people of Somalia shared a common culture and language, their society was organized along the lines of a segmentary lineage system, in which political allegiances were determined largely by clan and subclan attachments. In all, there were six main clans in Somalia and dozens of subclans.[9]

The civilian administration that assumed power after independence quickly fell prey to interclan wrangling and power struggles. That was not surprising. According to I. M. Lewis and James Mayall, both professors of international relations at the London School of Economics and Political Science, clan allegiances in Somalia were actually "sharpened rather than diminished" after independence because the creation of an alien political structure—the centralized state—"provided a new and enlarged arena for clan competition and conflict."[10]

Just nine years after independence, Somalia's government was overthrown in a bloodless coup led by Maj. Gen. Mohammed Siad Barre. Barre declared that clan allegiances would no longer dictate Somali politics. In reality, however, Barre began consolidating power in the hands of the Darod clan, particularly his own Marehan subclan, his mother's Ogaden subclan, and his son-in-law's Dulbahante subclan.[11] Barre also adopted a socialist model of centralized economic planning and moved Somalia into the Cold War orbit of the Soviet Union. He was rewarded with large arms shipments from Moscow, but eventually broke off ties with the Soviets when they refused to support his plan to annex territory in Ethiopia that was populated by ethnic Somalis.

Washington then moved to shift Somalia into its Cold War orbit. In August 1980, the Carter administration negotiated an agreement with Barre that permitted the United States to make use of the military facilities at the Somali port of Berbera, which the Soviets had previously used. In exchange, Barre received $20 million in credits for the purchase of U.S. military equipment, $20 million in general credits, and $5 million in budgetary support.[12] By that time, Barre's socialist experiment was in tatters and the International Monetary Fund called for the adoption of market-oriented economic policies, devaluation of the Somali currency, and liquidation of unprofitable state enterprises. After Barre postured and delayed for six years, a frustrated IMF finally withdrew from Somalia and declared it ineligible for further borrowing. By then, Somalia had already received billions of dollars in Western aid, including more than $800 million from the United States.[13] Meanwhile, Somalia's per capita gross national product had barely budged, earning it the title "The Graveyard of Aid."[14] Inflation was also spiraling out of control and Somali food production was on the decline.

Warlordism Replaces Dictatorship

As the economic situation continued to deteriorate and the marginalization of Somalia's other clans increased, Barre resorted to force to crush all opposition. Kidnapping, torture, and extrajudicial executions became commonplace. In 1988, Barre ordered bombs dropped on his own citizens when they demonstrated against his regime.[15] In 1989, government forces swooped down and arrested six outspoken clerics after morning prayers. Whole sections of their worshiping congregations were gunned down in the process, and innocent Somalis were rounded up by the hundreds, taken away, and murdered. More than 1,000 people died that day.

Two rebel movements—the United Somali Congress and the Somali National Movement—set out to overthrow Barre. In January 1991, they succeeded, but after the ouster clan rivalry broke out between the two groups. The USC, which was dominated by the Hawiyi clan, controlled southern Somalia, including the capital, Mogadishu, while the SNM, which was dominated by the Isaq clan, controlled northern Somalia. By March 1991, the SNM-controlled north declared its independence from the rest of Somalia. Then sub-clan factionalism surfaced within the ranks of the USC in the south. One faction was led by Gen. Mohammed Farah Aideed of the Habr Gidr subclan and another by Ali Mahdi Mohammed of the Abgaal subclan. Mogadishu became a divided city as the two factions sacked the country's armories and battled for control. Aideed dominated most of the southern section of the city, whereas Ali Mahdi's stronghold was in the northern section. Much of Mogadishu already lay in ruins as a result of their joint struggle to remove Barre from power. Meanwhile, most of the Darod clan associated with the Barre regime regrouped under the leadership of his son-in-law, Gen. Siad Hersi Morgan. But in northeast Somalia, the Mejertein subclan, led by Gen. Mohammed Abshir Musa, set up its own autonomous zone. And in the southern coastal town of Kismayu, Col. Omar Jess of the Ogaden subclan joined with Aideed to fight the Barre heir.

In all, more than a dozen factions were fighting and maneuvering for control in Somalia after Barre's ouster. The discord was certainly related to Somalia's acephalous clan structure. Indeed, as Rutgers University professor and Somali expert Said Samatar wrote during the initial wave of chaos, the "splintering of the opposition movements . . . into bewildering fragments . . . reflect[s] the schismatic nature of Somali society," and the "instability, anarchy, and murderous shiftings witnessed today in the Somali scene" are "inherently endemic" and "deeply embedded . . . in the very warp and woof of the Somali world."[16]

In November 1991, heavy fighting broke out between Aideed and Ali Mahdi in Mogadishu. The Red Cross called the clash a "human disaster of the worst magnitude," and aid workers estimated more than 1,000 people had been killed and 5,000 wounded in the first two weeks of fighting.[17] "Basically, these are people who don't know how to play well together," explained one foreign official working in Mogadishu, "and people [who] don't play well together probably shouldn't have anti-aircraft weapons."[18] Clan elders tried in vain to negotiate a cease-fire between Aideed and Ali Mahdi, but the fighting continued for months as the quantity of guns and ammunition in Somalia quickly surpassed that of food and medicine. Relief organizations soon began to see their supplies plundered by Somalia's warlords, each of whom was committed to keeping his own militia fed.

For much of 1992, Somalia was effectively in a state of anarchy as Aideed, Ali Mahdi, Morgan, Jess, and others battled to a stalemate. There was no operational government to speak of in Somalia, no police force, and no basic public services. The bombed-out carcasses of Soviet-made T-51 tanks littered the streets. Armed thugs and bandits roamed the countryside looting and pillaging. Food shortages made the situation even more desperate. By late summer 1992, the United Nations decided to try to facilitate the delivery of humanitarian relief. On August 28 the UN Security Council passed Resolution 775, which authorized the deployment of 500 Pakistani soldiers to guard the food stockpiles as they arrived from overseas. Known as the UN Operation in Somalia (UNOSOM), the relief effort proved futile because Somalia's rival warlords repeatedly plundered the relief convoys before they reached the starving masses. As a result, UNOSOM simply perpetuated the warlords' ability to fight on, while the population at large continued to go hungry. By fall 1992, more than 300,000 Somalis had died of starvation and 700,000 had become refugees.[19]

Operation Restore Hope

Coming under increasing pressure from the media and some corners of Congress to do something about the failing UN mission, the Bush administration broached the idea to the United Nations of sending in the U.S. military.[20] Smith Hempstone, the U.S. ambassador to Kenya, cautioned in a confidential cable to his State Department superiors that the United States should think "once, twice, and three times" before getting involved in Somalia. He further warned that Somalis are "natural-born guerrillas" who would engage in ambushes and hit-and-run attacks. "If you liked Beirut," he warned, "you'll love Mogadishu."[21]

On December 3, 1992, the UN Security Council unanimously approved Resolution 794, which authorized "all necessary means to establish . . . a secure environment for humanitarian relief operations in Somalia."[22] Within a week, the first of 21,000 U.S. troops began landing on the beaches of Somalia. They were joined by 16,000 troops from other countries. In President Bush's address to the nation officially announcing the start of the operation, which was called Restore Hope, he stressed: "Our mission has a limited objective—to open the supply routes, to get the food moving, and to prepare the way for a UN peacekeeping force to keep it moving. This operation is not open-ended." The U.S. military's central command even removed civil affairs and military police units from the deployment to ensure that no "encumbering activities" emerged during the operation that would prolong America's stay.[23] Bush stated further that the United States had no plans to "dictate political outcomes" in Somalia, and high-level administration officials exuded confidence that American forces would be out in less than six months.

Unfortunately, the United Nations began putting pressure on Washington to enlarge its responsibilities in Somalia to include disarming the warlords and laying the groundwork for a police force.[24] Meanwhile, proponents of the intervention, including those in the incoming Clinton administration, began clamoring for the need to redefine U.S. national interests and international law to allow for more such operations in the future.

A New President

On January 20, 1993, Bill Clinton was sworn in as the 42nd president of the United States. Soon after settling in, he ordered an internal study on the topic of post-Cold War peacekeeping. Word soon began leaking that Clinton's foreign policy team was prepared to take interventionism to an entirely new level. In fact, according to the former editor of *Foreign Affairs*, William Hyland, "early drafts [of the study] reportedly advocated a rapid expansion of UN operations; the United States would be committed to support such operations in all dimensions—military, economic, and political."[25] Characteristic of the thinking that went into the study was UN ambassador Albright's claim early in the administration that "state-building operations" and the "rescue of failed societies" were "essential" to facilitating democracy and in America's "best interests."[26]

The Clinton administration wasted little time moving ahead with a "state-building operation" in Somalia. On February 17, 1993, Clinton's deputy assistant secretary for African affairs, Robert Houdek, testified before the House Foreign Affairs Subcommittee on Africa about the effort. "We are moving to a new phase of our efforts in Somalia," he explained, "from the job of re-establishing a secure environment to get relief to the most needy to the challenge of consolidating security gains and promoting political reconciliation and rehabilitation." [27] Within days of Houdek's testimony the United Nations proposed a $253 million rehabilitation package for Somalia. The package included large-scale public works projects to rebuild roads, clear irrigation canals, and construct sanitation facilities. It also included $20 million for vocational training for Somalia's fighters if they laid down their weapons, and another $20 million for seeds and basic tools for Somali farmers as well as for assistance for nomadic herders to rebuild their stocks of camels, sheep, goats, and cows.[28]

By March, the Clinton administration had initiated plans to send as many as 60 U.S. Agency for International Development and U.S. Foreign Service specialists to Somalia. Their job would be to fan out to Somalia's cities and towns where they would establish reconstruction programs and help rebuild local governments.[29] The administration also sent two experts from the U.S. Justice Department to Mogadishu to assess the prospects of reestablishing a functioning police force there. The two returned and proposed a six-month, $12.7 million budget to jump-start a new police department.[30] On March 12, the scope of the administration's goals in Somalia became even clearer. UN ambassador Albright informed members of a House Appropriations subcommittee, "The key to the future of Somalia will be the establishment of a viable and representative national government and economy."[31]

Meanwhile, Somalia's warlords were attempting to exact as much political advantage for themselves as possible from the intervention. They were also siphoning off large amounts of cash from the multitude of nation builders who began descending on Mogadishu. Relief workers, reconstruction experts, and UN personnel were all charged exorbitant rent to live and work in properties that, in one way or another, were controlled by the principal warlords. The local drivers, translators, and office personnel who were hired were also almost always affiliated with the area clan and paid part of their earnings to the local warlord. On many occasions, factional skirmishes during this early period of intervention were actually over the spoils of nation building, not clan politics. Even more troubling, Somalia's warlords would turn around and use their new-found cash to buy more guns and ammunition.

Made in Washington

The Clinton administration's formal transition to a nation-building operation in Somalia began on March 26, 1993, with the passage of UN Security Council Resolution 814. Although the resolution was ostensibly designed to shift responsibility for Somalia from the United States back to the United Nations—as President Bush had originally urged—the wording of the resolution was actually written by U.S. political and military officials in Washington. In fact, according to Walter Clark, professor of peace operations at the U.S. Army's Peacekeeping Institute, and Jeffrey Herbst, professor of politics and international affairs at Princeton University, Resolution 814 was "written by the United States, mainly in the Pentagon, and handed to the UN as a fait accompli."[32]

The terms of the resolution stressed "the crucial importance" of disarming Somalia's warlords and their militias, and laid out the nation-building tasks of political reconciliation, economic rehabilitation, and restoration of Somalia's police and judiciary.[33] The U.S.-drafted resolution, a senior Clinton official later touted, was directed at doing something that "has never been done before in the history of the world"; it was directed at "re-creating a country."[34]

In addition to dictating the nature and scope of the effort to re-create Somalia, Washington also took the helm of the mission, which was to be redesignated the UN Operation in Somalia II (UNOSOM II). At Washington's urging, Jonathan Howe, a former senior U.S. military officer, was named the UN secretary-general's Special Representative for Somalia. Howe's inner circle was made up of American experts and it was his job to oversee all the civilian aspects of UNOSOM II. The civilian personnel in the mission numbered about 3,000.[35] On the military side, Washington insisted that Lt. Gen. Cevit Bir be named the chief commander of the 21,500 peacekeepers due to remain in Somalia as the UNOSOM II force, including 2,600 noncombat, logistical support troops from the United States.[36] Although Bir was not an American, the Clinton administration selected him for the position because he was from a NATO member country—Turkey—and had years of experience in the top echelons of the American-led alliance. Bir also clearly understood the nation-building mission Washington had in mind for Somalia. "We are here to re-establish a nation," he proclaimed on arriving in the war-torn country.[37] Bir's deputy, moreover, was an American, Maj. Gen. Thomas Montgomery. Montgomery exercised independent command over the 1,400 U.S. combat troops deployed in Somalia and he maintained frequent contact with Special Representative Howe.[38] The third in command and the operations officer was U.S. Army Col. Edward Ward.[39]

In short, the United States held effective control of UNOSOM II, even though it was officially a UN mission. Elisabeth Lindenmayer, a UN peacekeeping official in Somalia, conceded that the unprecedented role of Washington in a UN mission meant that certain concessions had to be made. "With the joining in of the big boys, things have obviously changed," she said. "They are used to doing things in their way. . . . It's a different kind of game. We are all trying to adjust."[40] But from the very beginning, the Italians and the Pakistanis, two of the largest contingents in the UNOSOM II force, were not as amenable and reportedly looked to their own governments for instructions and on occasion refused to follow Washington's presumptive orders. In response, a spokesperson with the UN secretary-general's office remarked: "It is unacceptable to the United Nations and the secretary-general . . . for the national contingents to seek instructions from their member states or their national capitals. They are under the force commander and they are supposed to follow his orders."[41]

"A Bright New Chapter"

UNOSOM II officially took control in Somalia on May 5, 1993, when U.S. Marine Lt. Gen. Robert B. Johnston ordered the American flag lowered over the command headquarters and his Turkish successor, Gen. Bir, ordered the UN colors raised. The ceremony, held in the sweltering heat and humidity of the Somali afternoon, lasted less than 25 minutes and only a handful of Somalis attended. Bir thanked the American-led forces for laying "a firm foundation" for the United Nations and promised, "We are ready to continue hope for all of Somalia."[42] Washington's chief nation builder in Somalia, Special Representative Howe, added that the day's transition opened "a bright new chapter in the history of the recovery of this nation."[43]

Others were less optimistic about UNOSOM II's prospects. Mogadishu is now "a bit like Belfast," observed Red Cross relief coordinator Geoff Loane, referring to Northern Ireland's capital, where British troops had been stuck battling the Irish Republican Army for more than two decades.[44] UNOSOM II, he explained further, is "almost an antiterrorist presence, a show of force with the ability to pull the trigger if necessary."[45] Others warned that Mogadishu might turn out to be more like Beirut.[46] During that conflict, the United States was gradually sucked into Lebanon's civil war on the side of one faction. Having lost their neutrality, U.S. Marines increasingly became targets of violence. Within five months, 241 were killed when a truck bomb was driven into their barracks. The U.S. mission to reconstruct Lebanon quickly collapsed.

A similar scenario was unfolding in Somalia. At first Aideed welcomed the outside intervention. As the commander most responsible for ousting the Barre regime, he felt it was only natural that he would become Somalia's new leader. His view was reinforced when the Americans, and later the United Nations, established their headquarters in his sector of Mogadishu. To his dismay, however, their proximity meant that the foreign peacekeepers were more likely to be disarming his militia, which advantaged his chief rival, Ali Mahdi.[47] Meanwhile, Ali Mahdi understood that he was weaker militarily than Aideed, so he maneuvered to use the United States and the United Nations to his political advantage. He soon began forging numerous links with influential Americans and UNOSOM II personnel, and he played along with their nation-building plans.[48] Consequently, tension grew even more between Aideed and the UN forces, which he came increasingly to see as an emerging ally of Ali Mahdi.

In late May, tensions between Aideed and the United Nations came to a head over the question of local peace negotiations. Aideed had initiated his own round of negotiations, arguing that peace in Somalia would be achieved by Somalis themselves, and not by well-intentioned foreigners. Without the participation or authorization of UNOSOM II, he called a peace conference in Mogadishu. Days later, UNOSOM II organized its own competing peace conference in the southern port city of Kismayu. UNOSOM II invited Aideed's chief rival, Ali Mahdi, but excluded Aideed's local ally, warlord Col. Jess. Aideed interpreted the United Nations' move as an overt threat to his power.[49] Adding to that already tense environment, a pro-Ali

Mahdi radio station announced on June 5 that UNOSOM II was going to take over the country's radio stations and other "institutions which are the causes of present instability."[50]

That same day, Pakistani troops paid an unannounced visit to an ammunition storehouse near Aideed's main radio station, Radio Mogadishu, and at one point actually entered the station.[51] Fearing the imminent takeover of Radio Mogadishu, Aideed's forces ambushed the Pakistanis later that day, killing 24. Instead of consulting with other nations participating in the operation or waiting for the results of an independent inquiry into the events surrounding the ambush, Special Representative Howe responded as if he were the sheriff of Mogadishu, declaring Aideed an outlaw and offering a $25,000 reward for his arrest.[52] Within 24 hours, the United Nations passed Security Council Resolution 837, authorizing military operations against "those responsible for armed attacks against UN Forces." With that move, Washington's nation-building mission was expanded to include a war against Aideed. An internal UN inquiry published months later admitted that "opinions differ, even among UNOSOM [II] officials on whether the weapons inspection of 5 June 1993 [that precipitated the ambush that left 24 Pakistani soldiers dead] was genuine or was merely a cover-up for reconnaissance and subsequent seizure of Radio Mogadishu." By the time the report was issued, however, UNOSOM II had already singled out Aideed as its principal enemy. Many Somalis, consequently, came to view UN peacekeepers as just another clan, with its own set of enemies and allies, fighting to get its way. The round of warfare that broke out between UNOSOM II and Aideed would last four months and produce thousands of casualties.

Rising Frustrations

On June 12, 1993, Washington moved to destroy Aideed's power base and militia. For several days, U.S. warplanes bombed the warlord's weapons depots, combat strongholds, and radio station, the last of which was then seized by U.S. infantrymen.[53] The day after the raids began, an angry Somali crowd gathered to protest the attacks. Nervous Pakistani troops positioned in elevated, sandbagged bunkers opened fire on the crowd with automatic weapons, killing at least 14, including women and children, and wounding 20.[54] Some of the demonstrators were apparently shot as they tried to flee the gunfire, and victims lay in their own blood as UN armored vehicles drove by making no effort to help the wounded. "There was a man whose arm was almost severed," reported Paul Watson, a correspondent with the *Toronto Star*. "He was basically mush from the hips down. The guy was still alive when the UN trucks passed by, but they just kept on going."[55] Among the dead was a two-year-old boy who was standing more than a half-mile from the shooting scene when a high-velocity bullet struck him in the abdomen.[56] "This is an absolute disaster," lamented one UN official. "Before this, we had the moral high ground."[57]

Confounding Washington's game plan even further, Aideed refused to confront directly the U.S.-led assault against his faction. "I'm still amazed that we haven't had any response" from Aideed, explained one frustrated U.S. officer. "The idea was to have him draw out his weapons so we can destroy them."[58] UNOSOM II, nevertheless, pressed even harder, and on June 17, UN troops, backed by U.S. air power, seized Aideed's headquarters. But Aideed's defiant militia fought back for six hours in fierce street battles that left five UN soldiers dead and 44 wounded. At least 60 Somalis, including civilians, were also killed, and two American missiles slammed into the office of the French aid group International Action against Hunger, killing one relief worker and injuring seven others.[59] Despite all the casualties, and the fact that Aideed managed to escape capture, President Clinton depicted the operation as the beginning of the end for Aideed. We have "crippled the forces . . . of warlord Aideed," claimed Clinton. "The military back of Aideed has been broken."[60]

Meanwhile, Aideed's chief rival, Ali Mahdi, was invigorated by the punitive military strikes taken against his enemy. He even staged pro-UN rallies on his side of Mogadishu and echoed Washington's claim that Aideed was the main impediment to peace in Somalia. "After so many people have died, the world now realizes that the only obstacle to peace is Aideed," Ali Mahdi said in an interview after the strikes began, and if "the world realizes that Aideed is the only obstacle and has to be removed, that is good for all Somalis."[61] But many Somalis actually held Ali Mahdi as culpable as Aideed for Somalia's disintegration after the fall of the Barre regime, and Jennifer Parmelee, editor of the *Humanitarian Monitor*, a journal covering the Horn of Africa, observed that Ali Mahdi's "militias are every bit as blood-soaked as those of Aideed."[62] In fact, the power struggle between them had already left 30,000 people dead or disfigured, and Ali Mahdi eventually joined forces with Barre's brutal son-in-law, Gen. Morgan.[63]

Despite the difficulties that were being encountered, advocates of the nation-building mission nevertheless continued to push their policy prescription. In testimony before Congress on June 24, UN ambassador Albright justified the use of the U.S. military in the actions against Aideed by claiming that it was essential to "rebuilding Somali society and promoting democracy in that strife-torn nation."[64] Similarly, on July 29, the State Department's undersecretary for political affairs, Peter Tarnoff, told the Senate Foreign Relations Committee, "the process of nation building will take time" and "we owe it to ourselves—and to Somalia—to help."[65]

Skeptics, however, began asking tough questions about the prudence of the mission. Writing in the *Washington Post*, columnist Charles Krauthammer raised doubts about the sustainability of the mission, noting that the administration was "trying to justify American soldiers dying 7,800 miles from home in an operation with no conceivable connection to the U.S. national interest."[66] Former secretary of state Henry Kissinger went even further and asked whether "risking American lives" in the "absence of any definable national interest" could erode the American people's willingness to support military operations when they do matter.[67] On Capitol Hill there were grumblings as well. Sen. Robert Dole (R-Kans.) lamented, "I think there's no doubt about it, the mission has changed from humanitarian aid to what they call pacification and institution building." "Many of us thought the job was complete," he added. "We expected an announcement that more Americans would be coming home, not that there would be further troop commitments."[68]

"Who Are the Warlords Now?"

In early July 1993, U.S. troops began conducting house-to-house weapons searches and Italian soldiers reestablished a key checkpoint in a prelude to what Col. Ward, UNOSOM II's third in command, said would be an all-out effort to reclaim control of Mogadishu. "My personal opinion is that the UN has stayed behind these walls too long," explained Ward, and it has "waited too long to give something to the people of this city—roofs over their heads, schools for the kids, a judicial system in place." U.S. soldiers, he added, are prepared to get involved in "nation-building activities," such as constructing schools and rebuilding roads.[69]

Aideed's military back, however, was not really broken, as President Clinton had earlier claimed. Aideed was able to replenish his arms and ammunition from his stockpiles in central Somalia and from his base camps across the border in Ethiopia. Aideed refused to cooperate with what he saw as the erosion of his power, and his camp vowed to fight against what it referred to as "colonialism" and "hegemony."[70] By July 11, 70 more UN peacekeepers and Somali UN employees had been wounded or killed as a result of mostly hit-and-run attacks carried out by Aideed's forces.[71] Many of the attacks occurred in what were formerly some of the safest areas of Mogadishu, such as the port, the airport, and the road in front of the U.S. embassy. In one incident, four Norwegian peacekeepers were wounded when a rocket-propelled grenade was launched over the Norwegian embassy's wall.[72] In another incident, several Somali UN workers were found killed execution-style after they had distributed pro-UN materials.[73]

On July 12, 17 U.S. Cobra helicopter gunships and Blackhawk reconnaissance helicopters fired more than 2,000 rounds of 20-millimeter cannon fire and 16 missiles into a residential villa used as a command center by Aideed's faction. American infantrymen then descended on the premises and confiscated radios, documents, and small arms.[74] According to a UN spokesperson, the attack resulted in "no collateral damage whatsoever" to areas outside the villa compound and "no innocent civilians were injured in the attack."[75] With regard to the people inside the villa compound, the spokesperson said that 13 were killed and 11 were wounded. "All were adult males. All were armed."[76]

Despite the claim that the attack was carried out with pinpoint accuracy and that all of the death and destruction was limited to the villa compound, an American reporter on the scene, Scott Peterson, said that the raid was far bloodier than UN and U.S. officials acknowledged. "It was devastating," said Peterson. "There were bodies all over the place—they were mincemeat."[77] On the basis of a survey of two of Mogadishu's large hospitals, the International Committee of the Red Cross said at least 54 Somalis were killed in the attack and 174 wounded.[78] But the actual casualty toll was likely higher because other medical facilities in the city were not surveyed, and the Somali tradition is to bury their dead without first taking them to hospitals. Enraged by the apparent slaughter, Somalis rioted in the streets, killing three foreign journalists in the process.[79]

In neighboring Kenya, news of the U.S.-led bloodletting was met with the provocative newspaper headline, "Who Are the Warlords Now?"[80] Meanwhile, international support for the mission began to show its first serious cracks. In Rome, the Italian government criticized the UN operation for having too many Americans in decision-making positions and voiced concerns that the operation had shifted from its original humanitarian objective to "urban guerrilla operations."[81] In Bonn, the opposition Social Democrats said Chancellor Helmut Kohl's offer to send a contingent of 1,600 German soldiers to Somalia should be withdrawn. In Washington, Sen. Robert C. Byrd (D-W.Va.) broke with his fellow Democrats in the Clinton administration and called for the U.S. troops in Somalia to "pack up and go home."[82]

"Operation Destroy Aideed"

In the wake of Washington's helicopter raid on Aideed's villa command center, one columnist concluded, "What began last December as Operation Restore Hope has now become Operation Destroy Aideed."[83] Aideed's response to the operation was to urge his followers to rise up against the multinational UN peacekeeping force and what he called "foreign domination."[84]

On August 3, 1993, heavy fighting erupted in Mogadishu as Somali gunmen fired on UN peacekeepers, launched mortars at the UN's headquarters, and attacked a UN military airfield.[85] The following day a land mine concealed in a street puddle near the American embassy injured a U.S. soldier and an American civilian contractor.[86] On August 8, four American soldiers were killed when their Humvee ran over another land mine.[87] An American spokesperson blamed Aideed for planting the explosive devices and claimed that the escalation of attacks "reflect[ed] Aideed's frustration over his shrinking support base."[88] The attacks actually signaled Washington's inability to defend against Aideed's low-intensity guerrilla campaign, which was increasing the U.S. troops' level of frustration.

On August 12, hundreds of Somalis at a pro-Aideed rally pelted a U.S. Army patrol with rocks and fired gunshots at the soldiers.[89]

U.S. military officials denied suggestions the American soldiers provoked the Somalis, but journalists at the scene gave a different account. They said that the first shots fired came from the U.S. troops, and that some Somalis in the crowd fired back at the convoy in response. They also said the Americans opened fire after their three-vehicle convoy had passed out of rock-throwing range. "Those guys were in no danger at the time they fired," said Michael Maren, a correspondent for the *Village Voice* newspaper. "It was after the Americans started firing that a couple of shots went off from the crowd. It was clearly a provocation."[90]

By late August, President Clinton sent an additional 400 U.S. combat troops—elite Army Rangers—to Somalia to help capture Aideed.[91] Washington, however, continued to encounter frustrating setbacks. A raid conducted on August 30 mistakenly captured UN aid workers.[92] On September 9, when an angry Somali crowd turned on troops fighting Aideed's militia, a U.S. helicopter fired on the crowd and killed about 200 Somali civilians. U.S. Army Maj. David Stockwell, chief spokesperson for the multinational UN force in Somalia, told reporters, "There are no sidelines or spectator seats. The people on the ground are considered combatants."[93] By September, Gen. Joseph Hoar, head of the U.S. central command, wrote a strongly worded letter to the State Department's undersecretary for defense policy, Frank Wisner, and the chairman of the Joint Chiefs of Staff, Gen. Colin Powell. "Control of Mogadishu has been lost," he wrote. "If the only solution for Mogadishu is [the] large-scale infusion of troops and if the only country available to make this commitment is the United States, then it is time to reassess our commitment."[94] In a follow-up message to Powell, Hoar warned that U.S. troops in Somalia were doing much more than originally planned and that no end appeared in sight.[95]

The turning point in Washington's manhunt for Aideed—and indeed its entire nation-building operation in Somalia—came on October 3–4, when a major U.S. assault on Aideed's positions in Mogadishu resulted in the shooting down of a U.S. Blackhawk combat helicopter. Eighteen U.S. Army Rangers were killed and 76 were wounded in the firefight that ensued. More than 1,000 Somalis, including women and children bystanders, were killed by American forces during the fighting.[96] The Blackhawk pilot was taken prisoner, while another crew member's dead body was dragged through the streets of the Somali capital. The disturbing video of that event was broadcast on television throughout the United States.[97] President Clinton's initial response was to justify the soldiers' deaths by claiming that they "lost their lives in a very successful mission against brutality and anarchy."[98] He also announced, "You may be sure that we will do whatever is necessary . . . to complete our mission."[99] Days later, when it became clear that the American public and Congress were not persuaded, Clinton reversed his Somalia policy: U.S. troops would be withdrawn within six months. The administration's hunt for scapegoats then began.

The Blame Game

After leading the hunt to capture Aideed, the White House turned to blaming the United Nations for the October 3–4 loss of American lives. When meeting with the families of the U.S. Rangers who were killed, Clinton said he was surprised to learn that Aideed was still being pursued.[100] Elsewhere, he said that the effort against Aideed "never should have been allowed to supplant the political process that was ongoing when we were in effective control, up through last May."[101] Members of Congress, too, were pointing their fingers at the United Nations. Rep. John Murtha (D-Penn.), chairman of the House Defense Appropriations Subcommittee, for instance, complained that the United Nations had "sucked in" Washington to hunt for Aideed.[102]

Despite Washington's attempt to pin the blame on the United Nations, the military operations directed against Aideed were repeatedly endorsed and often pushed by top American officials.

- Of the 17 UN Security Council resolutions that had been passed pertaining to Somalia, including Resolution 837, which authorized military operations targeting Aideed, all received Washington's affirmative vote.[103]
- In early summer 1993, the CIA backed the view, publicly articulated by Clinton, that Aideed was a disruptive force who would interfere with Washington's nation-building objectives in Somalia.[104]
- The American head of the UN operation in Somalia, Special Representative Jonathan Howe, lobbied for more U.S. forces to go after Aideed. The August 24 decision to send an additional 400 U.S. Army Rangers was approved by President Clinton,

Secretary of Defense Les Aspin, and National Security Adviser Anthony Lake.[105]

- On September 6, two weeks after the administration dispatched the 400 Rangers per Howe's request, Robert Gosende, the senior U.S. State Department diplomat in Mogadishu, sent a classified message to Washington requesting even more U.S. troops to conduct weapons sweeps.[106]
- The deadly October 3–4 operation against Aideed was commanded by U.S. Army Maj. Gen. William Garrison, who was reporting directly to U.S. central command, not to the United Nations.

Moreover, even while the peacekeeping operation was falling apart, administration officials intensified their rhetoric in support of nation building generally and the war against Aideed specifically. In early August, UN ambassador Albright identified Aideed as the chief obstacle to Washington's "humanitarian and political goals" in Somalia and declared that he "must be stopped." She recommended that Aideed's forces be "disarmed, retrained, and reemployed," that "democratic institutions . . . be established" in Somalia, and that "development aid . . . be delivered and efficiently used." This, she assured the administration's skeptics, would "lift" Somalia from a "failed state to an emerging democracy."[107] Later that month, Secretary of Defense Aspin called upon the world to step up efforts to map a detailed plan for Somalia's recovery and argued, "We must make real progress towards taking the heavy weapons out of the hands of the warlords."[108] Roughly five weeks later, after the 18 Rangers were killed, Clinton would openly contradict those statements. Somalia is not America's responsibility, he declared. "We have obligations elsewhere."[109]

Support, What Support?

So what went wrong in Somalia that culminated in such a dramatic policy reversal on the part of the administration? According to former Brookings Institution scholar Richard Haass, "when the costs in terms of American lives and dollars suddenly climbed, domestic public and congressional support for the intervention dissolved," and the Clinton administration concluded that "agreeing to exit by a specific date" was necessary.[110] But public and congressional support did not "dissolve." It was either weak or never there.

For the most part, the American public was opposed to the kind of mission the Clinton administration was pursuing in Somalia. According to a *Time*/CNN poll taken shortly before Clinton took office, 82 percent of Americans approved of the presence of U.S. troops in Somalia. But a Gallup poll taken at roughly the same time qualified that support, revealing that 59 percent of Americans believed that the U.S. role in Somalia should be "limited to delivering relief supplies." Only 31 percent said they believed that that U.S. role should be expanded "to bring a permanent end to the fighting."[111]

After Aideed attacked Pakistani UN soldiers on June 5, 1993, most Americans did approve of retaliating against him, but a CBS/*New York Times* poll revealed that 42 percent worried that it would lead the United States to be "bogged down" in Somalia.[112] By late summer, an NBC/*Wall Street Journal* poll showed that only 36 percent of Americans thought the Somali mission was "under control," whereas 52 percent thought the United States was "too deeply involved in Somalia."[113] A *New York Times*/CNN poll, furthermore, showed that 69 percent of Americans believed that U.S. forces in Somalia should "only be responsible for making sure that food is delivered." Less than half, 48 percent, thought U.S. troops should be in Somalia at all, down from the 82 percent high before the Clinton administration started its nation-building effort, and a scant 22 percent said U.S. troops should be used for "disarming the rival warlords."[114]

Disarming belligerents and nation building, however, was precisely what Washington was attempting to do. "In many ways the American people were misled," admitted an American civilian official working in Somalia that summer. "Nobody recalled hearing about this nation building thing [in the beginning]—that kind of snuck up on the American people."[115] Another American official, acknowledging the shallowness of public support for Clinton's Somalia policy, conceded, "I think we need to bring this to an end as rapidly as possible."[116] Alas, the administration did not follow that advice, and after the calamitous Ranger operation of October 3–4, public support for keeping U.S. troops in Somalia dropped another 13 percentage points, down to 35 percent, according to a *New York Times*/CNN poll. But that last drop was small relative to the 34-point plunge in public support that had occurred between January and mid-September 1993. In fact, according to Texas A&M

professor James Burk, "77 percent of the decline in public approval of the mission occurred *before* the Rangers lost their lives" on the streets of Mogadishu.[117]

Congressional support, too, did not suddenly dissolve. It was already waning before October 3–4. The Senate resolution authorizing the initial deployment of U.S. troops in Somalia came on February 4, 1993, more than two months after President Bush sent them in to deliver food relief.[118] The House version was not passed until May 25.[119] As the security conditions in Somalia began to deteriorate that summer, members of Congress began to express concern about the expanded role of U.S. troops in Somalia under UNOSOM II. Sen. Robert Byrd complained that the "mandate to disarm the warlords and rebuild civil society . . . was never addressed, never debated, or never approved by this [Senate] body."[120] Sen. John McCain (R-Ariz.) announced: "We went to Somalia to keep people from starving to death. Now we are killing women and children because they're combatants. It's got to stop. It's got to stop and it's got to stop soon."[121] Between February 1993 and November 1993, an estimated 15 bills and resolutions were introduced on Somalia, most of them calling for the withdrawal of U.S. troops.[122] On September 9, 1993, the Senate voted 90-7 to require President Clinton to seek congressional authorization before November 15 to continue the mission. The House passed an identical bill three weeks later by a vote of 406-26.[123] The White House did not take Congress's concerns seriously, and when Clinton's secretary of defense, Les Aspin, finally testified in October, members found his presentation of the administration's Somalia policy incoherent. "Never have I heard a more confused, disjointed, vague defense of American foreign policy in my professional career," remarked one member of Congress.[124]

Killing with Kindness

From the very beginning, the intervention in Somalia was plagued by unintended consequences. For instance, as early as December 1992 there were reports that the influx of foodstuff was hurting Somali farmers who were trying to get back on their feet. Many found themselves unable to compete with the cheap food that was suddenly flooding their country.[125] Operation Restore Hope also drew weak and malnourished people to refugee camps where food relief was distributed, but where, too, conditions were highly unsanitary and disease was readily contracted. The U.S. Centers for Disease Control and Prevention found that in the area of Bardera, the mortality rate had actually doubled among the general population in the first month of the U.S.-led deployment, and it had quadrupled among children under age five.[126]

U.S. troops would also disarm the local gunmen whom humanitarian relief agencies had hired to guard their aid shipments. With the guards disarmed, relief agencies became more vulnerable than before to theft because the most violent and resourceful bandits were able to keep themselves armed. Both Doctors Without Borders and the Red Cross reported that more of their vehicles were looted or shot up after the intervention than before.[127] Moreover, Somali gunmen who had previously viewed relief workers as a valuable source of semilegitimate income, came instead to see them as prime targets for robbery.[128] During the first three months of the intervention, three foreign-aid workers were killed, compared to only two during the preceding two years of chaos and civil war.[129]

The immediate political consequence of the intervention was that it forced the warring factions to recalibrate their power calculations. As Rakiya Omaar and Alex de Waal, formerly with the human rights organization Africa Watch, pointed out right after the first U.S. troops landed:

> True, Somalia's two strongest warlords, Mohammed Farah Aideed and his rival, Ali Mahdi Mohammed, agreed to cease hostilities on Friday, but in the preceding two weeks several important but low-key peace initiatives were called off. For example, until last weekend, the town of Baidoa was a success story. A delicate web of negotiated agreements had allowed the area to return to a modicum of stability. . . . In the last few days, this has all gone up in smoke. The militia led by warlord Aideed rampaged through the town, displacing thousands of people and forcing aid agencies to evacuate their staff. Why? Because all the agreements so painstakingly worked out no longer hold force. The only question that matters now is, who will gain from the U.S. occupation and who will lose? In this atmosphere, clan negotiators are paralyzed with uncertainty, while the warlords' eyes gleam with the chance of fresh adventures out of the sight of the Marines.[130]

Besides Baidoa, 11th-hour violence erupted elsewhere in Somalia as well. In the southern port city of Kismayu, more than 100 religious leaders, business executives, and other prominent residents were assassinated on the eve of the American landing. The killings were directed by Col. Jess in a move to eliminate educated Somalis who might support the Americans. All the assassination victims were members of the Harti subclan, which viewed Jess's militia as an occupying force. Hundreds more died in clan battles and looting raids that ensued.[131]

After the U.S. Marines had deployed, the focus of many Somalis turned to maximizing the spoils of the intervention. In fact, a *New York Times* story published two months into the intervention reported,

> Diplomats and development officials who have met with the factions still find them mostly interested in the spoils of war and in patronage, worrying about who gets to control revenue from the port, or demanding international assistance to rebuild government bureaucracies for them and provide money for government salaries.[132]

That languid way of thinking was rooted in Somalia's long and destructive dependency on foreign aid. In fact, prior to Somalia's collapse, foreign aid constituted a full 70 percent of the country's national budget.[133] To this day, explains Centre for Defence Studies scholar Karin von Hippel, "Many Somalis erroneously believe that a restored central government, based in Mogadishu, will once again cause the foreign aid floodgates to open at similar levels to those prior to state collapse. Mogadishu therefore remains the most hotly contested piece of real estate in the country."[134]

In addition, when the United States initially intervened to deliver famine relief, it disrupted the power structures of Somalia's warlords, who maintained their supremacy by brutally controlling the food supplies. Thus, as scholars have pointed out, in overseeing food deliveries, "the United States immediately stepped into the muck of Somali politics."[135] Indeed, prior to the intervention, food in Somalia was a source of power, and those who controlled it could reward their allies and starve their enemies. But after food became abundant and secure, Somalia's warlords were faced with a new political reality. What they did next depended on how they thought they could maximize their power within the changed political setting.

Picking Good Guys and Bad Guys

Because the famine in Somalia was largely created by political conditions, the logic of nation building dictated that Washington try to prevent the recurrence of the conditions that led to it in the first place. That effort drew Washington even deeper into Somali politics. At first Washington's approach, led by U.S. envoy Robert Oakley, was to arrange high-profile meetings with Somalia's principal warlords, leaving them with the impression they were equally legitimate. By late March 1993, after two weeks of UN-organized negotiations in Ethiopia, the 15 main factions fighting for control in Somalia agreed on a plan for forming a transitional government and for disarming within 90 days. The proposed transitional government would be headed by a 74-member Transitional National Council, which would consist of one representative from each of Somalia's factions, five from Mogadishu, and three from each of the country's 18 regions.[136]

But from the start the negotiations were flawed. Western negotiators tried to force through solutions and did not respect the Somali customs of peacemaking or *shir*, which could take months, involve the composition of poems and discussion about past feuds, and conclude with an agreement on compensation.[137] As Africa expert Gérard Prunier observed, "Elegant, well-paid, and highly educated UN officials" refused to "bend to the ways" of the Somalis. Instead, the Somalis "had to adapt to Western ways and make peace in a civilized fashion . . . by sitting at tables in air-conditioned rooms and putting their signatures at the bottom of a little piece of paper." The trouble was, explained Prunier, the Somalis

> had absolutely no idea, intention, or even understanding of what the international community was so keen on. The lack of what a Western magistrate would call "proper procedure" invalidated in [the Somali participants'] eyes the meaning of the whole process. They collected their per diem for sitting in Addis-Ababa, went shopping, met their friends living in exile in the Ethiopian capital, and then went home. As one of the participants . . . was to remark: "The speeches were nice, the slogans were really good but the whole thing was

> quite meaningless." [They] had no feeling that they had actually pledged anything by putting their signature on the UN-sponsored document they had been asked to sign.[138]

Washington made blunders of its own, such as distributing leaflets that mistakenly translated the English words "United Nations" into the Somali words for "Slave Nation."[139] Millions of the leaflets, which depicted an American soldier in helmet and flak jacket shaking hands with a Somali man, were dropped from the Somali skies. The erroneous message reinforced many Somalis' fears that Washington's motives were less than pure.

Many officials affiliated with the U.S.-led UNOSOM II mission also behaved as if they were Somalia's new colonial masters. "Many Somalis feel that the United Nations is now imposing itself on Somalia, that it is effectively an occupying force," observed Sharon Pauling, an Africa policy analyst with Bread for the World, a relief group involved in aid to Somalia. "Increasing numbers feel their views are not being considered when it comes to what national reconstruction should look like or where UN troops should be deployed. Basically, they're feeling excluded."[140]

Many Somalis were, therefore, deeply suspicious of the U.S.-led nation-building mission. Within that context, several attempts were made at persuading Somalia's warlords to lay down their weapons and sue for peace. The warlords, however, faced competing motives. If they agreed to disarm and then their rivals defected from the agreement or cheated, they would be at risk of losing all their power. Many warlords worried, furthermore, that any negotiated arms agreements would collapse after the United Nations left. They therefore preferred to err on the side of caution and kept their weapons.

Like the violence that had earlier spiraled out of control, the warlords' behavior was not motivated only by their sense of uncertainty. It was also motivated by their sense of opportunity. Indeed, each warlord was convinced that he could survive longer than his enemies under the dreadful stalemate conditions that prevailed in Somalia. But since each warlord thought in those terms, the stalemate continued. As University of Chicago political scientist David Laitin explains, Somalia's stalemate was perpetuated not so much by each warlord's desire to defeat his rivals, but by his desire to outlast them; that is, the principal warlords continued fighting "because each leader strategized, if the war was costing more for the opponents . . . they would sue for peace first."[141]

With the Clinton administration's fateful decision to launch a war against Aideed, Washington unintentionally fed right into the Somali logic of violence. Many Somalis—approvingly and unapprovingly, depending on their clan allegiance—came to view UNOSOM II forces as the newest party in their war, and that view only helped fuel the conflict between different Somali factions. In fact, dozens of factional chiefs and subchiefs immediately began jockeying for power and Western largess after the U.S.-led military campaign commenced against Aideed. Aideed, meanwhile, portrayed himself as the aggrieved party and his stature was raised as a folk hero. He also launched a low-intensity guerrilla war against the multinational presence in Somalia. Senior administration officials strongly defended their moves against Aideed, which they described as "necessary police actions."[142] But T. Frank Crigler, the U.S. ambassador to Somalia from 1987 to 1990, had a different view. "Unfortunately, we've allowed ourselves to be sucked into choosing sides and picking good guys and bad guys."[143] Crigler also warned the House Foreign Affairs Subcommittee on Africa, a full two months before the deadly October 3–4 incident in Mogadishu, that "we are turning triumph into tragedy, applying brute military force to a situation that calls for quiet diplomacy, patient mediation, steadiness, and understanding."[144]

Casting U.S. troops in the role of helicopter-borne enforcers whose aim it was to impose peace on the Somalis at gunpoint had predictable results: Aideed violently resisted while Ali Mahdi and others—who would benefit from Aideed's departure from the scene—encouraged it. To the very end, Ali Mahdi tried to exploit Washington's animus for Aideed. In fact, in late October 1993, after Clinton's announcement that the United States would pull out by a date certain, he organized a demonstration on Aideed-controlled turf in southern Mogadishu. UN officials speculated the event was designed to provoke Aideed in hopes that an incident would cause the United States to stay. The clash that resulted between the forces of Aideed and Ali Mahdi broke a 19-month-old truce. Washington did not change its mind, but the bloodletting was started anew.[145]

Peace Conferences and UN Mismanagement

Between 1991 and 1995 no fewer than 17 national-level and 20 local-level peace conferences were organized to address the Somali conflict.[146] Many of them were sponsored by the United Nations and many of them were a waste of time. Not only did a "conflict constituency" exist that had a vested interest in prolonging the conflict, but most of the warlords also had an exaggerated view of their own importance.[147] Thus, who got to attend the conferences and with how many representatives were politically charged questions that became a source of tension between rival clans. Moreover, as former UNOSOM II political adviser Ken Menkhaus pointed out,

> Somali political figures frequently viewed peace conferences more as vehicles for enhancing their own status *within their clans* than for advancing the cause of peace. . . . Aideed, Morgan, Ali Mahdi, and others all had to cope with [clan] elders, rival [intraclan] political figures, disgruntled subclans, clerics, intellectuals, and ambitious militia leaders laying claim to authority over some or all of the clan's political dealings. All of these political players thus viewed peace initiatives—especially well-funded, high-visibility, internationally sponsored peace conferences—as an excellent tool for elevating their own status within the clan.[148]

Meanwhile, amid UNOSOM II's efforts to negotiate a peace, $3.9 million in cash vanished from its guarded headquarters in Mogadishu in what investigators said was an inside job. The money, which was to be used to pay bills and staff salaries, was kept in a cabinet with a faulty lock. The UN bureaucracy in New York had delivered a steel safe to store the money, but no combination number was included.[149] Additional UNOSOM II money was lost as a result of waste, mismanagement, and fraud. For example, $369,000 was paid on a fuel distribution contract for services never rendered. Another $540,000 was paid to the same distributor for unnecessary deliveries. A further $160,000 was squandered buying water on the open market instead of purchasing it through a wholesale contract.[150] In response to those incidents and others, the UN's inspector general issued a report that found a "lack of fair and competitive bidding" and "improper evaluation of vendor's proposals resulting in the wrong choice of contractor."[151] The report recommended a new manual for the UN's procurement office, as well as better training for its officers. It also called for better controls of extended sick leave by UN employees "to prevent fraud and abuse" in that area as well.[152]

Collision Course

All the costs, miscalculations, and finger-pointing notwithstanding, President Clinton claimed that the operation in Somalia was a success because, "We saved close to one million lives."[153] The actual figure was probably closer to 100,000.[154] Moreover, the death rate in Somalia was already falling dramatically before U.S. troops arrived in December 1992, and the monthly death rate had dropped to 10,000–15,000 during the first month of Operation Restore Hope.[155] In a similar vein, the *New York Times* reported that when U.S. troops arrived they found that the worst of the starvation was over: "In the nearly three weeks since the troops landed, it has become clear that because so many of the hungry died before the foreign forces arrived, emergency food is perhaps a less critical issue than was originally outlined."[156] According to many sources, moreover, some regions of Somalia were actually producing an agricultural surplus at the time the United States intervened.[157]

From the start, Washington misunderstood the unresolved nature of the Somali conflict and pursued policies that paved its way, step by step, into the vortex of Somali politics. That, combined with the fact that public and congressional support for nation building was never very strong, meant that a collision course was set well before the October 3–4 deaths of the 18 Rangers. Rather than acknowledging those realities, however, Clinton scolded the United Nations for the American casualties and denounced the "poison" of isolationism at home.[158]

Yet the facts remain: the original intervention of U.S. troops disrupted the political setting in Somalia, and it was the U.S.-led campaign against Aideed that both encouraged Ali Mahdi and triggered an Aideed backlash that led to the embarrassing withdrawal of American troops. Those events, however, underscore a more basic problem: It is impossible for an intervening party, acting alone or in concert with others, to keep its nation-building activities from altering the power calculations of rival factions that are still maneuvering to outlast each other, as they were in Somalia. Invariably, something the outside party does will be seen as a benefit to one side's interests and as a danger to the other's. They will respond accordingly. Ten years before Mogadishu, the consequence of that problem was painfully demonstrated in Beirut, and like Beirut, the lesson was the same: Nation building is a fool's errand when no political will exists among the warring sides to reconcile and when the cost of influencing political outcomes—intentionally or unintentionally—exceeds the threshold of what the American public and Congress are willing to tolerate.

In an important 1994 *Foreign Affairs* article, Columbia University political scientist Richard Betts spotlighted that very same lesson. The notion of an "impartial intervention," he explained, is a "delusion," especially when the belligerents have reached a stalemate.

> Stalemates rarely seem solid to those with a strong stake in overcoming them. Belligerents conjure up one set of military stratagems and schemes after another to gain the upper hand, or they hope for shifts in alliances or outside assistance to tilt the balance of power, or they gamble that their adversary will be the first to lose heart and crack.[159]

Betts added that the intervening party must understand that wars, at bottom, are about "Who rules when the fighting stops?" and, thus, imposing peace is not about being impartial—which is impossible—but about "kill[ing] people and break[ing] things" and ultimately deciding "who will rule afterward."[160] "By the same token," he warned, the intervening party "should not mix in the dangerous business of determining who governs without expecting deadly opposition. An intervention that can be stopped in its tracks by a few dozen fatalities, like the U.S. operation in Somalia was, is one that should never have begun."[161]

Postscript: Necessity Is the Mother of Invention

By 1997, two and a half years after the last U.S. troops departed, commerce was booming in Somalia, the markets were full, and people who had previously eked out their existence with the barrel of a gun had gone into business importing, exporting, and transporting goods. Though Mogadishu was divided into three sectors controlled by individual warlords, hundreds of people every day crossed from one sector to another to do business. Currency markets, private schools, and hospitals had popped up. There were even two competing telephone systems operating in Mogadishu.[162]

In summer 2000, Abdulkassim Salad Hassan was elected the new president of Somalia. It seems that almost a decade after the fall of the Barre regime and the subsequent outbreak of brutal fighting between rival clans, the people of Somalia finally had enough murder, hunger, and anarchy. On a practical level, many Somalis also came to see the creation of a national government as a necessary step to ending the exploitation of Somalia's rich fishing fields by foreign fishing fleets and the illegal sinking of toxic garbage off the Somali coast.

Hassan's election was the product of a peace summit organized by Ismael Omar Guelleh, the president of Somalia's geographical neighbor to the north, Djibouti. For three months, he hosted about 2,000 delegates whom he had invited to the town of Arta, 15 miles south of the Djibouti capital.[163] The summit-goers reached an agreement on the composition of an interim parliament, and that parliament elected the 58-year-old Hassan to be Somalia's head of state for a three-year term. Some $150 million belonging to the old Somali state was transferred to the new government, and police and security forces were being recruited in Mogadishu.[164]

Warlords such as Hussein Aideed—the son of the late warlord Mohammed Farah Aideed, who died of battle wounds in 1996—boycotted the Arta meeting and declared their opposition to the Hassan presidency.[165] Meanwhile, the political leaders of the breakaway regions of Somaliland and Puntland in the north of the country said they were waiting for peace to be restored in other regions before meeting with the new president.[166] Optimistic Africa experts interpreted the fact that the Arta conference was able to produce concrete results without the participation of the warlords as a promising sign that the warlords' influence was finally waning.[167] What should be most notable from Washington's perspective, however, is that Somalia's recent political and economic improvements were achieved, not by way of foreign military occupation, but by way of Somalis who have found that they can do things when they need to.

3. Haiti: Voodoo Nation Building

Since its bloody birth in 1804, Haiti has been the object of outside concern, if not trepidation. In the 19th century, fear of Haiti, generated by a violent slave revolt there and the possibility that it could spread throughout the slaveholding parts of the Western Hemisphere, led to its international isolation. In sharp contrast, Haiti in the 20th century became a kind of international laboratory for foreign countries determined to transform it into a prosperous and democratic society. Despite multiple efforts and billions of dollars, however, little, if anything, has changed.[1]

The most recent attempt began in July 1994, when, at Washington's urging, the United Nations passed Security Council Resolution 940 authorizing the United States to use "all necessary means" to restore democracy to Haiti.[2] President Clinton then dispatched 20,000 U.S. troops to the island country and spent $3 billion trying to get the job done.[3] It was not the first time that U.S. soldiers had embarked for Haiti to nation build. U.S. Marines intervened in 1915, when they remained for 19 years, and again in 1961, when they stayed for two years. Like those two previous attempts, Clinton's attempt also came up short.

Today, Haiti remains one of the poorest countries on earth. Its long-term prospects are dim; its politics are turbulent and unpredictable; and its elections are models of technical incompetence and political chicanery. After all the effort, capped by the Clinton administration's determination to restore democracy, why has so little been accomplished? That is a simple question. But the answer—or rather, answers—most certainly are not.

Haiti Bound

For decades, Haiti was ruled by the two-generation regime of François "Papa Doc" Duvalier and his son Jean-Claude "Baby Doc" Duvalier. In February 1986, amid increasing political turmoil, the reign of the Duvaliers finally came to an end when Baby Doc and family fled to France. Haiti's political turmoil, however, did not end with the departure of Baby Doc. One government after another was overthrown. In 1990, the newest military junta to gain control organized elections. A last-minute candidate, Jean-Bertrand Aristide, won the presidency, but he was overthrown by another military junta the following year. The sudden regime change caused little concern within the Bush administration. Indeed, according to Secretary of State James Baker, the return of a civilian government in Haiti would be a positive thing, but it did not warrant the use of U.S. military force.[4]

Haiti, however, became a campaign issue during the 1992 presidential race, with candidate Bill Clinton condemning as cruel the Bush administration's policy of turning back boat people fleeing the increasingly oppressive conditions in Haiti. When upward of 150,000 Haitians prepared to leave Haiti aboard boats in the first days of the Clinton administration, however, Clinton changed his tune. In a radio address broadcast throughout Haiti, Clinton warned Haitians, "Those who leave Haiti by boat for the United States will be intercepted and returned to Haiti by the U.S. Coast Guard."[5]

After Clinton reversed his position on Haiti's boat people, he faced sharp criticism from within his own administration and certain quarters of the U.S. Congress. "We are not serious about assuming our role in the world as the last superpower to be a force for good in guaranteeing the human rights of human beings everywhere," denounced Rep. Major Owens (D-N.Y.) on the floor of the U.S. House of Representatives, and, he added, the "Congressional Black Caucus thinks we've had enough."[6] Clinton attempted to counter the criticisms by pushing for an international trade embargo on Haiti and putting a freeze on its international assets. The administration's rationale was that internal pressures created by the sanctions would compel the military junta to allow Aristide to return to power, thus solving the boat people problem.

In July 1993, after a few months of sanctions, the Clinton administration pressured junta leader Gen. Raoul Cédras to sign an accord at Governors Island, New York, consenting to Aristide's return. Clinton declared the accord a turning point in Haiti's history and for the "principle of democratic rule."[7] But that accord soon proved not to be worth the paper it was printed on because the Haitian junta decided that Aristide's return was not in its best interest. The military prevented Aristide's prime minister from reassuming power and assassinated several of Aristide's supporters. In October 1993, the junta sent a mob of government-paid thugs to the Port-au-Prince harbor to prevent a U.S. Navy support ship, USS *Harlan County*, from landing with its complement of UN peacekeepers sent to help oversee the transition back to Aristide. When the ship arrived, only nine days after 18 U.S. Army Rangers were killed in Mogadishu, Somalia, President Clinton decided not to force the issue with the dockside mob and had the USS *Harlan County* reverse its engines.[8]

President Clinton insisted that he was "dead serious" about enforcing the Governors Island Accord, but a second U.S. ship bound for Haiti was cancelled.[9] The administration next turned to the United Nations, which passed a resolution tightening sanctions. Members of Clinton's foreign policy team, such as National Security Adviser Anthony Lake, and congressional liberals began pushing for a stronger line on Haiti. The president's rhetoric intensified over the course of the next several months, and in July 1994, the Clinton administration persuaded the UN Security Council to authorize the American use of force to restore Aristide to power.

With a UN resolution in hand, Clinton issued his final warning to Haiti's military junta on September 15, 1994: "Your time is up. Leave now or we will force you from power."[10] Some question existed, however, about the legality of threatening an invasion. The administration claimed that Haiti was "a threat to international peace" and thus the United States should be allowed to invade under Chapter VII of the UN Charter. Under pressure, the UN Security Council, including Russia, accepted that reasoning, which saw the vote as reinforcing its long-maintained prerogative to intervene in its "near abroad," too. But in reality, it was an exaggeration to suggest that Haiti was a threat to international peace.[11] No one seriously believed that the Haitian military intended, or was even capable of, attacking any other country, or that the events there, though tragic, imperiled the stability of the region. Nevertheless, Clinton sent former president Jimmy Carter, along with Sen. Sam Nunn (D-Ga.) and the chairman of the Joint Chiefs of Staff, Gen. Colin Powell, to Haiti to persuade Cédras to give up power or face a U.S. invasion. At the very last moment Cédras capitulated, the military junta gave up power, U.S. troops landed in Haiti unopposed, and Aristide returned.

Transition to Nation Building

After six months of occupation, the Clinton administration transferred formal responsibility for the intervention to the UN Mission in Haiti (UNMIH) and downsized the American military presence to 2,400 soldiers, or about half of the 6,000-strong UN force deployed in Haiti until the end of June 1996.[12] According to its mandate, UNMIH had three primary goals: "the professionalization of the Haitian armed forces and the creation of a separate police force" and "establishing an environment conducive to the organization of free and fair legislative elections."[13] Foreign countries, including the United States, pledged $1.2 billion for infrastructure projects, judicial reform, and other programs.[14] Meanwhile, the U.S. Agency for International Development provided up to 60,000 temporary jobs for Haitians.[15]

In July 1996, UNMIH was replaced by the UN Support Mission in Haiti (UNSMIH). It was essentially a U.S.-Canadian operation, although a Pakistani battalion remained behind after Washington agreed to pay for its operating expenses.[16] The American contingent, operating separately as the U.S. Support Group Haiti, numbered 450 soldiers, mostly engineering and medical specialists. The Canadian and Pakistani contingents totaled 1,300 personnel.[17] According to UN Resolution 1063, which authorized UNSMIH, "institution-building, national reconciliation, and economic rehabilitation in Haiti" were added to the list of mission objectives.[18] Two other UN missions—the UN Transition Mission in Haiti and the UN Civilian Police Mission in Haiti—followed later, carrying Washington's involvement in Haiti into 2000.

From the beginning, the Clinton administration and its allies claimed that the nation-building efforts in Haiti were a success. Sen. Claiborne Pell (D-R.I.), for example, declared that Haiti's June 1995 local elections represented "an important step in the building of democracy" in Haiti and that "the Haitian people were able to freely exercise their right to choose their local legislators and municipal officials."[19] But the fact of the matter was that widespread irregularities occurred during the election; some polling stations never opened, while others ran out of ballots; voter registration lists were often incomplete; and some candidates were left off the ballots altogether.[20] Haiti's December 1995 presidential election, which was won by Aristide's handpicked successor, René Préval, did not fare much better. According to Ernest Preeg, a former U.S. ambassador to Haiti, the election

> was seriously flawed in a number of respects. The provisional election council was challenged by opposition parties. The media was harassed, with a few members beaten, and they were effectively silenced. It was a very brief election campaign. All the centrist and conservative parties boycotted the election. They had won a third of the vote 5 years earlier.[21]

The situation only worsened, and by early 1999, a wave of political assassinations and political bickering paralyzed the already moribund Haitian government. President Préval then dissolved the parliament and began ruling by decree.[22] The commander of U.S. troops in Latin America, Gen. Charles E. Wilhelm, was not impressed. He told a closed session of a House appropriations subcommittee that the United States should end its military presence in Haiti, arguing:

> As our continuous military presence moves into its fifth year we see little progress toward creation of a permanently stable internal security environment. In fact, with the recent expiration of parliament and the imposition of rule by presidential decree we have seen something of a backsliding.[23]

Haiti was also becoming increasingly hostile to Americans. In 1998, the Haitian parliament passed a law ordering all foreign troops out of the country.[24] Even more worrisome, on April 23, 1999, gunmen opened fire on dozens of Marines as they prepared for a morning run at the front gate of the U.S. military compound.[25]

By the end of Clinton's second term, it was clear that Haiti was not the foreign policy success the Clinton administration claimed. Haitians were poorer, hungrier, and less literate than when the president dispatched 20,000 U.S. troops to restore democracy.[26] Lawlessness, banditry, and corruption were also on the rise, and Haiti's 2000 parliamentary elections were dubious at best. Even Clinton's ambassador to Haiti, Timothy Carney, admitted that "Haiti has not met the unrealistic expectations of the international community since 1994." More important, he correctly identified—albeit in the tempered language of a diplomat—the primary reason for the failure:

"The modest advances in the economy . . . and the spotty record in the transition toward democracy reflect Haiti's history and political style."[27]

The Curse of History

Haiti is an anomalous country. Geographically, it is in the Caribbean and, by extension, the Western Hemisphere. But it is not part of Latin America, much less Anglo-Saxon America. Despite its French colonial past and predominantly Creole-speaking population, it has little cultural claim to Europe or, mythology aside, to Africa. In the first century of its independence Haiti was a pariah nation, shunned by countries that feared its bloody slave rebellion could spread to their colonial possessions. That isolation stunted Haiti's development. Severed from Europe and North America precisely in the century that industrialization and material progress began to take place, Haiti was prevented from absorbing the fruits of that advancement, in contrast to other Caribbean colonies such as Jamaica and Barbados.

France remained aloof from Haiti until 1838. The United States, for its part, did not recognize Haiti diplomatically until 1862, when the federal government no longer had to accede to southern wishes on anything related to the slavery issue. The major South American republics did not get around to formal relations with Port-au-Prince until the third decade of the 20th century. Haiti remains largely disconnected from Latin America and the Caribbean to this day, and it has yet to experience any significant or sustained economic growth in its more than two-hundred-year history.

A wide range of observers, who have usually been sympathetic to the plight of the Haitian people, have argued that the country's economic, political, and social problems could be rationally reversed.[28] But the unvarnished facts, stripped of any gloss of Whiggish optimism about the inevitability or even the possibility of progress, are daunting. During the late 17th and 18th centuries Haiti was a French colonial possession called Saint-Domingue. Saint-Domingue was no ordinary colony because it soon became the wealthiest and technologically most advanced outpost of any major colonial power in the world, including the 13 stripling colonies belonging to the British crown on the Atlantic coast of North America. Needless to say, the wealth created in Saint-Domingue was not evenly distributed (nor was it in the southern American colonies) because much of it was produced through forced labor as the slaves worked first sugar and then coffee plantations.[29] The dark side of the picture, of course, was that the whole system of wealth creation depended on slavery. Conditions were harsh and helped unleash a slave revolt that began in 1791 and ended 13 years later after more than 100,000 people had been killed—men, women, and children—with both sides acting in equally barbaric fashion.[30]

The ruination of Haiti's economy was further entrenched by the political malfeasance of the country's subsequent rulers. Governments in postcolonial Haiti were, for the most part, either harshly dictatorial or short-lived and chaotic. The brief periods of relatively good government were just that—brief—and now long forgotten.[31] Haitian governments were also increasingly corrupt as the main business of government became the extraction of revenues for the personal gain of Haiti's rulers and their inner circles. Haiti, in short, institutionalized a highly developed predatory state that proved incapable of fostering economic growth through incentives for individuals or of overseeing the administration of public services like education or justice. As a result, the vast majority of Haiti's citizens fell into utter helplessness and destitution.[32]

Each instance of Haitian failure, some analysts have argued, can be found in the histories of other societies, including our own.[33] Moreover, the argument runs, where countries have overcome political and economic backwardness, the change has been relatively recent.[34] Those apologetics, however, do Haiti little good. They also certainly misread a society that from beginning to end has exhibited a kind of gross dysfunctionalism that is difficult to find anywhere to the same degree. That bleak assessment, however, requires documentation and detail. Without them, the enormity of Haiti's interlocking problems cannot be understood, nor can the failure of nation building be explained.

Haiti's Economic Dysfunction

Poverty—even extreme poverty—is hardly novel in human history. Until recently, few people, other than a handful of early Utopians, thought it would ever be otherwise. Until the 18th century, the vast majority of human beings lived out their brief lives in Hobbesian fashion: "solitary, poor, nasty, brutish, and short."[35]

In Haiti most human beings still do. Nothing exemplifies this situation more than the data, which, while abundant, still abound with problems. Depending on the source, basic indicators such as per capita income, growth of GDP, unemployment, and literacy rates vary widely. None, however, gives an observer a reason for optimism.

Even the most optimistic numbers remain daunting. The best estimates are only approximate and suggest the following: Haiti has an illiteracy rate ranging between 47 and 85 percent. It may have been 90 percent 25 years ago, and nearly 100 percent before the American occupation of 1915, but no one is quite certain.[36] Haiti's current per capita income seems stuck around $250 per year with approximately 85 percent of the population living in direst poverty. That statistic ranks Haiti with the likes of Mozambique and other impoverished African countries. But even the numerical comparison to countries like Mozambique often is misleading. Mozambique suffered from decades of civil war and Marxist misrule. Today, the country is at peace; has accepted, for the most part, capitalist ways; and has the natural resources soon to surpass Haiti.

Haiti's economic growth patterns are less encouraging. They reveal—to the extent data are available—that over the last two centuries Haiti has never experienced any period of sustained, rapid, and positive economic growth, with the possible exception of the American occupation from 1915 to 1934. In contrast, spurts of growth occurred in former economic basket cases like South Korea and Taiwan, which have emerged in recent decades as world-class, export-driven economic tigers.

Recent decades in Haiti have been particularly depressing.[37] For instance, between 1965 and 1980, the economy grew by 0.9 percent, which is statistically insignificant. That dismal rate, moreover, is exacerbated by the fact that on a per capita basis growth was actually negative because Haiti's birthrate is the highest in the Western Hemisphere. Nevertheless, that period—the best years of the long father-and-son regime of the Duvaliers—now looks something like an economic golden age because in the years immediately following the Duvalier era, Haiti's GDP shrank by 2.4 percent. The worst, however, was yet to come. Between 1991 and 1994 a military junta ran affairs, to the intense displeasure of the Bush and Clinton administrations. Washington imposed devastating economic sanctions, which led to a precipitous decline of, at the least, another 30 percent in GDP. Since the Clinton-led "restore democracy" effort in 1994, matters have improved only slightly. According to the Inter-American Development Bank, per capita GDP figures improved 1.4 percent between 1994 and 1998 and only 0.5 percent in 1999. Those minor improvements, moreover, were mainly caused by the lifting of sanctions and a temporary influx of international aid dollars, not by systemic changes.[38]

Even more discouraging, Haiti's prolonged plunge into an economic abyss is not the end of its problems. The country is not only dirt poor, but also lacks the means and resources for creating wealth. Its once commercial reserves of bauxite, for example, are depleted. Deforestation has left Haiti's mountainsides bare of trees and has led to serious erosion of already scarce arable land: the equivalent loss according to one World Bank estimate of 15,000 acres per year. Reforestation projects invariably only supply more wood fuel for Haiti's peasants. Today, international donors could more cheaply import wood to Haiti than engage in reforestation programs, which have so far proved futile.[39]

Haiti, with its high population density, is also facing a population-to-arable-land ratio that is truly Malthusian. Thomas Malthus's gloomy forecast for humanity's future has, of course, been held in check by technological innovation, which, among other things, has created better seeds and more disease-resistant crops. By one estimate, however, Haiti today is less technologically advanced in agriculture than it was in 1790. So far, efforts to transfer technology and improved agricultural skills have failed despite the best efforts of international agencies.[40] Haiti's land impoverishment, in fact, is not static, but worsening. According to one estimate, the amount of arable land available to each farmer has dropped from 0.38 hectares in 1950 to an estimated 0.16 hectares in 2000.[41]

It is therefore not surprising that Haiti became a net importer of food beginning in 1980 and since then has become even more dependent on imports. Indeed, thanks to Haiti's chronically shaky currency, some 10 percent of the population is fed through international charities, and that percentage has been rising. As an unintended consequence, the importation of free food, rice in particular, has further depressed the one relatively productive part of agriculture, farming in the Artibonite Valley north of Port-au-Prince.

Decline in Haiti's agricultural sector is matched in its ailing industrial sector. That sector can be divided into two parts, each with its own special problems. First, the assembly-export sector, which—in Haitian terms at least—once flourished, has been shattered by the country's political instability since the fall of the Duvaliers. The sector, which once featured hundreds of *maquiladora*-style plants where imported parts and raw materials were turned into everything from textiles and toys to baseballs, generated hundreds of millions of dollars ($362.9 million in FY 1988) in exports, chiefly to the United States. Export assembly plants also accounted for 46,000 jobs in 1990, but shrank to 8,000 by mid-1994. To be sure, those jobs have often been derided as low wage, but that criticism missed the point. Despite Haiti's many disadvantages, comparatively low wages attracted foreign investment. Second, by Haitian standards, the pay rates were quite generous. Finally, economic history suggests that as skills are acquired and a sector grows, wages will rise as employers compete for a limited number of skilled workers. But that was not to be the case in Haiti, thanks largely to political turmoil that was compounded by international sanctions. Many foreign investors pulled out and moved their operations elsewhere in the Caribbean, often relocating to Haiti's next-door neighbor, the Dominican Republic.[42]

There are recent signs of a partial recovery in the assembly-export sector. Haiti, however, probably will never regain what was lost. Foreign investors remain skeptical of a country that never seems able to stay on the same track for any length of time, especially when opportunities for investment abound in other countries that have increasingly sought market solutions to their development problems.

Haiti's industrial export sector is also in disarray. During the Duvalier era, that portion of the economy was protected by high tariffs and other competition-killing state policies. Industries like cement, soybean oil, and sugar refining became either state-owned or private monopolies, where prices were kept high, quality low, and profitability—except for those in a position to skim off the top—uncertain. After the Duvaliers fled in February 1986, the new and very temporary government of Gen. Henri Namphy took a few, limited steps to address the problem, but the wavelet of reform soon went flat.[43] That was all supposed to change with the restoration to power of ousted president Jean-Bertrand Aristide in 1994. Under heavy pressure from the donor countries—the United States, Canada, and France—as well as the World Bank and the International Monetary Fund, the new government was to privatize this sector rapidly. In fact, there was nothing rapid about it. Aristide, for one, hesitated to do or even say anything. Ideologically, he distrusted markets and foreign investors. Moreover, within his own party, Lavalas, the bright flame of statism still burned brightly, and Aristide no doubt understood that if he were to extend his time in office, he could not alienate his core constituency. Finally, a substantial part of Haiti's elite—the national bourgeoisie—was also opposed to reconstructing these inefficient enterprises because they might be deprived of their rent-seeking activities.[44]

All that Hamletesque hesitation left privatization to Aristide's successor, René Préval, who faced serious problems of his own, including a recalcitrant parliament whose mandate ended in January 1999. Nevertheless, Préval made some, albeit slow, progress privatizing a flour mill and a cement plant, but did so in the face of vocal opposition from former president Aristide, who had once more regained his populist voice. Compounding the problem, those limited sell-offs did not have the force of law—only of presidential decree.[45]

Haiti's deeply flawed economy was further underscored by the fact that public foreign capital had been pouring into the country since the departure of the military junta led by Gen. Cédras in 1994. The United States alone has contributed some $2.2 billion, making Haiti one of the highest per capita aid recipients in the world. Other donor countries and international financial institutions like the World Bank have been equally generous. In addition, nongovernmental organizations and Haitian remittances abroad have contributed more billions in this period. Even more funds are in the pipeline, which could be disbursed when and if the Haitian government ever gets around to keeping its promises on implementing economic and administrative reforms.[46]

Yet, despite all that money and effort on the part of the international donor community, relatively little has changed for the better economically in Haiti. The economy remains stagnant with astronomically high rates of unemployment, and the infrastructure is crumbling while corruption flourishes to the extent that the World Bank, for example, has washed its hands of any new projects in Haiti. Worse, little on the horizon would suggest matters will improve, particularly under a government dominated by Lavalas's economic illiterates.[47]

Haiti's Political Dysfunction

The sources of Haiti's poverty are many, but they are not confined strictly to the economic factors already discussed. Take Haiti's political culture. Political culture, as usually defined, consists of a cluster of shared attitudes, values, and beliefs that are embedded in a society. That political culture plays a large, if not a dominant, role in the shaping of any society was once fiercely controversial—usually on irrelevant grounds—but such is no longer the case.[48] Clearly, attitudes, values, and beliefs *do* have a substantial impact on a society. But that does not mean that cultures cannot change. They can and do, at times more quickly than many would believe possible. Australia comes to mind. Its first generation of settlers were convicts, and although many were guilty of relatively minor offenses, much of the population were the dregs of London with scarcely the mix of values and beliefs that foster hard work, honesty, discipline, and socially constructive behavior. The second generation, perhaps in rebellion, adopted precisely such values.[49]

Unlike in Australia, in Haiti there has yet to be any happy reversal of fortunes in any generation. Some observers doubt whether Haiti is even a nation, and see it rather as a society divided by race, class, and cultures. In any case, not only does Haiti's political culture undercut economic and political development, but also, in Haiti expert Lawrence Harrison's apt phrase, it actually "chokes" them off.[50] Indeed, in Haiti one can speak of multiple political cultures, but none have much relation to creating and distributing wealth or democratic governance. That has been true since the French ran Saint-Domingue.

Contrary to the usual impression that Haiti's colonial society was a simple two-class arrangement—white masters and black slaves—it was much more complicated than that. White society, for example, was an odd mix of planters, many of the most successful being Huguenot; an artisan middle class; and a large group of Europeans that can only be described in Marxist fashion as lumpen proletariat, the kind of riffraff, thieves, and prostitutes that festered in Paris slums. Between the whites and the large slave population were a freed class of mixed-race mulattos, many of whom owned land and slaves as well but who did not possess all the rights of Frenchmen, which they justifiably resented.[51]

To this potent mix was added the French Revolution, which began in May 1789 as broadly, but peacefully, reformist but soon degenerated into a true revolution, both violent and radically transforming. Alarmed at the anti-monarchical trend in the *métropole,* the royalist white planters entertained ideas of independence from France—a move that soon sparked thoughts of revolt among slaves who hated both the white and *affranchi* elites. In the end, the near genocidal conflict (certainly in intent, if not result) lasted for 13 years and did nothing to fundamentally change the hierarchical nature of Haitian society. Replacing the whites—all of them—were the mulattos, who alone were in a position to run the country, albeit at a very basic level. The only threat to their rule came from a new class of *noire* who although black had the same low regard for the mass of blacks as the mulattos did.[52]

The experience of the colonial and immediate postcolonial period molded Haiti's political culture and still shapes it today. It gave the barely viable, but newly independent, nation not one society but two, so different, in fact, they did not even speak the same language. The wealthy mulatto elite, as has been often noted by observers over the decades, was Roman Catholic, French-speaking, and formally highly educated and adopted the values of the French planter class. The impoverished *noire* masses spoke Creole, practiced voodoo, were illiterate, and had no choice about how they earned their living. The few both feared and despised the many; the many, in turn, feared and envied the few. As a consequence of this acute division, the elite, who were no more than 5 percent of the population, believed their way of life, even their lives, depended on wielding repressive authority. There never was, nor is there now, a sense of noblesse oblige among either the mulatto elite or arriviste blacks.[53]

The elite's other values, too, are instructive. One was a lack of trust in anyone outside the immediate family. That mistrust, of course, extended to foreigners. In remembered Haitian history, foreigners are white and, whether French, British, Spanish, or American, have attempted to occupy and rule Haiti for themselves. Another value was that the pursuit of wealth, based on having connections and being an insider, was an appropriate way to conduct one's life. Taken together, those values militated against the possibility of developing an elite capable of establishing representative institutions able to execute and adjudicate laws fairly.

The black majority is no more capable of providing a basis for a positive political culture. For good reason, the many felt powerless, unable to control their own lives or their children's. That, perhaps, is why voodoo maintains such a stubborn hold on most Haitians. Voodoo—with no ethical content—provides through rituals access to spirits and gods who can protect the individual from further harm or even make good fortune possible. Moreover, with little or no access to advanced education, the black masses' view of the world is static.[54] In a vicious cycle, Haiti's poverty and instability help to reinforce these basic values, which make it all the more difficult for positive change to take place. As generations of well-intended foreigners keep discovering, the problem is often worsened when outsiders try to make things better.

Washington's Haitian Experiments

Sadly, there is no science of nation building, although philosophies on the subject abound. As for an art, the results in Haiti do not paint an encouraging picture. And even if there were a connect-the-dot manual, political constraints and limited resources would often restrict the ability of nation builders to finish the job. Yet that commonsense view rooted in experience has rarely prevailed when it comes to dealing with Haiti. At critical times, the world—and the United States in particular—has succumbed to the temptation to "do something" in Haiti. Washington has made three major attempts in Haiti to try to change the island nation's ways. None succeeded, and what few limited gains were made were reversed after the period of American attention abated. The three attempts were the period of U.S. occupation, launched by the Wilson administration, that extended for 19 years from 1915 to 1934; the Kennedy administration's effort at reshaping Haiti through the Alliance for Progress from 1961 to 1963; and Operation Uphold Democracy, which extended over both Clinton administrations, from 1994 to 2000. Though each effort was quite different, their failures were not caused by any want of effort. In fact, many of those who worked in Haiti exerted huge efforts at great sacrifice to make the country more prosperous, more stable, and more democratic. But, hard as they might try, the well-intentioned do not and cannot always succeed.

Wilson Goes to Haiti

Woodrow Wilson's initial decision in 1915 to intervene in Haiti with U.S. Marines was primarily strategic, not humanitarian. Haiti at the time was in its familiar turmoil, but what proved decisive to the president was the war in Europe. Although America remained neutral, Wilson had little regard for Imperial Germany and less for German interests in Haiti (which stretched back well into the 19th century). With Haiti's finances in a greater-than-usual state of disarray, the American president feared Germany would use Haiti's failure to pay off its foreign debt as an excuse to exercise its naval force at the strategic expense of the United States. In 1915, the Panama Canal had been open only for a year and Haiti lay astride the strategic Windward Passage. American leaders were sensitive about approaches to the canal and the various chokepoints that litter the Caribbean. Similar moves into Nicaragua and the Dominican Republic by Wilson at roughly the same time reinforce that point.[55] Three years later the war was over and Germany was a shattered military power. Nevertheless, the United States remained in Haiti for another 16 years.

After the pressing strategic concerns were allayed, Washington turned to what would now be called nation building, or at least making Haiti stable enough to shut the door to future interventions by other major powers. Haiti's finances were put in order with the help of City National Bank. Haiti's basic infrastructure (virtually nonexistent outside the capital) was substantially improved. More than 500 miles of roads were constructed. Schools were built. Sanitation was considerably improved. Telephone and telegraph service were upgraded. Agriculture was not ignored either. A school of agronomy was built; irrigation was repaired; and experimental farms were established. Much of this was done by the U.S. military, the Marines in particular, with the Philippines serving as a kind of model. But the experience with the Philippines was over a much longer period—1898 to 1946—and although the archipelago today is no paragon of democratic and market virtue, it never was an abyss to the same extent as Haiti. Moreover, Filipinos took to American ways, including adopting the English language, still the country's real lingua franca; Haitians, high and low, never did.

It would be a mistake, however, to conclude that the American occupation experience in Haiti was confined to public works like schools. The Marines, after all, were a ready fighting force, and fight they did—in the hope of providing Haiti much needed political stability. Their chief target was northern warlords and their followers, the *cacos*, who periodically disrupted national life by marching south to Port-au-Prince and imposing their own leader as president while helping themselves to what was available in the national treasury. In that regard, the Marines, at least, enjoyed some success.

If Haiti were to remain permanently free of warlordism, American policymakers rightly saw that a professional armed force had to be created. As in Nicaragua and the Dominican Republic, the Marines trained a new officer corps that would form the *Garde d'Haïti*. The new force was to be professional, politically neutral, and, it was to be hoped, more humane than Haiti's earlier armed forces. The *Garde* at the time was Washington's chief hope that Haiti would no longer pose any problems after the Marines left in August 1934. Alas, that would not be the case.

Kennedy Takes on Haiti

When the United States left Haiti in 1934, the country did not immediately slide back into the total chaos that prevailed during the preintervention years, but stability proved elusive and democracy a formality as one president after another sought to extend his term only to be overthrown eventually. Nor did Haiti's military act as a scrupulous defender of constitutional order; it led three military coups in the decade following World War II. Nevertheless, in 1957, Haiti staged its first plausibly competitive democratic presidential election. Although it was marked by violence and came on the heels of five short-lived governments during the 10 months preceding it, the election produced a fair result; that is, the winner actually got more votes than any other candidate. Unfortunately, the winner was the soon-to-be infamous François "Papa Doc" Duvalier.

By early 1961, the Duvalier terror machine was apparent to all in Washington. The once highly vaunted student of American public medicine, cabinet officer, and promoter of black pride ("negritude") quickly descended into a voodoo-laced hell of repression that spared no enemy, real or imagined. Yet the Kennedy administration thought it could lift Haiti from its miasma. Again, the initial motive was strategic. As the then (and now) poorest nation in the Western Hemisphere, Haiti seemed particularly vulnerable to communist-style subversion. After all, the republic was a mere 50 miles from revolutionary Cuba, which had already sent a small boatload of Fidel Castro's *barbudos* in a vain attempt to overthrow Duvalier in August 1959. As Castroite guerrilla warfare became more sophisticated in the early 1960s, Haiti could prove an easy target for communist agitators and insurgents. Or so John Kennedy's Latin American team worried, especially after the disastrous failure at the Bay of Pigs in April 1961.

The Alliance for Progress, a program of aid to Latin America, was launched in March 1961, with all the bells and whistles that usually accompany U.S. government-sponsored benevolence. Kennedy's soaring rhetoric promised a 10-year, $20 billion effort to transform the Latin American and Caribbean nations into prosperous, stable, and democratic states. To do all that by 1970 proved to be a tall, perhaps impossible order.[56] That is not to say many in the administration did not work hard to achieve those goals. Even disorderly Haiti would be the focus of a major reform push, Duvalier or no Duvalier. Efforts were made, for example, to raise Haiti's vague budgetary procedures to international standards—meaning Haiti's rulers could no longer pocket funds kept off-budget and unaccounted for, a technique that both Duvaliers perfected. But the biggest U.S. expenditure of time and money was on a bit of institution building. More than a quarter-century had passed since the U.S. Marines had whipped the tattered Haitian military into the semblance of a professional-looking force. Standards had long slipped, however, with most of the Marine-trained officers in retirement—or dead. Duvalier's (perhaps justified) fear of professional officers meant that those who were not retired or forced to retire were often murdered, and he sought to counterbalance any threat of a military coup with a new volunteer force—the dreaded *tonton macoutes,* which remained firmly under his direct control.

Meanwhile, the United States had, beginning in the latter years of the Eisenhower administration, already decided to do something about Haiti's vulnerability to Cuban subversion by sending a naval training mission to the country. What the advance U.S. survey team, under the command of Marine Maj. Gen. James P. Riseley, discovered was discouraging. According to Riseley's report:

> There appears to have been little progress made in the development of the Haitian army since the end of the American occupation in 1934. In fact, it is evident that the present Haitian soldier is apparently less proficient than were the members of the *Gendarmerie d'Haïti*. The condition of the individual equipment and facilities indicate a lack of organizational ability and an absence of systematic training. These defects appear to be more serious than any major deficiencies in equipment.[57]

Considering that most of the country's army rifles were rusted, inoperable ruins, Riseley was engaging in cautious, bureaucratic understatement in describing the combat readiness of a force that could barely muster a corporal's guard for any purpose, in which training consisted, at best, of firing a hundred rounds from a bolt-action Mauser rifle. Riseley, however, had more worrisome news to offer his superiors in Washington:

> The active participation of the army in political affairs in the past few years has involved a number of officers. The present government is busy trying to eliminate officers who might be considered inimical to the government. In this and recent campaigns, some 30 percent of the officer corps has been retired or otherwise eliminated. Many of these are the older and more stable elements of the army. With their departure, the younger officers question the desirability of a military career where the future is evidently so uncertain. The real basic need of the Haitian Armed Forces is to eliminate from it all political activity and to make the military a rewarding and appealing career.[58]

When the 52-man U.S. Naval Mission finally got to work, it began with a typical Marine can-do attitude. But it was not long before the Marine officers found themselves faced with an impossible challenge. Not only did they confirm the utter dilapidation of the Haitian armed forces outlined in Riseley's earlier report, but they also encountered other problems. The Haitian general staff resisted the Marine program of retraining. They were adamantly opposed to Marine instructors carrying out their assignments at provincial posts for fear that Port-au-Prince would lose control of the process. Moreover, the Marine advisers suspected (correctly) that many Haitian officers resisted professionalization because it would interfere with their life's real work, which was making money from businesses, licit and illicit. Haitian officers also had difficulty in accepting advice, any advice, from foreigners, especially the feared and distrusted *blancs*. That attitude carried over to the enlisted men, who were often unpaid and therefore had no incentive to train hard.[59]

After four grueling years of attempts at reform, the United States Naval Mission withdrew. Despite its best efforts, failures were frequent and successes ephemeral. The military mission aside, the Kennedy administration at the beginning of 1962 decided Duvalier's support of the U.S. struggle against Castro's Cuba was somewhat dubious, and that the grasping dictator had pilfered much of the money that was supposed to help the country build. Heavily conditioned aid then followed, but Duvalier accused the United States of bad faith. The final straw came in the form of Duvalier himself, who saw the growing American presence as more hindrance than help to his grip on power. Indeed, the thought of hundreds of well-trained, professional army officers who had absorbed American political values was highly unappealing to him. The climax came in July 1963 after months of intense suspicion. Duvalier had suspected (rightly) that Haitian army officers were seeking his overthrow. Because most of the plotters had been close to the U.S. Naval Mission, and fueled by a story that appeared in the *Washington Star* that suggested the Marines were part of the plot, Papa Doc deduced the Marines were behind the effort. By mid-summer 1963, U.S.-Haitian relations reached rock bottom and the U.S. mission was terminated.

Even more than Washington's earlier intervention, the U.S. Naval Mission was doomed to failure from the start. In 1934 when the Marines left, Captain Williamson observed,

> Law and order had been restored, the national infrastructure had been modernized and the treasury had been replenished. . . . The fact remains that the streets of Port-au-Prince were safe, the countryside was peaceful, roads and bridges linked cities and towns, and a telephone system provided communication from one end of the country to the other. Of equal importance, customs and tax revenues were controlled to ensure they ended up in government accounts and not in the pockets of politicians.[60]

In contrast, and despite the Kennedy administration's efforts, the Haitian military was not transformed into a professional, apolitical force, which would become all too clear to a new generation of Haiti watchers when President Jean-Bertrand Aristide was overthrown by a military coup in September 1990. Nor was any other Haitian institution successfully reformed, even on a temporary basis. The Duvalier regime continued for another 15 years after the death of Papa Doc in 1971, when his son, Jean-Claude "Baby Doc" Duvalier, assumed power and ran the country just as badly.[61]

Clinton Goes to Haiti

A generation would pass before U.S. policymakers once again assumed a central position in Haiti—with equally poor results. To be sure, Haiti proved an embarrassment and provided unwanted difficulties for administrations from Kennedy's to Clinton's, but most of the administrations in between attempted to deal with discrete problems, such as illegal immigration, rather than attempt to mastermind any tectonic changes in the wrecked republic.

By the time of the Clinton administration, however, Haiti was again proving a tempting target for Washington's nation builders. Although coups had become a rare thing in Latin America and the Caribbean, and democracies were taking root everywhere in the early 1990s, Haiti's elected president Jean-Bertrand Aristide was ousted by a military coup in early 1991. Meanwhile, the Clinton administration had made the idea of "democratic enlargement" central to its foreign policy, and soon, as *Newsweek* magazine reported, Clinton's Haiti policy came to be dominated by a group of Haiti hawks,

> moralists who form a liberal web knotted together during the administration of Jimmy Carter. They all speak the same language, the Carteresque "human rights first" policy. All hated the Central America policy of the 1980s. . . . And because Clinton eventually got the Pentagon he wanted—led by technocrats with no powerful say in policy—nobody was there to counterbalance the Haiti Hawks.[62]

The approach the administration eventually took to Haiti was unique. It seemed more interested in gaining UN cover than the approval or consent of the U.S. Congress or the American people—a decision that alienated many Republicans and some Democrats and guaranteed their antagonism toward the operation. Sen. Orrin Hatch (R-Utah) captured the sentiments of many members of Congress when he said,

> We do not have any vital interest in Haiti. . . . The administration is playing a high stakes game that commits the United States to an invasion of a sovereign nation and that opens up an indefinite stay of U.S. forces on that island. There is no consensus in Congress or among the American people for intervening in Haiti, or for a prolonged occupation of that country.[63]

From the start, the Clinton administration's nation-building experiment in Haiti was a dubious undertaking. When U.S. troops serving under a UN authorization arrived in Haiti in the early morning hours of September 19, 1994, their primary mission was to restore Aristide to the National Palace and allow him to finish his term in office. But replacing an unelected junta with an elected president did not exhaust the mission given to the U.S. soldiers, advisers, and eventually multinational peacekeepers in Haiti.[64]

Well-meaning foreigners had already pushed Haiti even further backward with the blunt-force sanctions they had earlier imposed. In the four-year period between Aristide's ouster and his return, Haiti's GDP dropped perhaps another one-third, while its population continued to grow, and its arable land diminished. Foreign investors had fled to safer climes, like the Dominican Republic next door. As a result, Haiti's unemployment rate shot up to astronomical proportions. Encouraging even more corruption in Haiti may not have been the intention of those who wanted to do something about Haiti, but the effect of the sanctions on corruption was real enough. Illegal foreign trade and smuggling further enriched Haitian officials already well-versed in the arts of international commerce not approved of by the World Trade Organization. Even more destructively, inflation, especially steep increases in the price of basic commodities like food, imposed an additional harsh burden on Haiti's already impoverished population. The misery of the private sector was mirrored in the public sector, where basic tax-based services, like elementary school education and the provision of clean water, simply collapsed.[65]

The effects of the sanctions, to be sure, were disastrous, but any hope for a quick recovery after they were removed proved to be farfetched. Despite the promise of hundreds of millions of dollars in aid by a variety of donors, the restored Aristide refused to make even the most elementary economic reforms. State-owned enterprises were not privatized or even restructured, the Haitian budgetary process was never made transparent, and legal reform—the key to investor confidence—is still to be carried out. Accordingly, foreign investors were no longer enticed by the prospect of Haiti's low labor costs, but were instead frightened away by its fundamental defects.[66]

Of course, international aid workers went about cleaning up the country, repairing roads and generators, and removing trash. By October 1995, U.S. Civil Affairs soldiers had completed 332 infrastructure rebuilding projects and were continuing to work on 375 others.[67] Washington also commenced several major institution-building projects: (1) replacing Haiti's discredited military with a professional and accountable national police force, (2) establishing an honest and working judicial system, and (3) supporting a series of elections that would return control of Haiti's destiny to ordinary Haitians.

Haiti's Broken-Down Police Force

A state can either provide order or be itself a source of lawlessness. Under the Duvaliers and their creatures, the *tonton macoutes*, it was the latter. In return for administering terror for their superiors at the National Palace, the *tontons* were allowed to inflict crimes ranging from extortion to murder for personal gain. The Clinton administration had hoped that a new, smaller, more professional army of some 1,500 would assume the task of being the nation's guardian against any foreign threats while a national police force would be trained that would, for the first time in Haiti's history, play the part of the good cop. In fact, it would be President Clinton himself who would underline the critical nature of building a new security force. In remarks made in Haiti's National Palace on March 31, 1995, the president admonished some of its new members:

> Let me say to the members of the new, permanent police force who are with us today, you are the guardians of Haiti's new democracy; its future rests on your shoulders. Uphold the constitution. Respect democracy and human rights. Defend them. That is your sacred mission and your solemn obligation.[68]

Nevertheless, newly restored President Aristide objected to reviving any sort of national army and thus the first part of Washington's plan came to naught. Aristide's motive was clear enough given what he endured during his first term in office—he wanted no armed force that could possibly challenge his present and future. As for a police force, the international effort has been mighty, but results are far from satisfactory, and the question of what happens when the international assistance eventually ends leaves room for doubt about the survivability of that effort as well.[69]

The Clinton administration hoped originally that a well-trained police force of 6,500 could be put into place by mid-1996, and 9,500 to 10,000 by 2003. Six years after Washington's 1994 invasion, that hope too seems forlorn. First, the numbers. The Haitian National Police never had more than 5,000 members, and half of them are limited to patrolling in the Port-au-Prince area. Recruiting has been extremely difficult. Many of those taken from the old forces proved unacceptable and were weeded out from the permanent force. Despite the platoons of UN police trainers—many of them from Francophone nations—the training process has been slow. Moreover, by 1997, 700 new policemen had been either dismissed or suspended for either human rights violations or sheer incompetence.[70]

According to a recent report from the U.S. General Accounting Office, the situation has since worsened. For example, the total number of officers dismissed from duty has reached 1,100, leaving only 3,500–4,500 remaining on duty, and that in a country of nearly 8 million people. In contrast, El Salvador, which has severe crime problems of its own, has 19,000 internationally trained policemen in a nation with 6 million people. Meanwhile, the numbers of Haitian policemen continue to shrink because of long working hours (12 hours a day, 6 days a week), poor discipline, and better pay opportunities in the private security industry, which, ironically enough, has been burgeoning because Haiti's law enforcement system is so bad.[71]

Those shortcomings, however, are only the beginning of a long laundry list detailed by the GAO.

> On October 7, 1999, the Secretary [of State for Public Security] resigned from his position, which remains vacant, and left the country. According to U.S. officials, the Inspector General—who was conducting investigations into human rights violations, narcotrafficking, corruption, and other offenses allegedly committed by police officers—unexpectedly left the force

> in April 2000 and has not been permanently replaced. . . . Since the departure of the Inspector General, investigations of police misconduct have dramatically decreased, opening the door to increased corruption within the force.[72]

Training has been inadequate and follow-up training all but nonexistent. The Haitian police also desperately needed equipment, which was often late in coming, thanks to the cumbersome international aid bureaucracy. When it did finally arrive, proper maintenance and upkeep once again became a familiar problem. Not surprisingly, Haiti's crime rates have not fallen since the new police force was fielded. In fact, they have exploded. And that, of course, raises a far more troubling issue: What will become of the Haitian police force when foreign assistance ends for good? After the Haitian government reassumes full responsibility, a familiar pattern will likely reemerge. Police will not be paid because of either budgetary shortfalls or skimming at the top. With no pay, most policemen will return to their customary practices: extortion, theft, and involvement in narcotics trafficking.

Legal Malpractice

The police problem, however, only parallels those attached to Haiti's system of justice. "System," perhaps, is not the right word. To be sure, even an effective police force will be stymied if the courts and prisons do not function. In Haiti, they never have, except at the most primitive level. As many observers have noted, Haiti's judiciary consists largely of illiterate judges who work without even the basic tools, like copies in hand of the criminal, civil, and penal codes. Justice is delivered ad hoc when it is delivered at all. Even if most judges could read, they could not read French, which is the official language of the courts because the codes are not available in Creole, the everyday language of 85 percent of the population. As for legal record keeping, it simply does not exist.

Those shortcomings are only the tip of the iceberg of deficiencies that have traditionally plagued the Haitian justice system. As William O'Neill, an international lawyer, observed in 1997:

> Haitian justice lacks everything: financial resources, materials, competent personnel, independence, stature, and trust.

> Court facilities are a disgrace: courthouses are often indistinguishable from small shops or run-down residences in Haitian cities and towns. Judges and prosecutors, ill trained and often chosen because of their connections or willingness to comply with their benefactors' demands, have traditionally dispensed justice to the highest bidder or to the most powerful. Until mid-1995, when some training began, no judge or prosecutor in Haiti had received any specialized training. Law schools are woefully inadequate and lack such rudimentary necessities as decent classrooms and law libraries; furthermore, cronyism reigns, professors are ill trained, students are ill prepared, and passing grades are bought and sold.[73]

Nor does that exhaust O'Neill's list of Haiti's judicial problems. Since 1994, Haitian authorities have resisted the notion of training by foreigners at all. In fact, the chief justice of the Haitian Supreme Court refused a French offer to train his judges in France because he said they already knew everything that they needed to know.[74]

In the three years since O'Neill made his observations, the U.S. General Accounting Office has reported that no significant improvements have been made. But that failure is not the result of lack of efforts to help. Donor nations have pumped huge sums of money into legal reform—the United States alone has contributed $97 million. Law books have been purchased, and some prosecutors trained.[75] Overall, however, little has changed. Those in control of Haiti, it seems, do not want a viable and independent judiciary. It is no wonder, then, that the courts and prosecutors have shown little interest in solving major crimes, including violence committed against the political opposition.[76]

With legal standards so low or even nonexistent, no one should be surprised that court decisions can be purchased, and are, by the better off. The sense that anything is for sale and that strict accounting in government accounts is nonexistent has led to ongoing and widespread corruption. State-owned enterprises are routinely looted by those who are in a position to take advantage of loose budgetary oversight. Funds from foreign-aid programs that are not closely monitored simply disappear into the pockets of government ministers and their colleagues.

Democracy, Haitian-Style

At the heart of the democratic process are elections, and they, above all else, have been the center of international efforts to turn

Haiti into a modern democratic nation. Few are fully aware of the sheer enormity of that undertaking. The view in Washington was that after the Duvaliers had departed, working democratic institutions could be set up. But that view mistakenly presumed that the Duvaliers were the sum and substance of Haiti's political pathology. The Duvaliers, in fact, were only a symptom of Haiti's history. Before the election of François Duvalier in 1957, Haiti had rarely experienced the direct election of a president. Haiti's past presidents (or kings and emperors) were self-selected through the use of force and served until turned out by another office seeker. Parliaments were either self-selected or chosen largely by a tiny electorate within Port-au-Prince's mulatto elite. All of Haiti, in other words, was a rotten borough. The country thus had no experience in democratic electioneering before, during, or after the long night of the Duvaliers.[77]

Consequently, the results since the Duvaliers left the political scene fit the Haitian norm and are not an aberration. Since February 1986, no fewer than 10 elections have been held. None can be judged a success by accepted international standards. The first, in November 1987, was an outright and bloody disaster. The 1990 election, which Aristide entered at the last moment, has been judged the fairest in Haiti's history. But that is not saying much. Aristide clearly had popular support but the other candidates were inept and often obscure, and there is no evidence that the ballots were ever actually completely counted.

The other seven elections held since 1987 were variations on the two mentioned above. Turnouts tended to be as low as 5 or 6 percent. The elections were invariably punctuated with violence and irregularities leading opposition parties to drop out of the race. Notably, these problems emerged regardless of whether the elections were held under a military or a democratic government. For example, the 1995 parliamentary elections—the first under a democratic regime—were outright shambles. As Robert Pastor, an election observer, has written:

> More than 2,000 legislative and municipal officers were at stake and twenty-seven political parties competed. The elections were nothing less than an administrative disaster, with an insecure vote count. Virtually all the political parties except the Plateform Lavalas (PPL), which was associated

> with the government, condemned the election and called for its annulment even before the results were announced.[78]

Five years later, the electoral process is in no better shape. The latest rounds of parliamentary elections were held in May 2000. The balloting was delayed because the Lavalas party members in the parliament wanted their elections to coincide as closely as possible with the presidential race scheduled for late November 2000, hoping a coattail effect would propel Aristide back into the National Palace. At first, observers from the Organization of American States pronounced the elections free and fair. But that imprimatur was quickly overturned by Haitian reality. Opposition parties filed complaints about how independent observers were turned away from polling areas and how armed men stole ballot boxes. Moreover, surrounding the vote was an increasingly ugly atmosphere of violence in which at least 15 persons were killed, including a prominent opposition journalist and his wife. According to State Department officials, other opposition politicians received telephone calls complete with recorded machine-gun fire.[79]

The Provisional Electoral Council was not immune from threats either. Its headquarters suffered a grenade attack wounding six innocent bystanders just before the May election. After the vote, two council members were forced to resign, and one, Léon Manus, fled to the United States in fear for his life after he refused to confirm what the government wanted in election results.

The legitimacy of the elections became more serious when it became clear that the declared winners of eight senate contests had not actually received the required 50 percent of the vote in the first round of voting. The Organization of American States then called for a recount, a move supported by Washington. But that effort was to no avail. The government, through Aristide's Lavalas party, after purging the two council members got the rump Provisional Election Council to ratify the original results and announce there would not be a recount. Lavalas assumed an overwhelming majority within both chambers of parliament.[80]

Thus, after years of effort and millions of U.S. taxpayer dollars, elections in Haiti were no more honest, fair, and free than they were in the past. Clinton administration officials threatened to impose economic sanctions once again if Haiti did not mend its undemocratic ways. As Luis Lauredo, U.S. ambassador to the Organization of American States, made clear, "In the absence of meaningful change, the United States will not support the presidential and legislative elections of November 26, financially or through observer missions." It was ironic, however, that the threat was aimed at the very people the Clinton administration helped restore to power in September 1994.[81]

Despite Washington's threats, the Haitian government went ahead with presidential elections on November 26, 2000. Aristide was voted back into the National Palace, but the election was marred by voter apathy and a broad-based boycott. Voter turnout was as low as 10 percent in some areas, and all of Haiti's major opposition political parties refused to participate in the election because the parliamentary elections held six months earlier had been rigged in favor of Aristide's party.[82] What is more, those small-party candidates who did choose to run against Aristide did not actually campaign for fear of reprisals. As in previous elections, there were also widespread reports of preelection violence and voting irregularities, such as some polling stations closing early while others closed late, voters voting where they were not registered, and polling stations running out of ballots.[83]

Plowing the Sea

In the summer of 2000, Luigi Einaudi, a seasoned diplomat and now assistant secretary general of the Organization of American States, observed, "With Haiti, the international community feels as if it has plowed the sea and invested uselessly."[84] After the island nation's questionable presidential elections in November, one U.S. official went further and explained: "Haiti is considered a failure. . . . There's a sort of psychology at work that we were never able to crack. . . . The problem with Haiti is they want us to fix it, and that's not the way you get things fixed."[85]

In sharp contrast, President Clinton and his top officials had been insisting that Haiti was an American foreign policy success.[86] But if Haiti should teach Washington anything at all it is that an ambitious nation-building program alone is not a sufficient condition to transform a country into a self-sustaining, democratic member of the family of nations. Other domestic variables can cancel out the effort, rendering it futile. Haiti simply is not ripe for nation building. It does not possess the human and physical capital or the natural resources to rise above extreme poverty. Nor does it have the political stability or legal institutions to inspire investor confidence, foreign or domestic. Few, if any, in the Haitian government favor a working market economy or even understand what the term means, and no political culture prevails with widespread acceptance of the habits, beliefs, and values that sustain democracy or democratic institutions. "There is always a limit," admitted a State Department spokesperson referring to Haiti in the final weeks of the Clinton presidency. "You can't impose democracy."[87]

4. Bosnia: The Making of a Potemkin State

The General Framework Agreement for Peace in Bosnia-Herzegovina, drafted at Wright-Patterson Air Force Base in Dayton, Ohio, in November 1995 and formally signed in Paris on December 14, 1995, halted the bloodiest armed conflict in Europe since World War II.[1] Widely referred to simply as the Dayton Agreement, the document's goal was to build a unitary, multiethnic Bosnian state in the wake of three and a half years of ethnic warfare.

Half a decade later, that goal is no more realistic than it was the day the war ended. Today, Bosnia is essentially divided into three mono-ethnic regions with three separate militaries. The Bosnian national government exists mostly on paper, and the vast majority of Bosnia's Muslims, Serbs, and Croats still will not vote for each other's political candidates. Ethnic reintegration is anemic, and nationalist political parties continue to dominate the political arena.[2] Moreover, international reconstruction aid and domestic institutions have been plagued by corruption, and the West has begun resorting to increasingly high-handed and illiberal measures to force Bosnia's three rival ethnic groups to live under the fiction of a single government.

That sorry state of affairs should have been expected. According to University of Chicago political scientist John Mearsheimer, "History records no instance where ethnic groups have agreed to share power in a democracy after a large-scale civil war. . . . The democratic power-sharing that Dayton envisions has no precedent."[3]

It would be a mistake, however, to suggest that the Dayton Agreement is without any successes. The fighting *has* stopped, and so far more than 3,600 pieces of heavy weaponry have been removed under the terms of the Agreement on Armaments Control. Moreover, Bosnia has largely met the requirements of the Agreement on Conventional Armaments, which provides for a 2:1 allocation of weapons

Table 4.1
DIVISION OF ARMAMENTS IN BOSNIA

Type of Armament	Muslims and Croats	Serbs
Tanks	273	137
Airplanes	41	21
Helicopters	14	7
Armored Vehicles	227	113
Artillery (> 75mm)	1,000	500
Total	1,555	778

SOURCE: Miroslav Lazanski, "Zbogom Oruzje," *NIN*, June 21, 1996, p. 22.

between the Muslims and Croats on one hand and the Serbs on the other (Table 4.1).[4]

But those few successes reveal the Dayton Agreement for what it really is: a complicated cease-fire, not a durable solution to Bosnia's problems. The country is still deeply fractured, officially divided into two semiautonomous "entities" separated by the Inter-Entity Boundary Line. One entity, the Muslim-Croat Federation, is made up of two rival enclaves that maintain a tense coexistence with each other. The other entity, the Republika Srpska, is almost entirely populated by Serbs. What is less obvious about the Dayton Agreement, however, is that it is part of the problem, yielding results that weigh against a self-sustaining peace and thus the eventual withdrawal of U.S. troops.

To the very end, however, nation builders in the Clinton administration continued to embrace the idea that good intentions plus the deliberate application of American political, economic, and military power could transform Bosnia. Indeed, four and a half years after NATO arrived in Bosnia, Secretary of State Madeleine Albright insisted that the Dayton Agreement was still a workable proposition. "Our goal in Bosnia remains a unified, multiethnic state," she told a May 24, 2000, gathering of the North Atlantic Council. "The trends are positive. . . . [and] NATO's commitment remains strong."[5]

The Road to Dayton

Bosnia was one of the six republics making up the Socialist Federal Republic of Yugoslavia, which began disintegrating in summer 1991 when the republics of Slovenia and Croatia declared their independence. Germany then paved the way for tragedy in Bosnia by officially recognizing the independence of the two breakaway republics and pressuring the other members of the European Union to do the same. As Misha Glenny explains in *The Fall of Yugoslavia,*

> The death sentence for Bosnia-Herzegovina was passed in the middle of December 1991 when Germany announced that it would recognize Slovenia and Croatia unconditionally on 15 January 1992. So distressed was [Bosnian President] Alija Izetbegovic by this news that he traveled to Bonn in a vain effort to persuade [German Chancellor Helmut] Kohl and [German Foreign Minister Hans-Dietrich] Genscher not to go ahead with the move. Izetbegovic understood full well that recognition would strip Bosnia of the constitutional protection it still enjoyed from the territorial claims of the two regional imperia, Serbia and Croatia.[6]

Germany thought it was helping matters and expected that its recognition would stem the tide of war. Instead, it exacerbated a volatile situation in Bosnia, which had large minority populations of Croats and Serbs. Indeed, when Bosnia's government declared independence from Yugoslavia in April 1992, both Serbs and Croats found themselves living adjacent to Serbia and Croatia, respectively, but governed by a Muslim-led government. War broke out soon after and was fought among Bosnia's three major ethno-religious groups: Roman Catholic Croats, who made up 17 percent of the population; Eastern Orthodox Serbs, who made up 31 percent of the population; and Muslim Slavs, or Bosniaks, who made up 44 percent of the population. The Croat and Serb factions fought to break away from Bosnia and merge their territories with those of Croatia and Serbia, respectively. Bosnia's Muslims, on the other hand, fought to create a single Bosnian state where they would be the largest ethnic group.

Although some of the most ferocious fighting during the war was between the Muslim and Croat factions in 1993 and 1994, the war between them formally ended with the signing of the U.S.-engineered Washington Agreements in August 1994, which created the precarious Muslim-Croat Federation of Bosnia. Thereafter, both Muslims and Croats concentrated their firepower on the Serbs.

In October 1995, following U.S.-NATO bombing the month before, U.S.-led negotiations produced a cease-fire between the warring Muslim-Croat and Serb armies. Several weeks later, a peace agreement was hammered out in Dayton. The resulting peace plan formally ended the war and instituted a new national constitution for Bosnia. According to that constitution, Bosnia is one country with two entities and three co-presidents—one Serb, one Croat, and one Muslim. As part of the settlement, it was also agreed that NATO would deploy 60,000 ground troops in Bosnia to implement the military aspects of the agreement, such as segregating the warring factions and demilitarizing a buffer zone four kilometers wide between them. Twenty thousand of NATO's troops would be American.

Bait and Switch in Bosnia

In his November 1995 television address making the case for sending U.S. troops to Bosnia, President Bill Clinton assured the American public that the operation he was proposing had a "clear, limited, and achievable" mission and that the total deployment "should and will take about one year."[7] The president also claimed, "If we leave after a year, and they [the Bosnians] decide they don't like the benefits of peace and they're going to start fighting again, that does not mean NATO failed. It means we gave them a chance to make their peace and they blew it."[8] Deputy Secretary of State Strobe Talbott soon after added, "There will be no 'mission creep'—from purely military tasks into 'nation building'" in Bosnia.[9]

Throughout 1996, the Clinton administration continued to lead American voters to believe the one-year deadline was still intact. Even 10 months into the deployment, State Department spokesperson Nicholas Burns adamantly denied there were any plans not to withdraw American troops from Bosnia on time.[10] As far as Americans were concerned on the eve of the presidential election, Bosnia was a nonissue. Within two weeks of winning reelection, however, the president suddenly announced a change in his Bosnia plan. U.S. troops numbering 8,500 would stay until June 30, 1998, another 18 months. Clinton said the policy shift was necessary to overcome an honest error on his part. "Quite frankly," he explained, "rebuilding the fabric of Bosnia's economic and political life is taking longer than anticipated."[11]

Benchmarks and Mission Creep

In December 1997, one year into his 18-month extension, Clinton traveled to Bosnia to announce that U.S. troops would not, in fact, be coming home by his second exit date. But instead of setting a third exit date, the president said certain criteria or "benchmarks" would have to be met in Bosnia before U.S. soldiers could hope to return home. The first benchmark was that multiethnic political institutions would have to be created that were strong enough "to be self-sustaining after the military operation." Clinton also stated that an independent judiciary must be created and that the political parties must give up control of the state media, which he called "instruments of hate and venom."[12]

Sen. Robert C. Byrd (D-W.Va.) later noted that requiring that such benchmarks be met before U.S. troops could be withdrawn "reads more like a nation-building strategy," not the purely military tasks the Clinton administration originally outlined in 1995. In fact, claimed Byrd, the idea that Bosnia must first have multiethnic political institutions, an independent judiciary, and a free press before U.S. troops can exit is simply "a formula requiring the completion of a new integrated democratic state. That is what nation building is. I didn't buy on to that. The U.S. Senate has not bought on to that."[13]

Responding to questions about the administration's decision to make the U.S. troop commitment in Bosnia open-ended, a senior Clinton administration official stated: it is "part of our strategy to convince the opponents [of the Dayton Agreement] they cannot wait us out. . . . If they believe they can outlast the international community, then they will be hard to move."[14] Secretary of State Albright later defended the president's decision: "We set the [original one year] deadline because we believed it. We didn't set the deadline just to fool the American people. That's the last thing we would do."[15] According to the memoirs of the chief U.S. negotiator at Dayton, Richard Holbrooke, however, it was obvious from the beginning that setting a deadline for U.S. troop involvement would give the Dayton Agreement's opponents in Bosnia the impression that they could "outwait" NATO. "Everyone closely associated with implementation knew this from the outset," explains Holbrooke.[16]

Outside the administration, advocates of the Bosnia intervention were largely in favor of nation building.[17] Others supported the idea of nation building, but did not think the implementation of the

Dayton Agreement went far enough. Writing in the *Washington Quarterly*, for example, journalist Charles Lane said he considered the West's implementation of the Dayton Agreement "insufficiently imperial" for that purpose.[18] Similarly, in the journal *International Security*, researcher Jane Sharp claimed that the West's "unwillingness" to deal forcefully with the Bosnians would greatly hamper nation building.[19] Several critics, however, argued that practical limitations meant adhering to the Dayton Agreement was unlikely to produce a durable peace and some form of partition of Bosnia should be considered.[20] Writing in *Survival*, the quarterly journal of the London-based International Institute for Strategic Studies, for example, Dartmouth College political scientist Robert Pape explained,

> [It has been said that] Dayton is failing because it allows too much Serb independence and because the West has not tried hard enough to obtain the real agreement of the local parties and to enforce its integration provisions. The real problem is the opposite: none of the parties will accept the multiethnic Bosnia envisioned by Dayton and nor can they be made to do so. . . . Partition is Bosnia's future and no Western policy can avoid it. Rather than allow ethnic boundaries to be written in blood after [NATO] leaves, the West should help to manage a peaceful partition while it still has troops on the ground.[21]

An Open-Ended Commitment

Today, more than five years after the Dayton Agreement was signed, the United States has an expensive, open-ended nation-building commitment in Bosnia. There are 4,400 U.S. combat troops still in Bosnia trying to implement the Dayton Agreement, plus more than 400 U.S. support personnel in Croatia, Hungary, and Italy.[22] The General Accounting Office says that Washington has spent approximately $11.8 billion on the operation so far: $9.9 billion for the military aspects and $1.9 billion for the nonmilitary aspects (Table 4.2).

According to a high-ranking Western official involved in overseeing the implementation of the Dayton Agreement, NATO troops will have to stay in Bosnia another 10 years.[23] A senior U.S. official thinks it may take longer. "I'm sure that in 20 years, there will be a multiethnic state [like that called for in the Dayton Agreement, but the] lesson of the last two years is that you cannot force these

Table 4.2
ESTIMATED U.S. COSTS FOR MILITARY AND NONMILITARY ASPECTS OF BOSNIA PEACE OPERATION, FISCAL YEARS 1996–2000
(Dollars in millions)

Fiscal Year	1996	1997	1998	1999	2000	Total
Military Aspects	$2,520	$2,283	$1,963	$1,538	$1,603	$9,907
Nonmilitary Aspects	560	500	301	295	211	1,867
Total	$3,080	$2,783	$2,264	$2,833	$1,814	$11,774

SOURCE: United States General Accounting Office, *Balkans Security: Current and Projected Factors Affecting Regional Stability* (Washington, D.C., April 2000), p. 86.

things. They will just take time."[24] When President Clinton visited Bosnia in December 1997, he asked a group of young Bosnians at a Sarajevo café, "What's the most important thing the United States can do?" "Stay!" cried out a young woman. Then a man added, "The next 50 years, please."[25]

The prospect for political and ethnic reintegration is not promising.[26] For starters, Bosnians have no history of independence or sense of shared national identity.[27] Indeed, over the course of the past five centuries Bosnia was, in turn, part of the Ottoman Empire, the Austro-Hungarian Empire, a monarchist Yugoslavia, and a communist Yugoslavia. Moreover, the current international boundaries of the Bosnian state have a flimsy historical legitimacy. They were purely artificial creations, imposed by Yugoslavia's leader, Josip Broz Tito, shortly after he consolidated his power at the end of World War II. The boundaries were meant to be internal lines of political and administrative demarcation within Yugoslavia, not boundaries that separated nations. They were also a deliberate exercise in political gerrymandering to dilute Serb political influence inside Yugoslavia by minimizing Serbia's size and placing large minorities of Serbs in other political jurisdictions.

Even the core of Bosnia's Muslim elite, who have the most to gain from the implementation of the Dayton Agreement, have not fully embraced the West's vision that multiethnic civil society should prevail over nationalist ideologies in Bosnia. As the Muslim representative to Bosnia's three-way presidency, Alija Izetbegovic, told the second congress of his Party of Democratic Action in 1997, "There is no turning back to a conflict-free and non-national Bosnia. The Bosniak [Muslim] people, now that it has become aware of itself . . . will never again give up its Bosniak identity as a nation, and Islam as its spiritual component."[28] Izetbegovic added that the best to be hoped for in Bosnia is to "harmonize the *unalterable fate of nationality*. . . . We will be satisfied if we have Croats in Bosnia instead of Greater Croats, and normal Serbs instead of Greater Serbs."[29] Of course, many Croats and Serbs interpret those words as an argument for their subjugation within Bosnia.

In election after election, moreover, Bosnia's Muslim, Serb, and Croat populations have shown themselves unwilling to break with their nationalist political parties, and 85 percent of Bosnians polled say they will not vote for candidates from another ethnic group.[30] Meanwhile, elected Bosnian officials have obstructed everything from designing a national flag and setting up joint institutions to reforming the economy and privatizing state-owned enterprises. On the local level, multiethnic administration in most Bosnian municipalities is a sham. Ethnic minority officials are typically ignored and relegated to the political sidelines. Many have been the targets of death threats and choose to reside in municipalities other than those where they serve so that they can live safely among their own ethnic group.

What is more, during the past five years there has been a constant din of ethnic violence and intimidation throughout Bosnia, including bomb attacks and shootings.[31] The most severe ethnic violence has occurred in and around the divided city of Mostar, where Muslims and Croats still live separately.[32] Mostar Croats continue to use Croatian money—the kuna—rather than the new Bosnian currency. Their mobile phones log on to the network run by the Croatian telecommunications utility, and mail is still likely to bear a stamp of "Herceg-Bosna," the Bosnian Croat zone created during the war.[33] The city is so divided, says Ferid Pasovic, general manager of Sarajevska Brewery, that "We sell in [Muslim] east Mostar, but it's easier to sell our beer in Libya than in [Croat] west Mostar."[34] Since 1998, more than 70 incidents in the area have been aimed at preventing Muslims from returning to the towns and villages surrounding Mostar, including an incident in which a group of 25 Muslims trying to return to their homes in Tasovcici was attacked by an angry crowd of Croat nationalists.[35] During the clash five explosions occurred,

Table 4.3
ESTIMATED TOTAL RETURNS, 1996–2000

Returnees	1996	1997	1998	1999	2000	Total
Refugees	80,114	111,650	106,000	28,180	14,046	339,990
Displaced Persons	102,913	53,160	19,440	29,935	30,281	235,729
Total	183,027	164,810	125,440	58,115	44,327	575,719

SOURCE: United Nations High Commissioner for Refugees, "Returns Summary to Bosnia and Herzegovina from 01/01/96 to 31/01/01," http://www.unhcr.ba/Operations/Statistical %20package/T5-RET01.PDF [accessed March 30, 2001].

two houses were set afire, and a grenade killed one Muslim and injured five others, including two Croat policemen.[36]

Not surprisingly, postwar ethnic reintegration in Bosnia has been less than encouraging. There were 2.3 million refugees and internally displaced persons when the Dayton Agreement was signed in December 1995.[37] By January 2001, only 235,729 internally displaced persons had returned to their prewar homes and only 339,990 refugees had returned to Bosnia from other countries (Table 4.3). What is important to note, however, is that most of those displaced persons and returning refugees resettled in areas where they would be in the ethnic majority. Only about 160,000 had actually returned to areas where they would be in the ethnic minority.[38] Over the same time period, more than 80,000 Bosnians moved from areas where they were in the ethnic minority to areas where they would be in the ethnic majority.[39] That means that only 80,000 more Bosnians today are living as ethnic minorities as when the war ended nearly five years ago. Those figures also illustrate that minority returns really account for only a small fraction of the total number of people actually uprooted by the war. Moreover, many who have returned across ethnic lines have ventured only a few kilometers from the Inter-Entity Boundary Line.[40] Even more telling, nearly 30 percent of the Croats who lived in Bosnia when the war ended have since left the country.[41] The remaining Croats now form only nine percent of Bosnia's population, or about half their prewar numbers.[42]

Such facts do not point toward the reintegrated Bosnia that the Dayton Agreement envisions, but toward ethnic separation. As

Kevin Mannion, former field officer of the UN's International Management Group in Bosnia, explained more than four years ago: "Returns of refugees are not going to happen, so why set impossible goals? We're trying to recreate something here that never really existed and most people never really wanted."[43] More recently, in an issue of *Foreign Affairs*, Harvard University professor of international affairs Stephen M. Walt pointedly asserted that "NATO has been unable to craft a workable formula that would secure peace and permit its forces to withdraw," and "by rejecting the possibility of ethnic partition and insisting that the long-term goal be a democratic and multiethnic Bosnia, the United States has committed outside forces to Bosnia for years to come."[44]

Still, some analysts cling to the idea that the West is successfully undoing the consequences of the Bosnian war. "Movement across the 'inter-entity boundary' . . . has never been so free," says one observer.[45] But the fact of the matter is that most of the people who are now crossing ethnic lines are either Muslims returning to the Brcko area, which is a special NATO-occupied municipality in eastern Bosnia that is part of neither the Muslim-Croat Federation nor the Republika Srpska; Serbs and Croats returning to Sarajevo, which has always been the most cosmopolitan city in Bosnia and, not coincidentally, where they have the best chance of finding employment because most international and aid organizations are based there; and refugees returning to designer villages, which are being built from the ground up by the West to increase the official numbers of "minority returns." What is more, most of the minority returns to the more rural areas of Bosnia are tolerated by the local majority only because the returnees tend to be elderly and thus pose no long-term demographic threat; that is, they are beyond child-bearing years and not expected to live much longer anyway.[46] All the supposed progress in returns, therefore, belies the fact that Bosnia's rival ethnic groups still largely do not want to live with each other. In the Brcko-area village of Velika, for example, Muslim refugees returned only because NATO troops are there. When asked by an American reporter if they thought civil war would resume if the troops left, their answer was bluntly matter-of-fact. They said, "Of course."[47] Their response raises the chilling question: Is the West actually building a nation in Bosnia or is it re-creating the conditions for another round of ethnic cleansing after the international aid money dries up and Western peacekeepers depart?

Washington Brings Democracy to Bosnia

Despite overwhelming evidence of hardened animosity and entrenched ethnic separation, Washington has resorted to increasingly high-handed and undemocratic measures to force Bosnia's Muslims, Serbs, and Croats to live under the fiction of one government. "Our job," summarizes America's top nation builder in Bosnia, Jacques Klein, "is to turn a province into a country—sometimes, whether the people like it or not."[48] Similarly, in the Muslim-Croat Federation, the lack of cooperation between Muslims and Croats drew the following response from another high-ranking Western official: "I don't care. I am simply not interested in who does not want the Federation: this is a concept we will implement. . . . We dictate what will be done."[49]

Today, thousands of aid workers, soldiers, and international diplomats run Bosnia as a virtual protectorate. According to the Soros Foundation's Sarajevo office, there are about 18,000 civilian nation builders in Bosnia.[50] Moreover, there are 20,000 troops from around the globe. Together, this legion of foreigners oversees reconstruction, provides security, and decides on everything from what churches may be constructed to what Bosnia's passports should look like.

High-Handed High Representative

With a staff of more than 300 specialists at his disposal, the top nation builder in Bosnia is Austrian diplomat Wolfgang Petritsch.[51] Known as the High Representative, Petritsch is the international official in charge of implementing the Dayton Agreement for the Peace Implementation Council—the multinational body overseeing the peace plan.[52] In December 1997, the Peace Implementation Council met in Bonn, Germany, and granted the Office of the High Representative a broad mandate to make decisions for Bosnian officials if they missed any Western-imposed deadlines. The Peace Implementation Council also gave the Office of High Representative the power to dismiss elected Bosnian officials who resist the West's efforts at nation building.

According to Spanish diplomat Carlos Westendorp, who was the High Representative at the time, his office did not need the Peace Implementation Council's approval to begin making decisions for the Bosnian people or dismissing elected officials. In fact, the month before the Peace Implementation Council meeting in Bonn, Westendorp told the Bosnian newspaper *Slobodna Bosna*,

> You see, if you read Dayton very carefully ... Annex 10 gives me the possibility to interpret my own authorities and powers. Therefore I do not need anything new, in the legal sense.... If they want to give this to me in writing at the Bonn conference it would be the best, and if not, I am going to do it anyway.

Westendorp went on to assert, if Bosnia's elected officials cannot

> agree about some decision, for example the passports, the license plates, the flag ... I will stop this process of infinite discussions. In the future, it will look like this: I will give them ... a term to bring a certain decision, that is to agree about some decision. If they do not, I will tell them not to worry, that I will decide for them.[53]

When asked how Bosnia's elected officials might react to his decrees, Westendorp told the paper, if they "show resistance towards the implementation of these decisions, and if they block Dayton systematically, I will ask for the resignation of those who are not cooperative." More bluntly, in a December 1997 interview with the Belgrade daily *Nasa Borba*, he explained to Bosnian officials, "So, if you do not agree, do not worry: I will do it for you. If you don't agree systematically, worry not again: I will liberate you from this duty."[54]

Undemocratic Measures

After the Peace Implementation Council meeting in Bonn concluded, Westendorp returned to Bosnia and began to rule by fiat. In 1998, when Bosnian authorities could not agree among themselves, Westendorp imposed a national flag, the music for a national anthem, a national currency design, and common automobile license plates.[55] He also exercised his power to dismiss elected Bosnian officials, removing Dragan Cavic, the number-two man in the hard-line Serbian Democratic Party (SDS), from his Republika Srpska assembly seat for making inflammatory statements about the crisis in Kosovo.[56] Westendorp also sacked Mehmed Alagic, the Muslim mayor of the western town of Sanski Most, and Drago Tokmacija, the acting president of the Croatian Democratic Union.[57] By August

1999, Westendorp had removed 13 Bosnian officials from power and imposed 46 different laws and executive orders.[58]

Westendorp's dominion over Bosnian politics did not end there. According to the *Economist*, "Westendorp's power to meddle politically would make a coup-rigging CIA operative envious."[59] Indeed, the magazine reported that the election of Milorad Dodik to the prime ministership of the Republika Srpska "was virtually engineered by [Westendorp's] office, which had a whip on the floor of the Serb parliament when it happened."[60] Moreover, Westendorp's staff directly participated in securing the outcome it wanted. As columnist Michael Kelly later recounted in the *Washington Post*,

> [Momcilo] Krajisnik's hard-line SDS and their allies, who control 39 of 83 seats, and the speaker's chair, had adjourned parliament late Saturday night and left the building in the hands of Dodik and 41 other . . . moderates. This left the moderates one vote shy of a majority. The missing vote was held by a member who had left early to drive to Zagreb. . . . When [Westendorp's deputy] heard about Dodik's situation, he requested NATO troops to intercept the missing delegate on the road and return him to the parliament. Now holding a one-vote majority, Dodik's supporters reconvened the parliament and voted in a new government while Krajisnik's forces slept.[61]

In August 1999, Austrian diplomat Wolfgang Petritsch replaced Carlos Westendorp as the High Representative for Bosnia. In his last speech before turning over the reins of office, Westendorp offered Petritsch some insight into the nature of nation building in Bosnia.

> My successor Wolfgang Petritsch, to whom I wish all success, has said that much can be achieved by a kind word. With this I agree, but would wish to quote from [a] famous historical figure, who said not just that much could be achieved with a kind word, but a kind word and a gun. This figure was Al Capone. Joke!!! I've been here too long. . . . I actually prefer Teddy Roosevelt's "Walk softly and carry a big stick." The gun or the stick in this context is the continuing presence of [NATO's Bosnia] Stabilization Force and the international community.[62]

By November, Petritsch used his "stick" and fired 22 elected Bosnian officials, including two leading figures in the principal Croat and Muslim parties. Alexandra Stiglmayer, a spokesperson for Petritsch, told a news conference, "The dismissed officials are not the officials that Bosnia needs."[63] Petritsch himself told Bosnian voters the removed officials "had blocked your road leading to a better future."[64] To protect them from being tempted to vote the wrong way again, he added that he would ban the removed officials from running for political office in the future. Petritsch assured his skeptics that Bosnians "don't believe in themselves," they "want me to do their job for them."[65] On September 8, 2000, he sacked another 15 public officials.[66]

In a further move, Petritsch placed a new draft election law before Bosnia's national parliament. Among other provisions, the law would require political candidates in the future to petition for nomination signatures outside the area where they are running for office. In other words, a party that draws support from a specific ethnic group will not even be able to appear on the ballot. In typical fashion, Petritsch indicated that he may simply impose the law if Bosnia's rival groups do not enact it.[67]

The imperious actions of Petritsch and Westendorp have caused many Western observers to express concerns. Some question the correctness of the methods used. "It troubles me," concedes one Western official. "I mean, here we are with [thousands of] foreign soldiers demanding that a country do what we want."[68] Still others worry that the High Representative's power does not always bring competence. In 1998, for instance, thousands of passports approved by High Representative Westendorp had to be destroyed after a glaring grammatical error was discovered in the Serbo-Croatian case endings.[69] Another concern is that the High Representative's power seems to know no limits. As one top aide has admitted, "We do not know what we can't do."[70]

Political Engineering

In addition to the High Representative, other Western authorities have used questionable tactics with regard to the democratic process in Bosnia. The extent of that activity first became evident with the September 1997 municipal elections. According to the *New York Times*,

> In many towns foreign officials disregarded the election results somewhat and ordered that the minority groups have

> enough seats on the local council to feel secure that the government would not abuse them. . . . Distributing power this way runs counter to the Bosnian political philosophy of winner take all. . . . It also, foreign officials concede, violates Bosnian law. But the 1995 Dayton Peace Agreement supercedes all Bosnian laws and increasingly Western governments are interpreting that agreement to impose their views of how the country should be run.[71]

Specifically, in the towns of Vares, Novi Travnik, Kresovo, Gornji Vakuf, Zepce, Foca, Prozor-Rama, Srebrenica, and Stolac, the Organization for Security and Cooperation in Europe chose the mayors itself and disregarded the local election results to create city councils with more ethnic diversity.[72] In Sarajevo, Western authorities decided that although the Muslim Party for Democratic Action won 70 percent of the city council seats, the mayor should be a Croat and a member of the Social Democratic Party.[73]

Western authorities have shown contempt for the democratic process in Bosnia in other ways as well. When Republika Srpska president Biljana Plavsic broke with the hard-line SDS in 1997 and espoused a moderately pro-Dayton line, Western officials openly favored her political ambitions. When she dissolved the parliament and called for new elections, the Republika Srpska's constitutional court ruled her actions illegal. Western authorities simply overruled the court's decision and began to organize elections anyway. When the parliament backed the court's decision and declared that Plavsic's dissolution of the parliament was illegal, Western officials ignored that as well.[74] U.S. State Department spokesperson James Rubin claimed that "challenges to [Plavsic's] actions are not legally valid," and that Serbs who fail to comply "are too stupid to realize that . . . a failure to follow through on the international community's demands will only make their people suffer."[75]

Armed NATO forces, backed by Apache helicopter gunships, then helped Plavsic purge policemen loyal to the hard-line SDS from stations in and around her stronghold of Banja Luka in northwest Bosnia. A short time later, NATO forces seized four important television transmitters controlled by the SDS after their operators refused to stop airing anti-Plavsic propaganda and criticizing the international organizations involved in implementing the Dayton Agreement. By December 1997, the Clinton administration had initiated an $88 million loan package aimed directly at strengthening Plavsic's support.[76] "It is crucial that the people who support Plavsic see there are benefits from doing so. This money is very carefully targeted; these are her towns," explained one senior administration official.[77] Other kinds of U.S. support were given to Plavsic as well, and tens of millions of additional dollars came in from European sources. Correspondent Philip Smucker described the nature and extent of the support in the pages of the *Washington Times*:

> Mrs. Plavsic's party was inundated with Western help, both direct and indirect. Funding came from the Organization for Security and Cooperation in Europe, the U.S. government, and the European Union to provide jobs and infrastructure. . . . NATO's Stabilization Force also provided satellite links for a pro-Plavsic TV station and beamed television pictures from a special U.S. airplane.[78]

As the September 1998 elections approached, however, Plavsic faced a tough reelection challenge from hard-line Serbian Radical Party (SRS) candidate Nikola Poplasen. Secretary of State Albright traveled to Bosnia two weeks before the election to try to buy more support for Plavsic.[79] Highlighting the economic benefits Bosnian Serbs would receive if they voted the way Washington wanted, Albright explained that the election offers a "clear, consequential choice," in which Bosnian Serbs "can decide whether this country will be a country that prospers from trade and investment or a country that stagnates in isolation."[80]

Signs of a Backlash

International officials began to panic when it became clear that Plavsic would be defeated by Poplasen and that hard-liners had won many other races. "It does not look good. . . . This is not what the international community wants," exclaimed one Western official.[81] Following the close of polling, the Organization for Security and Cooperation in Europe, the international body that supervised the elections in Bosnia, abruptly postponed releasing early results, prompting allegations by Serbs of Western vote tampering.[82] The OSCE also disqualified nine Poplasen allies running for either the Bosnian national parliament or the Republika Srpska assembly for violating election rules by appearing in television interviews over the election weekend.[83]

What is worse, Western officials began discussing the option of disregarding the election results altogether. Speaking anonymously, one Western diplomat said that extreme measures were a possibility. Specifically, he suggested that High Representative Westendorp might turn Bosnia into an outright protectorate.[84] Another plan considered would have divided the Republika Srpska into five cantons, thereby salvaging a political stronghold for Plavsic.[85] Although neither plan was adopted, Plavsic's allies still hoped that the West would do something to return them to power. Prime Minister Milorad Dodik, for example, noted that under the constitution, Poplasen would have two attempts to form a coalition government in the Republika Srpska assembly. If he failed, fresh elections will have to be held. "I expect a parliamentary crisis here and hope for more support from the U.S.," said Dodik.[86] On March 5, 1999, Poplasen was removed from power by High Representative Westendorp for "ignoring the will of the people."[87]

The overall failure of Washington's votes-for-dollars scheme, however, was not surprising. Indeed, toward the end of her campaign Plavsic complained that hard-liners were naturally exploiting Serb fears of foreign manipulation, "blam[ing] us for too much cooperation" with Washington.[88] Washington tried to put its best spin on Plavsic's defeat, claiming that the election produced a "mixed bag" because Bosnian Serb nationalist Momcilo Krajisnik was not reelected to Bosnia's collective presidency. U.S. special envoy Robert Gelbard, for example, claimed that "movement among the Bosnian Serbs was totally in favor of those who support implementation of the Dayton Agreement and against the hard-liners, including the really important victory of [Socialist Party of Republika Srpska leader] Zivko Radisic over Momcilo Krajisnik."[89]

But Gelbard's analysis was either strangely ill-informed or boldly misleading; it ignored the fact that Krajisnik's defeat was not a repudiation of his nationalist politics by Bosnian Serb voters, but a reaction to his ties to organized crime and possible involvement in the murder of a senior Serb police chief.[90] Gelbard also ignored the fact that Krajisnik would not have been defeated without the 200,000 or so votes his competitors received from Muslim refugees living outside the Republika Srpska. That practice of packing the voter registration rolls with voters who live elsewhere has been one of the continuing ways the West has tried to manage the outcomes of

Bosnia's elections. Indeed, instead of requiring voters to register where they currently live, the OSCE has strongly encouraged voters to register where they lived before the war. A sizable minority of Bosnian voters, and virtually all those who have left the country, have done just that. The result is vote dilution, especially by those now living abroad who have no intention of ever returning to Bosnia.

The Poplasen affair, however, was far from over. Though he was removed from the Republika Srpska presidency by High Representative Westendorp, Poplasen still served in the leadership of his political party, the SRS. On October 5, 1999, Westendorp and the OSCE sent a joint letter to the SRS that demanded Poplasen and two others be removed from party leadership positions or the SRS would be prohibited from fielding candidates in the next round of elections.[91] The SRS refused to comply and it was subsequently banned altogether from participating in the April 2000 municipal elections.[92] That unprecedented move clearly demonstrated the extent to which the High Representative's power to control Bosnian politics had grown. The SRS may have been an ardently pro-nationalist party, but it was not an insignificant political actor without popular support. It had won the previous presidential election in the Republika Srpska and held 13 percent of the seats in the Republika Srpska Assembly.[93]

Nationalists Continue to Dominate

Despite the disqualification of the SRS, the April 2000 municipal elections reconfirmed the nationalists' grip on power. In the Republika Srpska, the nationalist SDS took all but a handful of municipalities, and in Croat-controlled regions, the ruling Croatian Democratic Union (HDZ) captured every Croat-dominated municipality. In Muslim-controlled areas like Tuzla the nationalist Party for Democratic Action (SDA) lost some ground to the opposition Social Democrats, but that movement was not necessarily indicative of a backlash against Muslim nationalism. Instead, it was a backlash against *corrupt* Muslim nationalism. As the *Christian Science Monitor* rightly reported,

> A raft of ugly corruption scandals involving top officials undoubtedly hurt the ruling Muslim party [SDA], which had dominated not only political life but also the economy, the civil service, and the media in Bosnian Muslim-populated areas. Recently, the Tuzla canton's former prime minister

> [an SDA member], as well as its top justice and health officials [also SDA members], received prison sentences for pocketing state funds. Fraud cases are under way against dozens of others [in the SDA].[94]

In the face of such contrary evidence, High Representative Petritsch still managed to claim, "All the signs are that the people of Bosnia and Herzegovina are slowly turning away from the old wartime political agendas, which were determined by ethnicity, and towards those political parties that have taken up issues of everyday concern to the country's citizens."[95]

Bosnia's November 2000 national elections struck a further blow to the West's self-delusion that the fractured country was progressing toward a self-sustaining peace. The nationalist SDS retained a big lead in the Republika Srpska, crushing the Western-backed Independent Social Democrats of Milorad Dodik.[96] In the Muslim-Croat Federation the Muslim nationalist SDA had a strong running and the Croat nationalist HDZ won overwhelmingly in areas populated by Croats. The HDZ also said it no longer recognized the authority of Western officials running Bosnia and it organized a referendum demanding a separate Croat entity in Bosnia.[97] Three months later, the HDZ declared the Muslim-Croat Federation dead.[98] Its top leaders were promptly sacked by High Representative Petritsch.[99]

Education and Media Controls

The West's nation-building mission in Bosnia has not been limited to manipulating the political process. Deputy High Representative Jacques Klein, Washington's highest-ranking civilian nation builder in Bosnia, says the international community must overhaul the educational system there as well. According to Klein, Bosnians do not understand their own past: "Their history is either a nationalistic history, a Marxist interpretation of history, or what's worse, is an anecdotal history. 'My grandfather told me,' 'my uncle told me.' That means their leaders are making political decisions based on very false historic premises."[100] Thus, says Klein, the West must undertake to relieve Bosnians of their ignorance.

Right now, schools in Muslim-, Croat-, and Serb-dominated areas teach their pupils divergent versions of language and literature, but the differences are perhaps greatest in the teaching of history, in particular the causes and conduct of the Bosnian war. Muslims in

Zavidovici blocked a highway after the Croat authorities prevented their children from being taught the Muslim curriculum. Croat pupils in Bugojno cram into a makeshift classroom because the Muslim authorities have barred schools teaching them the Croat curriculum.[101] Some Western nation builders want to create a historical commission, headed by a foreigner, to write an official uniform account of the war for the classrooms of Bosnia.[102] Other experts recommend leaving all discussion of the war out of the textbooks entirely.[103]

In an October 1998 report to the UN's secretary-general, High Representative Westendorp announced that his office was working on the implementation of the "Textbook Review Project" to remove "offensive materials" from textbooks used in primary and secondary schools in Bosnia.[104] Bosnian and international experts were assembled to study school textbooks to "identify and eliminate elements likely to induce intolerance and ethnic hatred."[105] A project committee recommended that the term "crime" be replaced by "mistake" in a sentence printed in a grammar textbook used by 14-year-olds in Sarajevo. The committee decided that children traumatized by the war might read into the word "crime" connotations of wartime culpability and suggested that "mistake" might be less inflammatory. When the recommendation became public a major row developed. Muslim critics lambasted Westendorp for seeking to whitewash the past in pursuit of cosmetic ethnic reconciliation. But Westendorp said in a statement that the textbook reviews "are essential in creating the country envisaged in the Dayton Peace Agreement: a Bosnia and Herzegovina in which all its citizens feel fully accepted and respected regardless of their place of residence or their ethnic affiliation."[106] By August 1999, a spokesperson for the High Representative announced, "Offensive and objectionable terminology will no longer be included in the textbooks. . . . Deletion of items is to be completed by the start of the new school year."[107] In all, there was a 24-page list of phrases, paragraphs, and even whole pages that were deemed "offensive and objectionable." Teachers were then instructed to find them in every textbook and make sure students could not read the words anymore.[108]

Even this level of control has not satisfied Bosnia's nation builders. In April 1998, the Office of the High Representative created a media commission that has the power to shut down or fine radio stations, television stations, and newspapers it decides are engaging in reporting or editorializing that hinders the implementation of the Dayton Agreement. Called the Independent Media Commission, the body has an annual budget of $2.7 million, financed in part by the United States.[109] The IMC is headed by a non-Bosnian, and half the 30-person staff is made up of foreigners.[110] A U.S. State Department official has admitted that "there are obvious free-speech concerns," but Western diplomats hesitate to characterize the commission as a censorship organ.[111] On April 14, 1999, however, the IMC ordered Kanal S TV in the Republika Srpska off the air. According to the commission, Kanal S TV committed a "serious violation" when it aired an appeal from Sarajevo University students requesting their fellow citizens to join them in a protest against NATO's air strikes against Yugoslavia.[112] But the IMC is not limited to punishing media it does not like: it also has the authority to mandate certain coverage. Indeed, during NATO's air strikes, the commission required, "under direct order," Bosnian Serb television to carry a Serbian-language address by Secretary of State Madeleine Albright defending the NATO action.[113]

Following the April 2000 municipal elections, the IMC found five Bosnian TV broadcasters in violation of its "Code on Media Rules in Elections" and fined them. According to the IMC's enforcement panel, four of the stations were fined for violating the commission's rule on media silence, which forbids airing election-related material on election day. TV Bel was ordered to pay a fine for broadcasting contentious news on election day and reporting that Croats were boycotting the polls in the towns of Gornji Vakuf and Zepce. RTV BiH was fined because its news program announced that the SDS would be holding a press conference. ATV Banja Luka was ordered to pay a fine for reporting that two Republika Srpska politicians were being omitted from the vote registers. And HRTV Herceg-Bosna was fined for broadcasting on its early evening news a statement made by the HDZ.[114]

In the months leading up to Bosnia's October 2000 presidential elections, the West again tightened its control over the media. High Representative Petritsch, for example, summarily dismissed the board of governors of the main Bosnian Serb television station, RTRS, and appointed a new one.[115] "This decision is a direct result of the continued failure of the Republika Srpska Government and the RS

National Assembly to adopt new legislation for RTRS, in order to bring it in line with international standards for public broadcasting," he announced.[116] But Petritsch's move was also likely an expression of the West's increasing anxiety that the nationalists would win most of the elections yet again.

Bosnia's Economic Calamity

Shortly after the Dayton Agreement halted the fighting in Bosnia in late 1995, the World Bank announced it would raise $5.1 billion in reconstruction aid. Concerned with securing large pledges from the United States and other Western governments, bank officials claimed that the breakaway Yugoslav republic was intent on privatizing its economy as soon as possible. Bosnia was expected to respond quickly to privatization, explained the bank's director for Central Europe, Kemal Dervis. "This is not an economy like the former Soviet republics," he assured skeptics. "Yugoslavia was halfway to the market when the war started."[117]

A Failure to Privatize

Five years and billions of dollars in reconstruction aid later, Bosnia has yet to privatize any significant part of its economy.[118] In fact, officials at the International Finance Corporation, an arm of the World Bank, reported in late 1998 that the number of privatized companies in Bosnia was negligible. "It is closer to zero percent than one percent," explained Richard Rutherford, the principal investment officer with the International Finance Corporation in Europe.[119] Since then, nearly every privatization effort has run into controversy, and now 14 different, and sometimes competing, privatization agencies exist.[120]

One privatization plan was designed to cover about 2,000 small properties and businesses, such as apartments, shops, and hotels. The idea was to issue vouchers to the public, which could be used either to buy state-owned apartments or to buy shares of state-owned businesses. But that plan has been mired in scandal and disputes between Muslims and Croats over the share of vouchers each will receive to pay off more than $4 billion in war debts and back wages owed the veterans of their respective armies, which fought against each other from 1992 to 1994.[121] U.S. diplomats have blamed the leading Bosnian Muslim party, the SDA, for possible interference in the bidding process, and the furor has led the main privatization agency to cancel 34 future tenders. The U.S. Agency for International Development, which has spent more than $30 million in U.S. taxpayer money laying the groundwork for privatization, has suspended financial support for the Muslim-Croat Federation's program. Many American officials now doubt whether the entity's Muslim majority is truly dedicated to economic reform. Indeed, according to one senior U.S. official, the Bosnian Muslims "have been tremendously obstructionist in blocking . . . transparent, honest privatization laws . . . because they find it a lot easier to sit back and enjoy the benefits of international economic aid . . . [and] because they basically believe in state control and party control."[122] "If you want to know the reason why things have moved slowly, it is because the political parties are still deeply entrenched in everything. . . . They are not interested in real privatization," says U.S. diplomat Robert Barry, head of the OSCE mission to Bosnia.[123]

Without large-scale privatization there is little prospect for self-sustaining economic growth and direct foreign investment in the Muslim-Croat Federation. Indeed, the entity's tiny private sector accounted for 58 percent of total profits made in 1998, while state and mixed state-private ownership companies accounted for 88 percent of all losses.[124] The situation in the Republika Srpska looks even worse, because privatization laws have not even been fully enacted. This dismal outlook is worsened by the prospect that Bosnia must begin repaying the principal of its foreign debt in 2002.

An Entrenched Socialist Legacy

Another obstacle to economic growth in Bosnia is the legacy of bureaucratic socialism. The same functionaries who ran things before the war are still running things today.[125] Other remnants of the socialist era—onerous taxes and regulations—also continue to thwart business start-ups and foreign investment. "Things are still so rigidly controlled here that many businessmen can't get off the ground even if they have money and ideas," explains one reconstruction expert.[126]

Take the case of Morgon Sowden for example. Sowden, a British citizen, founded the popular Internet Café in Sarajevo but was forced to close his business after confronting exorbitant taxes, burdensome bureaucracy, and multiple layers of regulations. As the *Los Angeles Times* reported,

> Already well-versed in doing business in Eastern Europe after a stint in Prague, Sowden took an early gamble on Bosnia. Arriving just a month after the war ended, he expected hardships. . . . What he did not expect was layer upon layer of bureaucracy and the seemingly deliberate way the government had of making it impossible and expensive to do business. Make that governments, plural. In its post-war development . . . Bosnia has created jurisdictions at the city, canton, entity and state . . . levels, each of which has some form of taxation and regulatory powers. Because it's all new, laws at different levels sometimes contradict one another and are extremely complex. As a consequence, Sowden recently found himself hit with a retroactive tax bill going back to 1996. Authorities simply changed their minds about whether a particular duty was applicable to his business. . . . He was also assessed a payroll tax equal to a full 85 percent of his employees' salaries and seven taxes on alcohol totaling roughly 20 percent, and he must pay 36 to 51 percent tax on his profit annually—in advance. . . . Rather than continue to fight the bureaucrats and lose money, Sowden has decided to hand the popular café over to his 25 employees and walk away.[127]

Another small business owner, New Yorker Bethany Lindsley, opened up Sarajevo's first Tex-Mex restaurant, but she too complains of cost-prohibitive taxes and reams of regulations that do not allow her to make changes as simple as paying her employees weekly instead of twice monthly. "These problems are not from the war," she explains. "It's communism."[128]

Large businesses, too, bemoan communist-era obstacles. McDonald's Europe complains that Bosnia's communist legacy has overpriced Sarajevo real estate. Most of the property is still controlled by the government, it says, and in some cases the Bosnian government charges prices higher than in downtown Geneva.[129] Klaus Dieter Stienbach, who ran Bosnia's Volkswagen plant in the 1980s, says Bosnia's customs and tax forms are identical to the ones he filled out more than a decade ago. "Everybody is living and thinking in the past," he says.[130]

Even Bosnia's communist-era Payment Bureau, which collects and distributes taxes, performs treasury and audit functions, and gathers statistical data on the economy, still exists. A 1999 U.S. government report says that the Payment Bureau directly and indirectly costs the Bosnian economy more than $197 million a year.[131] That is some five percent of Bosnia's gross domestic product. "The current system makes possible bureaucratic intervention into all aspects of business life," the report says. Its activities "add no or little value in a free-market system, and create major obstacles to the development of free markets, and the financial intermediation process that supports free markets."[132] "You've got to be crazy to invest in this country where it is a given that if you obey the laws you're going to lose money," explains the OSCE's Robert Barry. "If the [economic] reform doesn't come," he adds, "if I were a[n international] donor, I wouldn't be putting money down a rat hole."[133]

The West Is Rebuilding Socialism

Bosnia's ongoing failure to implement a viable privatization plan and to reform multiple layers of taxes and bureaucracy has had a disastrous economic impact. Although Bosnia's economy is estimated to have grown 11 percent in 1999, most of that so-called growth reflected an influx of millions of dollars in international aid and the purchasing and employment power of the civilian army of nation builders working there, not an expanding national economy.[134] Bosnians may be building bridges and roads with aid money, but that activity only masks the underlying sickness of their economy. "There's really no economic growth," admits Peter Hanney, head of private business development for the Office of the High Representative. "There's no job creation."[135]

The reality is that Bosnia is in an economic coma. Most state-owned businesses are struggling to stay open. Many are completely dormant. Unemployment, which fell immediately after the war, is no longer improving significantly. Of Bosnian workers, 60 percent are unemployed today, but the actual unemployment rate may be as high as 80 percent in some areas.[136] Meanwhile, 50,000 to 60,000 of the Bosnians who are employed work for one of the 463 reconstruction and humanitarian organizations currently operating inside the country.[137]

Bosnia's resistance to privatization and bureaucratic reform, of course, was well known in December 1997 when President Clinton informed American taxpayers that they would have to pay for an open-ended military presence in Bosnia. The question today is: What have billions of dollars in aid and five years of military occupation produced? Ironically, after fighting the Cold War for 40 years, the United States now finds itself preserving and subsidizing the institutional remnants of a defunct communist state. As one U.S. official noted, "The goal is not to rebuild a socialist economy" in Bosnia.[138] Unfortunately, that is precisely what has been happening. In fact, a recent economic study of 155 nations ranked Bosnia the 14th least-free economy in the world, just ahead of countries such as Syria, Iran, Cuba, Iraq, Libya, and North Korea.[139]

Ethnic Politics and the Economy

The primary obstacle to privatization in Bosnia has been political foot-dragging. Many Bosnian officials are resisting privatization in order to protect a highly bureaucratic system of jobs and privileges, as well as to keep control away from their ethnic rivals. In most cases the heads of Bosnia's major state-owned enterprises are also members of the local ruling political party. For example, the main utility in the Muslim-Croat Federation, Elektroprivreda, is run by Edhem Bicakcic, vice president of the main Muslim party, the SDA. In the Republika Srpska, the major public utilities and largest companies are run by SDS leaders. In Brcko, for instance, the local telecommunications company is headed by SDS president Mladen Bosic, the local furniture factory is run by SDS official Bosko Maricic, and the Brcko Electric Company is run by a former SDS chairman.[140]

NATO Funds the Nationalists

Ironically, because so much property in Bosnia is still government-owned, NATO peacekeepers are paying millions of dollars in rent for buildings and land that are winding up in the coffers of Bosnia's nationalist political parties. In fact, the United States, Great Britain, Germany, and other NATO countries may be paying as much as $40 million a year to rent space from government-owned companies in Bosnia.[141] That money is then pocketed by the nationalist party that happens to exercise control over the local or regional government and its institutions. "Every important manager of these [government-owned] companies is appointed by the political parties," explains UN economist Didier Fau, and "they do what they are told."[142]

Still, NATO officials claim that they pay rent only to private companies. But an October 1998 report in the *New York Times* found that "interviews with company and local government officials, as well as financial experts working for Western governments in Bosnia . . . indicate that much of the [rental] money is going to the Bosnian . . . governments, which funnel it to political parties."[143] Some examples of rental payments made by NATO allies include the following:[144]

- The Bosnian company that received the most rent from the United States was paid $1.4 million for space at a coal-processing plant. The company's director says that the company is owned by the government of the Muslim-Croat Federation.
- The U.S. Army reports that it paid about $744,000 in rent for space at a private mining site. But the mine's director says that the company is owned by the government of the Muslim-Croat Federation, and that the rental payment was nearly three times what the U.S. Army claims.
- The headquarters of the British army in Bosnia is located in an unused sheet-metal factory near the town of Banja Luka. The financial director of the factory says that the factory is owned by the government of the Republika Srpska.
- In the town of Sipovo, the deputy mayor says that all the rent paid by British forces for an abandoned textile factory was transferred directly from the factory's bank account to the government of the Republika Srpska.
- German army records show that it paid $2.5 million to rent warehouses from a Sarajevo company owned by the government of the Muslim-Croat Federation.

What is puzzling about NATO's rental payments to government-owned companies in Bosnia is the obvious contradiction. NATO allies are effectively subsidizing the very nationalist political parties that Western civilian officials consider the principal obstacles to peace in Bosnia. Civilian money, too, has played a role in entrenching the power of Bosnia's nationalist politicians. Indeed, postwar money distributed by the OSCE for elections made its way into the pockets of some of the most notorious war criminals in the Balkans. Vojislav Seselj and his associates are said to have received more than $450,000, and the Party of Serb Unity, which was founded by the infamous Zeljko "Arkan" Raznjatovic, gladly took away $195,000.[145]

Fraud and Corruption

By mid-1999, the United States and other major powers agreed to provide the last installment of the World Bank's $5.1 billion Bosnia reconstruction program, to which Washington had already contributed more than $1 billion.[146] On May 18, 2000, the World Bank announced a new country assistance strategy that would distribute an additional $300 million over the next two to three years.[147] Unfortunately, allegations of corruption began surfacing soon after the first aid dollars began flowing into Bosnia back in 1996.[148] Indeed, just six weeks after the Dayton Agreement was signed, the Western media were reporting that local Bosnian authorities were trying to impose arbitrary "taxes" on humanitarian agencies delivering aid to refugees. "Anything we buy, we have to pay a war tax of 10 percent. We have built housing for refugees, and they're telling us, 'you have to pay for the water and electricity that your refugees are using,'" said Kevin Mannion, a field officer for the UN's International Management Group, the agency that would go on to oversee much of the World Bank's spending in Bosnia.[149] "We're trying to tell them, 'Don't be so corrupt, or at least don't be so open about it,'" explained one agency head who dealt extensively with municipal officials. "Every time you go into a place with a development project, the first thing the mayor wants to know is when he gets his new Mercedes."[150]

Several months later, the *Washington Post* reported that it was commonplace to skim the river of aid money streaming into Bosnia.

> The World Bank, for example, is funding a health project through a Bosnian company that is buying medicine at two to three times the market price, a senior Western aid official said. The difference, he said, is going into Bosnian pockets. Bosnian officials are [also] trying to tax every aid project they can find. The European Union, for example, is giving Bosnia millions of dollars' worth of equipment. In theory, the EU should not have to pay customs duty on the goods. But Bosnia's Customs Department is unwilling to process the goods quickly and suggests instead that the EU contract with "private" Bosnian companies, run coincidentally by off-duty customs officials, to clear the paperwork. All, of course, for a hefty fee.[151]

By 1997, it was becoming clear that rampant fraud surrounded the international aid program. Millions of dollars of international aid sent to Bosnia to finance reconstruction and to bolster the shattered country's fragile peace had gone astray. Much of the money, reportedly, had "been siphoned into private organizations and personal bank accounts by corrupt members of the Balkan state's multiethnic leadership."[152]

Western officials, too, were becoming more concerned with the situation. "There's no clean accounting, there are no open accounts. It's deplorable," lamented one Western diplomat in Sarajevo, adding, "It's really a miserable situation in which everyone is hiding how much they are spending because they are in effect preparing for the next war."[153]

By July 1997, allegations of fraud and corruption had become such a problem that British foreign secretary Robin Cook traveled to Sarajevo to discuss those and other issues with Bosnia's collective presidency. On the eve of his arrival, reports were circulating in the Bosnian capital that as much as $150 million of World Bank assistance was missing. During his meetings with Bosnia's three presidents, Cook said that the rampant corruption had to stop, and he cited their failure to publish proper accounts of where two and a half years of international aid had gone. "You must understand that neither our patience nor our resources are unlimited," he told them pointedly.[154]

Cook's scolding apparently had little effect. By March 1998, a delegation of Bosnian parliament members informed British officials and auditors that nearly $600 million in aid given by the United States, the European Union, and the United Nations had been embezzled since the Dayton Agreement was signed. Much of the fraud was conducted with the foreknowledge and cooperation of ministers and senior government officials in Bosnia, they added. They also reported that "tens of millions" of dollars sent to Bosnia for industrial reconstruction had gone into the pockets of government officials, mafia bosses, and criminals.[155]

In November 1998, U.S. officials admitted that politicians in Bosnia tolerated corruption. "Corruption exists," said U.S. diplomat Richard Sklar, adding that "all three national [army] corps tolerate corruption. Perhaps some politicians are corrupt [too]."[156] A few months later, the Office of the High Representative admitted that its anti-fraud unit discovered that $100 million was lost to domestic corruption between 1996 and 1999.[157] It was also discovered that Bosnian Muslim leader Alija Izetbegovic ignored the corruption of his son Bakir—one of Bosnia's wealthiest and most powerful men—who was found to be involved in shady dealings, most involving his role as head of the City Development Institute, which oversees occupancy rights for some 80,000 publicly owned apartments in Sarajevo.[158] Bakir also owns 15 percent of Bosnia Air, the state airline, and takes a cut of the extortion money paid out by local shopkeepers to Sarajevo gangsters.[159] Other examples of government corruption in Bosnia include the following:[160]

- Western diplomats say they have seen evidence that the former prime minister of the Tuzla canton diverted an estimated $30 million in public funds to his friends, squandering it on bad loans, needless painting of government buildings, overpriced pharmaceuticals, and official cars.
- The mayor in the city of Sanski Most diverted public funds to help build a racetrack and to back family members opening a bank. One Western diplomat said the mayor "ran [the city] like it was his own factory or property."
- Three officers of the Bosnian national bank transferred $7.4 million in public funds to a Croatian bank, where it disappeared. Meanwhile, Croat officials in Stolac are involved in a stolen-car market and smuggling ring.
- Scores of municipal officials who control Bosnia's border crossings routinely take bribes to let cigarette smugglers in; the practice has cost the government an estimated $100 million in taxes, according to federal officials and European Commission experts.

On August 17, 1999, nearly four years after NATO arrived in Bosnia, the *New York Times* reported that up to $1 billion in public funds and international aid money had been siphoned off by Bosnia's Muslim, Croat and Serb leaders.[161] The Muslim-Croat Federation, the greater recipient of Western dollars, denied that foreign-aid money had been stolen. The entity's government then established a commission to investigate corruption. The commission, composed primarily of American lawyers, studied the nature, causes, and consequences of corruption. On the basis of its analysis, the commission claimed that the *New York Times* "exaggerated" corruption concerning international aid, but recommended not taking any legal action against the newspaper and admitted that "domestic corruption in Bosnia is very real."[162] Foreign editor Andrew Rosenthal said the *New York Times* stood behind its reporting.[163]

In November 2000, it was revealed that Bosnian prime minister Edhem Bicakcic managed an illicit public fund that secretly disbursed tens of millions of dollars in tax receipts to favored companies, political allies, and Muslim veterans of the 1992–95 Bosnian war.[164] Although the fund was ostensibly established to create jobs, an official audit found widespread corruption and irregularities that extended to the top levels of the government. In 1997, the fund disbursed $39,500 in so-called "loans" to the Muslim-Croat Federation's president, Ejup Ganic, and to his cabinet. In 1998, $290,000 in "loans" were made to the defense ministry and another $39,500 went to Ganic and his associates.

Despite all their liberties with public funds, Bosnian officials continue to ask Western taxpayers to send them aid money for new government programs. In fact, more than four and a half years after the Dayton Agreement was signed, President Ganic appealed for $1 billion in additional aid and loans. "We have been spending money to keep the peace," he said. "Now we need money to build the peace."[165] The new proceeds, he explained, would be used to reengineer Bosnian society by paying refugees about $5,000 per family to return to and repair their prewar homes. Refugees returning to villages would also get a few cows or sheep and a tractor for every 10 households. In urban areas, returning refugees would be given money to build multiethnic factories and small businesses.

Naive Expectations

When U.S. Army General John Sylvester returned to Bosnia in 1998, after a two-year absence, children at a school for refugees sang him a song. "I was expecting the Bosnian version of *Mary Had a Little Lamb*," he would later recall, but instead the chorus ran, "we live only for revenge, to kill all the Serbs who have taken our families away from us."[166] Deputy High Representative Jacques Klein thinks there is a way to reduce this kind of hatred. Holding up a bright yellow-and-blue T-shirt featuring the Western-imposed Bosnian flag, Klein told reporters in October 1999 that he was seeking $1.2 million to distribute 300,000 of them to Bosnia's schoolchildren. "We need to build a consensus, especially among the young people . . . that they have a future here," so T-shirts that read "Our Flag, Our Country, Our Future" should be passed out to all the kids.[167]

Klein's T-shirts-for-peace program is only one of dozens of nation-building projects that have been proposed or carried out with the use of U.S. taxpayer money. Another is the open-air Arizona Market in eastern Bosnia. Outside the market's entrance is a sign paying tribute to American generosity and good intentions. The sign reads: "Our thanks to the U.S. Army for supporting in the development of this market."[168] Unfortunately, the sign is no longer a source of pride at the nearby U.S. military base. It has instead become an embarrassing symbol of wasted aid money because the market has become one of the largest havens for car thieves, drug traffickers, prostitutes, and tax cheats in the Balkans. The Pentagon funded roughly $40,000 of the market's start-up costs, and Western officials originally promoted the site as a cradle of local entrepreneurship that would hopefully provide an economic springboard for the rest of the country.[169] Today, the market is a den of criminal enterprise.

Other American nation-building programs have cost the U.S. taxpayer as well. The U.S. Agency for International Development, for example, has been forced to sue 19 Bosnian companies to recover some $10 million in bad loans. The loans, ranging from $100,000 to $1 million, are part of a $278 million revolving credit line established in 1996 by USAID to help kick start the Bosnian economy. One of the deadbeat companies is Hidrogradnja, one of the largest companies in Bosnia today. USAID, which has not made its total losses public, also had $4 million in the Bosnia and Herzegovina Bank in Sarajevo. The bank stole tens of millions of dollars from international agencies and 10 foreign embassies. The money, investigators say, was loaned to fictional businesses or given out as personal loans to friends of the two owners.[170]

Even Washington's program for removing land mines from the Bosnian countryside has been subject to corruption, including theft and contract rigging. Since 1997, the United States has contributed $3 million worth of mine-detection machinery, vehicles, bomb-sniffing dogs, and other equipment to the Bosnian Demining Commission. The equipment was supposed to be loaned to demining firms and returned to the commission when they completed their demining contracts. But much of the equipment was never returned, giving those firms that kept it an advantage in materiel when bidding for new contracts. Not surprisingly, the firms that kept the equipment have been linked to the Bosnian government officials who manage the country's demining program.[171]

"*E Pluribus Unum* Not Catching On"

Despite the circumstances, the Clinton administration insisted that U.S. policy would not be changed on Bosnia. "There will be no revision of the Dayton Accords," proclaimed Secretary of State Madeleine Albright in 1998.[172] Washington's unwillingness to rethink the Dayton Agreement may, however, be making things worse. Indeed, although its goal is to create a unitary, multiethnic Bosnian state, the Dayton Agreement actually attaches a premium to voting along ethnic lines. That pattern has been repeated in election after election as voters cast ballots for hard-liners or self-styled pragmatic nationalists to counterbalance the actual or perceived political power of their ethnic rivals, who, in turn, vote for nationalist candidates for the same reason. Such circular logic is built into the Dayton Agreement because it requires three ethnic groups, each of which fears the political ambitions of the other two, to operate under the fiction of a unified state. The political foot dragging and stalemates brought on by upholding that fiction have crippled Bosnia's economic recovery and perpetuated the central role of nationalists in the political discourse. In other words, the Dayton Agreement is itself an impediment to economic and political reform because it artificially preserves an environment of perpetual confrontation and political insecurity. Indeed, as Susan Woodward, a fellow at the London-based Centre for Defence Studies, points out:

> The Bosnian Muslims won their independent state, but they control less than one-third of the territory, including almost none of the external borders. The Dayton constitution . . . declares that this state continues "the legal existence under international law as a state" the former republic of Bosnia and Herzegovina, but it also obliged the Bosniaks to give up their power base in the offices and powers of the former republican government, to merge with Bosnian Croats in the Federation entity, to accept a weak common government, and to share power with two parties who oppose a single

> state. The Bosnian Serbs gained their own republic, but its existence was under daily challenge—by Bosniak leaders who denounced its legitimacy the moment Dayton was signed, and from the internationally supported right of return to prewar communities and the electoral rules allowing absentee balloting. . . . Finally, the Bosnian Croats gained recognition of their right to self-determination in the power-sharing arrangements and joint defense of the Federation, but they have been denied a separate republic within Bosnia and were obliged to dismantle their wartime Croatian Republic of Herzeg-Bosna (an order they managed to ignore despite their repeated promises to comply).[173]

In a similar vein, Brookings Institution scholar Michael O'Hanlon observes, the Dayton Agreement "keeps Muslim hopes for resettlement of refugees and ultimate reintegration of the country unsustainably high and therefore keeps the Serbs on edge and paranoid about losing wartime gains."[174]

Turning to even more intrusive and illiberal nation-building practices is the answer according to some, most notably High Representative Wolfgang Petritsch, who wants what he euphemistically calls "more energetic implementation" of the Dayton Agreement.[175] But that recommendation does not resolve the core issue: There is no *raison d'état* that holds the Bosnia nation-building project together. On the one hand, Serbs and Croats do not identify the Bosnian state the Dayton Agreement envisions as indispensable to their interests, and in many cases they believe that it is a threat. Bosnia's Muslims, on the other hand, find the idea of a Bosnian state indispensable, but have little practical ability to effectuate that goal under the Dayton Agreement. Any internal or external attempt to increase Muslim authority, however, will make Bosnia's Serbs and Croats feel less secure, and any attempt not to increase that authority will leave the Muslims feeling vulnerable. Much of Bosnia's political obstruction, and thus economic stagnation, is a byproduct of this security dilemma, and until Bosnia's rival factions feel safe behind the barriers of self-rule and their own laws—that is, have a *raison d'état*—it will continue.

An Impossible Fairy Tale

A failure to understand the dynamics of Bosnia's security dilemma has also led to nation-building programs that are counterproductive to both democracy and civil society. Nongovernmental organizations and international organizations like the OSCE have made a cottage industry of underwriting and publicizing cross-community cooperation and highlighting it as an alternative to ethnic separation. Unfortunately their actions politicize the activity, making it more threatening. As Leeds Metropolitan University political scientist David Chandler points out,

> The people whose lives involve cross-entity cooperation do not necessarily want to turn everyday activity into a political movement. The moment these actions become politicized they become an implicit threat to the status quo and create a backlash to a perceived threat that did not exist previously. As an experienced senior democratization officer related: "I'm surprised they tell us anything anymore. Inter-entity contacts are very common with businesses, etc. If I were a businessman I wouldn't report it . . . because it just creates problems." . . . People want to cross the Inter-Entity Boundary Line . . . but without drawing attention to themselves and without their actions being seen as threatening to the security of others.[176]

An added feature of the Dayton Agreement is that there has been little tendency to limit or roll back the powers of Western nation builders. Instead their powers over the past five years have grown considerably. The chief U.S. negotiator of the Dayton Agreement, Richard Holbrooke, says that this approach has been a success because "there have been no U.S. or NATO fatalities from hostile action" in Bosnia.[177] But the fact that Bosnian Muslims, Serbs, and Croats are not killing peacekeepers in the streets is not evidence that they support the Dayton Agreement or the West's increasingly imperious nation building. Rather, it is reflective of the fact that a widespread sense of powerlessness exists among Bosnia's populations, an observation that is confirmed by Bosnia's declining voter turnouts.[178] The West's nation-building programs have reinforced that sense by consistently and progressively disempowering the Bosnian people and their representatives, and by closing off any and all alternatives. In other words, the notions of democracy and self-government are being eroded by the very army of nation builders sent to help. Indeed, the West's implementation of the Dayton

Agreement through dismissals, political regulation, and media controls has done little to reassure political majorities that their interests will be taken into account. Instead, at the national, entity, and local levels, a clear pattern has emerged of political majorities *not* making policy.

Western nation-building efforts in Bosnia have also bred a culture of dependency. American business consultant Claude Ganz estimates that up to one-third of Bosnia's economy directly depends on foreign spending there.[179] Christopher Bennett of the Washington and Brussels-based International Crisis Group says, "It's surreal. Every day, more foreigners pour in to do every conceivable task, and the more they do, the less the Bosnians do themselves."[180] Bosnian foreign minister Jadranko Prlic agrees, noting that Bosnia is suffering from a "syndrome of international community dependency," in which local leadership largely does nothing significant on its own.[181]

Resentment has been another by-product of the West's increasingly imperious nation building. A leader of the opposition Socialist Party of Republika Srpska, for example, says the results of the 2000 municipal elections show that the people "do not want a protectorate" and that Serb politicians who collaborate with the West "do not have the majority of support from Republika Srpska citizens."[182] Though they are the main beneficiaries of U.S. dollars and diplomacy, Bosnia's Muslims have also expressed some bitterness. In a May 1998 interview, Deputy High Representative Klein criticized all Bosnian politicians for their lack of cooperation. But Bosnian Muslim leader Izetbegovic wrote an open letter condemning Klein's comments. "I was amazed by the amount of your arrogance," wrote Izetbegovic; the Dayton Agreement did not establish a protectorate in Bosnia and "you are not the protector."[183]

What complicates the matter of nation building still further is that Bosnia has no tradition of free markets, property rights, and the rule of law. Even former High Representative Carlos Westendorp finds that problematic. Indeed, says Westendorp, "the international community can do a lot of things, but you cannot produce entrepreneurs and people who really have a free-market economy mind."[184] Klein is even more blunt in his assessment of the Bosnian situation: "It's just a great old commie system that hasn't changed."[185] "The leaders on all sides have learned the words to use: *free enterprise, Western-style economy, dynamic, efficient,*" explains a French investment entrepreneur in Bosnia. "They say these things with great passion, but that is superficial. Nothing has changed from the days when this was a communist country."[186] To make matters worse, where commerce exists in Bosnia, much of it tends to be criminal in nature. Indeed, Western officials estimate that 40 to 60 percent of Bosnia's economy is now based on black-marketeering, which has fueled the rise of a wealthy criminal class that wields enormous political influence and opposes changing the status quo.[187] More ominously, a growing relationship exists among criminal gangs, corrupt politicians, and members of wartime security institutions, who profit from the fact that the Dayton Agreement perpetuates a security dilemma in Bosnia. Indeed, by simultaneously denying the Croats their own state, depriving the Muslims of a unified Bosnian state, and granting the Serbs a state within a state, the Dayton Agreement virtually ensures that legal jurisdiction and law enforcement issues fall victim to public controversy and political resistance.

As the nation-building effort in Bosnia makes clear, nation building involves more than heavy outside interference and a pliant civilian population. Domestic factors as well as the unintended consequences and contradictions of nation building itself can have a severely limiting effect. But the most overwhelming barrier to nation building can occur when the real and perceived security threats that led to conflict in the first place remain unresolved by the nation builder. That situation not only perpetuates a chronic atmosphere of political uncertainty, but also encourages aberrant political and economic activity. As such, the Dayton Agreement's muddled answer to the question "What kind of Bosnia should there be?" has virtually ensured that peace will not be self-sustaining, and that the conditions for a timely U.S. withdrawal are not really being created.

5. Kosovo: False Peace, Futile Mission

Adopted on June 10, 1999, UN Security Council Resolution 1244 lays out the military and political framework for the West's nation-building effort in the Serbian province of Kosovo. Specifically, the resolution calls for the deployment of an international "security presence" in Kosovo, as well as the establishment of an international "civil presence" to oversee the development of democratic structures that will "ensure conditions for a peaceful and normal life for all inhabitants of Kosovo" and pave the way for "substantial autonomy."[1] In other words, as Secretary of State Madeleine Albright explained the day the resolution was passed, "we would like to see Kosovo be a multiethnic society" that is both "democratic and self-governing."[2]

Separate from the debate over whether NATO's 78-day bombing campaign against Yugoslavia was well conceived or in America's vital national interest is the matter of the West's postwar occupation of Kosovo. In the two years since NATO arrived, most of Kosovo's Serbs, Gypsies, Goranies, Montenegrins, and other minority residents have been driven from or have fled the predominantly ethnic Albanian province, while those non-Albanians who are too old or too poor to leave have moved into NATO-protected enclaves that are growing ever smaller and more isolated. Meanwhile, Washington's de facto wartime ally, the Kosovo Liberation Army, has shown little concrete interest in autonomy within Yugoslavia or multiethnic democracy, and is currently fomenting an insurgency beyond Kosovo's borders. What is more, the war-torn province has become a playground for armed gangsters and drug traffickers who slip across the border into Albania and Macedonia with impunity.[3] All that notwithstanding, the UN's chief nation builder in Kosovo for the first 18 months, Special Representative Bernard Kouchner, managed to insist that "the Kosovo mission is a success. We are building a modern democratic society."[4]

In reality, however, Kosovo is a militarized protectorate of the West. Nearly 40,000 foreign soldiers, including 6,000 Americans, occupy Kosovo as part of the NATO-led Kosovo Force (KFOR), and under the United Nations Interim Administration Mission in Kosovo (UNMIK), Hans Haekkerup, who assumed Kouchner's job as the Special Representative for Kosovo in January 2001, now oversees more than 3,500 UN police, including 540 Americans, and 1,500 UN specialists who conduct the province's daily administration.[5] More than 330 relief and other nongovernmental organizations also are operating in Kosovo, bringing with them a small army of aid workers.[6] "This is just the beginning of a very long involvement of the international community," explained Kouchner during his tenure.[7]

So far UNMIK has taken over responsibility for Kosovo's health care, education, banking, telecommunications, mail delivery, and garbage collection systems.[8] It has also declared the German mark the local currency; it pays the wages of teachers, doctors, and civil servants; and it decides on matters such as how much vending licenses should cost to sell ice cream on Kosovo's street corners.[9] Gen. Klaus Reinhardt, NATO's former chief commander in Kosovo, says NATO and the United Nations have to stay in Kosovo for 10 years to get the economy and culture working again.[10] Former Finnish president Martti Ahtisaari, who helped negotiate NATO's terms for entering Kosovo, is even less optimistic. He estimates that two or three generations will need to pass before Kosovo becomes a normal society.[11]

In Washington, early proponents of nation building in Kosovo, such as Secretary of State Albright, insisted that Washington's task should be to build multiethnic democracy, and "with time and sufficient support, the cooler heads on all sides will prevail."[12] President Clinton's national security adviser, Sandy Berger, claimed that the United States "must stay the course" and do "for Kosovo and Southeast Europe what we did for Western Europe after World War II."[13] Outside the former administration, advocates of nation building have similarly argued that Washington should not leave Kosovo any time soon. The director of the Washington office of the Open Society Institute, for example, claims, "We'll get out of the Balkans the same way we got out of Western and Central Europe—after the establishment of democracy, the rule of law, human rights, open markets, and integration with the rest of Europe."[14] "That's the exit strategy," he adds, apparently overlooking the inconvenient fact that the United States has not actually gotten out of Western and Central Europe even though World War II ended more than half a century ago.[15] Indeed, there are still 63,000 U.S. troops in Germany alone despite the fact that Germany certainly has "democracy, the rule of law, human rights, open markets, and integration with the rest of Europe."[16]

Notwithstanding such dubious cheerleading, the Kosovo operation actually demonstrates that nation building involves much more than imperious foreign rule and copious amounts of international aid. Fundamental obstacles can exist, such as when a popular insurgency in the place targeted for nation building has not given up on its wartime objective. Kosovo is just such a place. Indeed, unlike the German and Japanese forces, which were utterly vanquished after World War II, the Kosovo Liberation Army was made nearly victorious by NATO's air campaign against Yugoslavia. Given that circumstance, the KLA has shown little interest in doing Washington's bidding, especially when it conflicts with the organization's own, primarily nationalistic, vision for the future of the Balkans. Consequently, the policy the Clinton administration devised for Kosovo is not producing the results it said would be necessary for American troops to eventually return home.

NATO Goes to War

On March 24, 1999, the U.S.-led NATO alliance launched Operation Allied Force against the Federal Republic of Yugoslavia, a country that presently consists of two republics: Serbia and Montenegro. The intense bombing that followed was meant to force Yugoslav president Slobodan Milosevic to agree to Washington's terms for peace in Serbia's southern province of Kosovo. In the 12 months prior to NATO's bombing, roughly 2,000 people, many of them civilians, died as a result of the fighting between Serbian special police, who were backed by Yugoslav government forces, and ethnic Albanian separatists known as the Kosovo Liberation Army.

Although the events leading up to NATO's air strikes against Yugoslavia are complex, the source of the underlying conflict in Kosovo is readily identifiable: the irreconcilable aims of the Milosevic regime in Belgrade and those of the KLA. Indeed, whereas the KLA's goal was to split off Kosovo from Yugoslavia, Belgrade rejected that idea and invoked its sovereignty over the territory. As the overwhelming majority of the province's population, most ethnic Albanians in Kosovo wanted independence or at least some kind of extensive political autonomy from Yugoslavia. In contrast, most Serbs rejected independence and extensive autonomy—which they viewed simply as the first step toward independence anyway—because Kosovo was the birthplace of their history, culture, and religion.

After 11 weeks of NATO bombing, all Serbian special police and Yugoslav government forces were expelled from Kosovo.[17] With that development, the KLA was brought substantially closer to its main wartime objective: separating the province of Kosovo from Yugoslavia.

But the Clinton administration would have none of that. "Our position is that we need to make sure that there is a high degree of autonomy and self-government here, and that the future status [of Kosovo] is something that we can look towards later," explained Secretary Albright in a November 1999 interview.[18] Today, the United Nations administers virtually all of Kosovo's day-to-day affairs. Special Representative Kouchner began the process by consolidating all Yugoslav state-owned enterprises and social services under his administrative authority and by deciding who would manage those companies and bureaucracies. Kouchner eschewed province-level elections and instead installed an unelected body called the Interim Administrative Council, whose members he handpicked himself.[19] Kouchner also set up a legal system under which KFOR soldiers are permitted to make arrests based on their own country's national laws and can bring the arrested individuals before a panel of UN-appointed judges who have the authority to make laws as they go, using the old Yugoslav legal code as only a guide.[20]

In the realm of media, Kouchner's United Nations staff, not local managers, took over the TV broadcasts after the Yugoslav authorities left the province.[21] Kouchner and the West's army of nation builders then began to evince the same appetite to control the media in Kosovo as their counterparts have in Bosnia. As early as August 1999, NATO forces shut down *Çlirimi,* an Albanian-language newspaper, for publishing an editorial critical of KFOR. The offending issues were confiscated by NATO troops and the publisher was arrested.[22]

Soon after the *Çlirimi* incident, the Organization for Security and Cooperation in Europe began drawing up a plan for wide-ranging media control in the province, including the formation of a media board that would be responsible for overseeing the media and, when it deems necessary, imposing penalties.[23] The OSCE plan, which envisaged strict media licensing and standards with powerful enforcement mechanisms, raised fears of censorship among local journalists in Kosovo. The director general of the Independent Media Commission in nearby Bosnia, however, argued that media regulation was needed because

> Broadcasting—especially television—has played a great role in the hands of propagandists in fomenting ethnic cleansing in Bosnia and Kosovo over the last decade. Authentic journalists in Kosovo need the protection and encouragement of a small, Western-style regulatory agency to establish reasonable limits on partisan political control of radio and television stations and on the incitement of violence and hatred."[24]

The Washington and Brussels-based International Crisis Group also backed the idea of media regulation in Kosovo. Though it warned that the controls must not be excessively broad or be allowed to become a permanent feature of the Kosovo media environment, the ICG maintained that "limited government regulation of media content in Kosovo is justified in the immediate post-conflict period, and while the region's media is becoming re-established."[25]

In June 2000, Special Representative Kouchner shut down the Albanian-language daily, *Dita*, for 8 days after a Serb UN worker the newspaper accused of being a former member of a Serb paramilitary group was abducted and murdered. Within weeks of the killing, the OSCE set up its media-control organ, which it called the Temporary Media Commission, and issued a stern warning letter to *Dita* when the newspaper republished the offending article after reopening for business. The warning letter also demanded an official explanation of what it called a breach of the OSCE's media code of conduct. *Dita*'s publisher publicly vowed to continue publishing the names of alleged participants in Belgrade's oppression and called the OSCE's Temporary Media Commission *Dita*'s "inquisitor." An OSCE spokesperson told the newspaper it had better apologize or retract the statement or it would face a $50,000 fine or even another closure.[26]

Two other publications have since been reprimanded for violating the OSCE's media controls. One of them, a Kosovo women's magazine called *Kosovarja*, was threatened with closure for an article it published titled "Nightmare Butchers," which criticized Gypsy collaboration with the Belgrade regime and named 11 Kosovo Gypsies it said had belonged to an anti-Albanian paramilitary group.[27] Worried by the ethnic animosities that more such articles might inflame, OSCE officials begin mulling over plans to ban articles that "denigrate" a specific ethnic group.[28] "The freedom of the press is not limitless," explained a spokesperson for the OSCE.[29]

In mid-August 2000, Radio S, a Serbian-language radio station in the ethnically divided city of Kosovska Mitrovica, was ordered to shut down its broadcasts. Western authorities cited licensing irregularities. But the real reason the station was shut down was because the United Nations disapproved of the station's content, which often characterized the United Nations and NATO as an "occupying force" and encouraged Serbs to boycott the UN-administered municipal elections scheduled for that October.[30]

No "Post-Colonial Sensitivities"

Though the authority of Western nation builders in Kosovo is extensive, it is not an unexpected development. Even before NATO's air campaign ended, advocates of nation building began calling for the foreign occupation and administration of the province. For example, Carlos Westendorp, the West's former top administrator in Bosnia, argued at the height of NATO's bombing that "a full international protectorate is required" for Kosovo. "Yes, this disregards the principles of sovereignty," he said, "but so what? This is not the moment for post-colonial sensitivities."[31] Westendorp was not alone in his imperious view. "The only viable course," editorialized one Western newspaper, "is to . . . establish a NATO protectorate in Kosovo." Another newspaper boasted, "We have argued from the start . . . for a land war to capture Kosovo and turn it into an international protectorate."[32]

After NATO ended its air campaign, the Clinton administration enthusiastically supported the idea of running Kosovo as a protectorate. In fact, it quickly endorsed a UN mandate broader than anything the international organization had undertaken before, and, unlike

Table 5.1
ESTIMATED U.S. COSTS FOR MILITARY AND NONMILITARY ASPECTS OF KOSOVO PEACE OPERATION, FISCAL YEARS 1999–2000
(Dollars in millions)

Fiscal Year	1999	2000	Total
Military Aspects	$3,000	$2,025	$5,025
Nonmilitary Aspects	256	302	558
Total	$3,256	$2,327	$5,583

SOURCE: United States General Accounting Office, *Balkans Security: Current and Projected Factors Affecting Regional Stability* (Washington, D.C., April 2000), p. 86.

the Bosnia operation, Washington avoided all promises against "mission creep" and talk of "exit dates."

In a clear indication of what was instead to come, the first regulation enacted by the United Nations stated: "All legislative and executive authority with respect to Kosovo, including the administration of the judiciary, is vested in UNMIK and is exercised by the Special Representative of the Secretary-General."[33] By August 1999, the U.S. ambassador to the United Nations, Richard Holbrooke, was encouraging UN officials in Kosovo, including Special Representative Kouchner, not to worry about the U.N.'s cumbersome bureaucracy in New York, but to focus on what they deemed necessary to successfully administer Kosovo. "Don't always ask—just do it," Holbrooke told them.[34]

So far, U.S. taxpayers have spent more than $5.5 billion on Kosovo (Table 5.1). Yet the prospect of rebuilding a democratic, multiethnic society there, even with Holbrooke's recommended "just do it" attitude, is not promising. To start with, it is not possible to rebuild something that never existed in the first place. For nearly 90 years, Belgrade ran Kosovo like a colonial backwater. Serbs and ethnic Albanians who lived there rarely intermarried and both ethnic groups eventually developed their own separate civic and political institutions. "Here [in Kosovo] I discovered hatred deeper than anywhere in the world, more than in Cambodia or Vietnam or Bosnia," once admitted Special Representative Kouchner. "Usually someone, a doctor or a journalist, will say, 'I know someone on the other side.' But here, no. They had no real relationship with the other community."[35]

The economy in Kosovo, moreover, is a wretched vestige of bureaucratic socialism. According to Tom Koenigs, the UN's director of civil administration in Kosovo,

> We are trying to transform this from a rotten socialist-command economy to a modern European market economy. We spent the first three-quarters of a year focused on emergencies—shelter, food, basic security, law and order, minority protection. The starting of an economy still has to come.[36]

But it is not at all clear that the desired economy will come. Kosovo was the poorest and most underdeveloped part of the old Socialist Federal Republic of Yugoslavia, which began disintegrating in 1991. In 1990, Kosovo's per capita gross domestic product was only $480, compared with $8,193 in the republic of Slovenia and $5,114 in the republic of Croatia.[37] In 1952, Kosovo's per capita GDP was 56 percent below Yugoslavia's national average; it dropped to 67 percent below by 1974 and 78 percent below by 1990.[38] During the mid-1990s, the economic conditions worsened still further, and 20 percent of Kosovo's population became wholly or partially dependent on humanitarian assistance for its survival.[39]

Except for public services run by the UN administration, few large enterprises have actually reopened in Kosovo. Formerly part of the Yugoslav command economy, most have no capital and no markets, and because Kosovo is still legally part of Yugoslavia, UN officials are prohibited from privatizing them because they are technically Yugoslav state assets. The Trepca mining and metals complex, which at one time employed 24,000 people, is one such enterprise.[40] Though many doubt that restarting the antiquated complex makes financial sense, Kosovo's Albanians, who believe that the mine is a national treasure wrested from the Serbs, are pressuring the United Nations to do so.[41]

Another major obstacle to economic recovery is the fact that Kosovo's political status is locked in limbo. As any economists worth their salt will explain, property ownership will not facilitate investment and economic efficiency unless owners and investors (foreign and domestic) have some reasonable expectation of profit. In Kosovo, the final status of the province has deliberately been left up in the air by Western policymakers. That basic uncertainty has discouraged investors from forgoing other consumption to sink their money into new ventures or to purchase properties to develop. The predictable result: dismal investor confidence and anemic economic development.

But Does NATO Do Windows?

Despite such discouraging factors, all kinds of nation-building projects continue apace in Kosovo. On April 15, 2000, NATO organized "Just Clean It" day across the province. A KFOR spokesperson explained the "purpose of the event is to gain support and interest from within the community so that children and adults appreciate the value of rubbish-free neighborhoods."[42] He added that staff from KFOR's headquarters and KFOR soldiers were organizing the cleanup around Pristina University and that the "British Light Division Band will be on hand to play music, and children who participate in the hard work will receive school bags, T-shirts, and refreshments."[43] While NATO troops clad in surgical gloves put trash into bright blue trash bags, Special Representative Kouchner used the event to warn that rats feeding off the rotting waste strewn around the provincial capital were becoming a health threat.[44] Gen. Reinhardt, KFOR's top commander at the time, led a contingent of NATO soldiers in combing grassland at the university, picking up cigarette butts, orange peels, broken glass, and plastic spoons. "We just want to set an example to clean up," explained Reinhardt.[45]

NATO's good deeds did not end there. KFOR soldiers report that there is more to their patrols "than tough soldiers with the rifle in ready-position."[46] They conduct what are called "social patrols," which aim at improving the well-being of local populations by providing assistance and comfort.[47] KFOR also has a Civilian-Military Cooperation (CIMIC) team, which, among other things, delivers wood stoves to "smiling teachers and children."[48] According to an officer with the team, CIMIC's work is mainly focused on three issues, "healthcare, culture, and education."[49] "Warm classrooms during the winter improve the conditions for education." He adds, "Remember that 60 to 70 percent of KFOR soldiers are parents. Therefore they feel that it's very natural to pay attention to the children."[50]

NATO is not alone in doing what amounts to social work in Kosovo. The U.S. Agency for International Development, which closed its Kosovo office three days before NATO began bombing, reopened for operations on April 1, 2000. So far USAID and its affiliated offices have spent more than $553 million.[51] USAID's Office of Transition Initiatives alone has funded more than 300 projects, ranging from purchasing start-up equipment for three Kosovo television and radio stations to buying equipment and materials for the Belanica Women's Sewing Group.[52]

The UN administration, too, is doing social work in Kosovo. "Prioritized public awareness campaigns, local capacity building and training, and community based events to promote human rights compliance and encourage tolerance between ethnic and social groups are high on UNMIK's agenda," explained Special Representative Kouchner in a letter to the European Parliament.[53] Kouchner also signed a decree on municipal elections that stipulated that at least one-third of political candidates must be women.[54] In May 2000, he organized a conference in Pristina called "Women in Elections and the Peace Process." More than 250 people attended the event that was, according to an UNMIK statement, "aimed at getting more women to participate in the elections this autumn, and to encourage their involvement in building a tolerant society in Kosovo."[55] After a two-hour plenary session, the conference divided into working groups to address topics such as "establishing a Kosovo women's advisory group to liaise with the UNMIK office of gender affairs."[56] In contrast to all the talk of peace and harmony, however, the reality of Kosovo was being catalogued at KFOR's daily press briefing being held nearby. The prior day's violence: a hand grenade was thrown from a car at a Serb's house in the town of Kosovo Polje injuring five people, an ethnic Albanian attacker struck a Serb man on the Head with an ax near the village of Dobrosin, a Molotov cocktail was thrown into an Albanian store near the town of Gnjilane, a KFOR checkpoint near Malisevo came under automatic fire by unknown assailants, and KFOR troops in Pristina were fired on.[57]

In an equally incongruous incident, UNMIK authorities designated September 9, 2000, Kosovo's official "Day against Violence," but Serbs were warned by "highly placed" UNMIK officials to stay away from the day's events out of fear they would become the targets of violence.[58] At the day's largest rally, Special Representative

Kouchner was loudly booed by a 6,000-stong ethnic Albanian crowd when he asserted, "Everyone in Kosovo is equal."[59] Later, when he repeated in the Serbian language a call for Kosovo's ethnic communities to work together, he again was met by a chorus of boos.[60]

A False Peace

Traveling through the Balkans shortly after NATO ended its air campaign, President Clinton declared: now that the war is over, "we must win the peace."[61] Obscuring the distinction between the physical presence of American peacekeepers in Kosovo and what specific policy aims they were being ordered to pursue, Clinton told U.S. soldiers that the United States must not walk away from Kosovo. In similar fashion, Secretary Albright proclaimed, "Having prevailed in war, our challenge is to secure the peace. This is proving, as expected, costly and hard. . . . But the cost and risks of quitting far exceed those of maintaining a peaceful Kosovo."[62] Albright, like Clinton, blurred the issue, equating quitting the administration's specific policy with quitting the peace. In reality, the peace Albright recommended maintaining in Kosovo was, and still is, a false peace. Indeed, unlike Bosnia, where the warring sides had been exhausted by three and a half years of civil war and three failed attempts at peace plans, Belgrade and the KLA had not yet fought each other to a similar standstill in Kosovo. As a result, the KLA saw NATO's bombing campaign against Yugoslavia not as a necessary means to end a brutal civil war, but as a means to advance its wartime agenda. "Without a doubt," concedes NATO's first commander in Kosovo, Gen. Michael Jackson, "the KLA had seen NATO and the air campaign as all part of what they were doing," which was creating an independent state.[63]

There is substantial evidence showing that the KLA and its supporters have not given up that objective. After a major NATO seizure of KLA weapons in June 2000, for instance, there were multiday demonstrations by ethnic Albanians calling for the withdrawal of NATO peacekeepers from Kosovo.[64] The protests were the first outright anti-NATO demonstrations held by Kosovo's Albanians since the arrival of peacekeepers 12 months earlier. Most of Kosovo's Albanians had viewed NATO as their savior, and such protests were previously unthinkable. But when NATO started tightening its leash on the KLA, the ubiquity of that support began to slip. In fact,

NATO's Civilian-Military Cooperation team released a summer 2000 report stating that the alliance was concerned its forces "had lost substantial credibility" in the eyes of the local communities and was becoming viewed as an obstacle to ethnic Albanian aspirations for independence. Many ethnic Albanians, moreover, are today tiring of the foreign-run government in Kosovo. They have nearly everywhere adopted the double-headed eagle flag of neighboring Albania as their own, and popular music now directs open threats at KFOR peacekeepers and UNMIK police. One song, sung in English to maximize the effect, warns NATO and UN personnel, "The future's gonna be the same as the past if you don't change your ways very fast / cause there is no bullet-proof vest to protect when I strike and blast."[65]

There were, however, earlier indications that the KLA and Washington's nation builders might not see eye to eye. In February 2000, NATO peacekeepers and ethnic Albanians openly clashed in the streets of the divided city of Kosovska Mitrovica. Ethnic Albanian militants, wanting to bring the entire city into their vision of what an independent Kosovo should look like, shot and wounded two French peacekeepers who were maintaining the city's line of separation. The French responded by killing one rooftop sniper and wounding at least four others. NATO soldiers subsequently arrested more than 40 people suspected of involvement in the bloodletting and released a joint statement with the United Nations that read: "What is clear . . . is that two young French soldiers, who came here as peacekeepers, are lying in hospital beds suffering from gunshot wounds inflicted on them by the very people that they came here to protect."[66]

On the political front, things were not going as smoothly as Washington's nation builders had hoped either. In June 2000, the KLA's former political leader, Hashim Thaçi, began a boycott of the Interim Administrative Council, the centerpiece of the unelected structure set up by Special Representative Kouchner to involve Kosovo's local leaders in decisionmaking. Thaçi said his new political party, the Democratic Party of Kosovo, had suspended formal cooperation with the Interim Administrative Council. That move followed the signing the week before of a memorandum of understanding between the United Nations and leaders of the Serb minority promising them better security and access to local public services in their enclaves. Members of Kosovo's ethnic Albanian majority expressed anger at the deal, which they said allowed the Serbs to have their own institutions. Specifically, the United Nations promised to "take special measures" to protect Serbs, including creating a neighborhood-watch system and a special committee to oversee protection of Serbian Orthodox religious sites. A senior member of Thaçi's party said they found the agreement unacceptable because the arrangement could be a first step toward dividing Kosovo into ethnic regions, which threatens ethnic Albanian aspirations to rule all of Kosovo.[67] Outside observers, moreover, speculated that the memorandum of understanding was a handy excuse and that Thaçi's decision was a sign of his growing impatience with the United Nations and NATO's interference with his efforts to consolidate power and create an independent state.[68]

Kosovo's "Declining" Murder Rate

Another early indication that Kosovo's peace is false and that the KLA and its supporters have not given up on their wartime objective was the widespread violence perpetrated against Serbs and other non-Albanians early on in the NATO deployment. In the first four months after NATO arrived, there were 348 murders, 116 kidnappings, 1,070 lootings, and 1,106 arsons aimed largely at Serbs and other non-Albanians.[69] The wave of ethnic violence was not without dramatic effect. As early as August 1999, Human Rights Watch estimated that more than 164,000 Serbs and Gypsies had been driven from or had left Kosovo because of the violence aimed at them.[70]

By April 2000, however, Secretary of State Albright approvingly reported, "The murder rate in Kosovo is now lower than in many American cities."[71] Similarly, in June 2000, National Security Adviser Berger touted, "The murder rate has declined by 90 percent in the past year."[72] Albright and Berger, however, failed to point out that the murder rate had fallen in Kosovo precisely because the province had been virtually cleansed of non-Albanian murder targets. Indeed, reports at the time estimated that as many as 240,000 non-Albanians, including Goranies, Croats, Turks, and Jews, had fled the province since NATO arrived.[73] In Kosovo's capital, Pristina, only 400 Serbs, of a prewar population of 40,000, were said to have remained.[74] Notwithstanding their dwindling presence, however, more than 25 murders, 45 aggravated assaults, and 100 incidents of arson were reported between February and June in which the victims were non-Albanian.[75] Reports also circulated that hundreds of Serbs and other non-Albanians had mysteriously disappeared or had been kidnapped.[76] The president of Médecins sans Frontières, a leading international emergency medical aid organization, complained that there "is no true environment of security [in Kosovo], there exists a climate of impunity."[77] The Belgian branch of that humanitarian group ceased operations in Kosovo in August 2000 because it said its doctors were "eyewitnesses to the daily harassment and terror against the Serb minority," and it "can no longer tolerate the serious and continuous deterioration of living conditions of the ethnic minorities in Kosovo."[78] Unfortunately for Albright and Berger, who were still trying to sell the idea that NATO's presence—rather than Kosovo's shrinking non-Albanian population—was responsible for the slowdown in ethnic violence, newspapers such as the London *Independent* were reporting:

> Trouble in Pristina comes fast, and almost always involves automatic weapons, organized crime, or ethnic hatred. Last Tuesday, two Serbian women in their twenties were strolling through the bustle of Mother Teresa Avenue, the city's central thoroughfare. It was 9:30 p.m. . . . Two gunmen opened fire on both women, hitting one in the chest and one in the legs. Totally ignored by Kosovo Albanians crowding down the street, they staggered bleeding into the arms of a British soldier. Their crime: being Serbs.[79]

Meanwhile, informed observers inside and outside Kosovo began to raise questions about the KLA's role in the ongoing violence and intimidation. *Time* magazine's Tony Karon, for example, concluded that members of the "Kosovo Liberation Army . . . appear to be animated by instincts every bit as violently racist and intolerant as their enemies in Belgrade, and simply started their own ethnic cleansing campaign as soon as they had the opportunity."[80]

Kosovo's Next Masters?

The Kosovo Liberation Army was founded in December 1993 on the radical fringe of Kosovo's political scene.[81] Just over two years later, the KLA made its violent debut, bombing several refugee camps housing Serbs displaced by the wars in Bosnia and Croatia.[82]

According to journalist Chris Hedges, who spent more than a year investigating the organization for the *New York Times*, the KLA

> splits down a bizarre ideological divide, with hints of fascism on one side and whiffs of communism on the other. The former faction is led by the sons and grandsons of rightist Albanian fighters—either the heirs of those who fought in the World War II fascist militias and the Skanderbeg volunteer SS division raised by the Nazis, or the descendants of the rightist Albanian *kacak* rebels who rose up against the Serbs 80 years ago. . . . The second KLA faction, comprising most of the KLA leaders in exile, are old Stalinists who were once bankrolled by the xenophobic Enver Hoxha, the dictator of Albania who died in 1985. This group led a militant separatist movement that was really about integration with Hoxha's Albania. . . . The two KLA factions have little sympathy with or understanding of democratic institutions.[83]

Throughout 1996 and 1997, the KLA expanded its militant operations in Kosovo, with numerous hit-and-run attacks on Serbian police and ethnic Albanians accused of collaborating with the Belgrade regime.[84] The KLA also received an unexpected boost in 1997 when the central government in neighboring Albania collapsed. In the ensuing chaos, Albania's army dissolved, the police abandoned their posts, and the government's arms depots were thrown open. Between 650,000 and 1 million light weapons and 1.5 billion rounds of ammunition were stolen.[85] An estimated 3.5 million hand grenades, 1 million anti-personnel mines, 840,000 mortar shells, and 3,600 tons of explosives also went missing.[86] Many of the plundered weapons headed straight into the hands of the KLA.[87]

There are also strong indications the KLA subsidized its activities with funding from organized crime and an Albanian drug-trafficking network that stretches across Europe.[88] In fact, as early as June 1994, the Paris-based Geopolitical Drug Watch issued a bulletin that concluded narcotics smuggling had become a prime source of financing for civil wars already under way—or rapidly brewing—in southeastern Europe.[89] The GDW, which compiles research from 80 countries, is regarded as Europe's most authoritative monitor of the international drug trade and its efforts are conducted in partnership with several national police agencies and underwritten by grants from the European Union in Brussels.[90] The GDW bulletin identified Albanian nationalists in Kosovo and Macedonia as key players in the region's accelerating drugs-for-arms traffic and noted that they were transporting up to $2 billion worth of heroin annually into Central and Western Europe "in order to finance large purchases of weapons" from black-market arms dealers in Switzerland.[91] At the time the report was written, more than 500 Albanians from Kosovo and Macedonia were in prison in Switzerland for drug- or arms-trafficking offenses, and more than 1,000 others were under indictment.[92]

Over the next few years, police forces in at least three European countries discovered evidence that drug money was funding the KLA.[93] In the Czech Republic, police tracked down a drug dealer from Kosovo who had escaped from a Norwegian prison where he was serving a 12-year sentence for heroin trading. A raid on the dealer's apartment turned up documents linking him with arms purchases for the KLA.[94] In Italy, a criminal court convicted an Albanian drug trafficker who admitted obtaining weapons from the Italian Mafia in exchange for illegal drugs.[95] In Germany, federal police agents froze two bank accounts of the United Kosovo organization when they uncovered deposits totaling several hundred thousand dollars from a convicted drug trafficker from Kosovo.[96] By 1999, Western intelligence sources estimated that more than $250 million in illegal drug money had been funneled into the KLA,[97] and an internal NATO report conceded:

> Some funds from the drug trade, in which the Albanians traditionally acted as couriers and more lately as suppliers, reportedly are being used to purchase weapons for the Kosovo insurgents. . . . The profitability of the drug trade and the Kosovo Albanians' extensive involvement in it suggests this activity is a significant source of income for the insurgency and other Albanian causes.[98]

From "Terrorists" to Partners

On January 7, 1998, the KLA for the first time took responsibility for attacks outside Yugoslavia, admitting that it had bombed two police stations in Macedonia three days earlier. In a faxed statement, the group said its armed forces complied with orders issued by its chief of staff to begin attacks in "operational zone number 2."[99] Over the next several weeks the KLA began a killing spree, gunning down unarmed people, including a physical education teacher, a bar manager, and a forest ranger.[100] It also conducted armed attacks on buildings housing the families of Serbian police in Kosovo.[101] By February 23, U.S. special envoy to the Balkans Robert Gelbard had little difficulty in denouncing the KLA in the strongest possible terms. The KLA, he said, "is, without any questions, a terrorist group," and "we condemn very strongly terrorist actions in Kosovo."[102]

Gelbard's remarks came just five days before a KLA attack on Serbian police left two policemen and five KLA members dead.[103] A few days later, Serbian police began a massive security sweep through central Kosovo that resulted in at least 20 deaths, including several civilians and four policemen.[104] Concerned that Gelbard's earlier remarks about the KLA were interpreted by the Milosevic regime as a "green light" to crack down on the KLA, the House Committee on International Relations asked him to clarify his views. Although the KLA has committed "terrorist acts," Gelbard told the committee, it has "not been classified legally by the U.S. government as a terrorist organization."[105] By the time Gelbard made that clarification, however, the situation in Kosovo had already been transformed. Indeed, what was once a matter of sporadic KLA attacks and indiscriminate Serbian responses had become a full-scale counterinsurgency, and by the end of March, more than 80 people, including many civilians, had died in clashes between Serbian authorities and the KLA.[106]

Over the course of the ensuing 12 months, Washington decided to embrace the KLA as a partner, and demanded that the Serbs meet in Rambouillet, France, to accept a peace plan with Kosovo's ethnic Albanians. Three former U.S. State Department officials—Morton Abramowitz, Marshall Harris, and Paul Williams—advised the ethnic Albanian delegation in Rambouillet, and Secretary Albright told the KLA that it would be made the official police force of Kosovo under Washington's proposed peace plan and be given training in the United States.[107] "We want to develop closer and better ties with this organization," explained deputy State Department spokesperson James Foley.[108] On Capitol Hill, Sen. Joseph Lieberman (D-Conn.) even managed to claim that the "United States of America and the Kosovo Liberation Army stand for the same human values and principles. . . . Fighting for the KLA is fighting for human rights and American values."[109]

The KLA Settles In

The KLA, however, had ideas of its own. When the Milosevic regime refused to sign the agreement produced at Rambouillet, NATO carried out its threat to bomb Yugoslavia. After Milosevic finally withdrew his forces from Kosovo in June, following 11 weeks of NATO bombing, the KLA swept across the province, organized its own provisional government, and set up a "Ministry of Public Order."[110] As quickly as NATO began deploying peacekeeping troops in Kosovo, the KLA began driving out the province's Serbs and other non-Albanians, seizing property and businesses, extorting money, and intimidating moderate ethnic Albanians.[111] Human Rights Watch, which for years had catalogued abuses committed by Serbian authorities in Kosovo, acknowledged the new reality in August 1999, noting "the most serious incidents of violence . . . have been carried out by the KLA." "The frequency and severity of the abuses," added the rights group, "make it incumbent upon the KLA leadership to take swift and decisive action to prevent them."[112]

KLA officials did no such thing. In fact, the abuses and killings continued, often committed by the "secret police" connected with the KLA's so-called Ministry of Public Order.[113] By December 1999, the Organization for Security and Cooperation in Europe published a damning report that cataloged the human rights violations committed in Kosovo since NATO peacekeepers had arrived five months earlier. Serbs and other non-Albanians, said the report, were the targets of "executions, abductions, torture, cruel, inhuman and degrading treatment, arbitrary arrests . . . house burnings, blockades restricting freedom of movement, discriminatory treatment in schools, hospitals, humanitarian aid distribution and other public services . . . and forced evictions from housing." In many of the cases, the report added, "there are serious indications that the perpetrators of [these] human rights violations are either members of the former KLA, people passing themselves off as members of the former KLA or members of other armed Albanian groups."[114]

The KLA was also implicated in efforts aimed at silencing moderate ethnic Albanians with a terror campaign of intimidation, kidnappings, beatings, bombings, and killings.[115] In October 1999, Kosovapress, a news agency tied to the KLA, issued a veiled death threat to Veton Surroi, editor of the popular Albanian-language newspaper *Koha Ditore*, when he criticized the widespread violence directed at

Serbs and other non-Albanians in Kosovo.[116] Surroi was singled out for expressing the following view in an editorial:

> Today's violence . . . is more than simply an emotional reaction. It is the organized and systematic intimidation of all Serbs simply because they are Serbs. . . . Such an attitude is fascist. It will dishonor us and our own recent suffering which, only a few months ago, was broadcast on television screens throughout the world. And it will dishonor the memory of Kosovo's Albanian victims, those women, children and elderly who were killed simply because of their ethnic origins. . . . [From] having been victims of Europe's worst end-of-century persecution, we are ourselves becoming persecutors and have allowed the specter of fascism to reappear. Anybody who thinks that the violence will end once the last Serb has been driven out is living an illusion. The violence will simply be directed against other Albanians.[117]

Kosovapress's response to Surroi's editorial was immediate. In a strongly worded column, it warned that he risked "eventual and very understandable revenge," claimed that "such criminals and enslaved minds should not have a place in the free Kosovo," and accused him of having a "Slav stink" about him.[118]

As worrisome, the KLA was linked to attacks across Kosovo targeting offices and members of the Democratic League of Kosovo (LDK), a political party whose leader, Ibrahim Rugova, was Kosovo's most popular politician before the war. LDK party activists who have survived severe beatings have said their attackers claimed to be from the "true KLA" or the "Ministry of Order."[119] One victim who did not survive his attack was Haki Imeri, a schoolteacher who had recently been appointed a member of a local board of the LDK. He was abducted and killed on November 2, 1999. He was last seen entering a car licensed to an intelligence officer with the KLA.[120] In another incident, Ismet Veliqi, a local LDK activist and schoolteacher, was abducted, beaten, shot, and left for dead on February 23, 2000. Veliqi said his assailants were ethnic Albanians who asked him during their attack, "Why do you still support Rugova?"[121] At the time of his abduction, there were five "unofficial" KLA Ministry of Order police stations still operating in Pristina alone.[122] On June 15, 2000, a moderate LDK politician, Halil Dreshaj, was shot and killed when two attackers forced their way into his home in the western

Kosovo village of Nabrdje. The victim's wife was quoted as saying the attackers wore uniforms with the red-and-black emblem of the Kosovo Liberation Army.[123] Special Representative Kouchner, however, blamed the murder on nonspecific "extremists" who "do not want us to succeed."[124]

The KLA "Demilitarizes"

According to Secretary of State Albright, Washington's peace plan for Kosovo had three main elements: "the KLA would disarm, the Serbs would pull their forces out, and there would be an international force that would go in there to help implement it."[125] The idea that the KLA would disarm was reiterated by the administration before and during NATO's air campaign against Yugoslavia. Testifying before the House International Relations Committee on April 21, 1999, for example, Secretary Albright claimed, "At Rambouillet, Belgrade rejected a plan for peace that had been accepted by the Kosovo Albanians, and that included provisions for disarming the KLA."[126] In the weeks before NATO's bombing ended, State Department spokesperson James Rubin said Washington was working with Moscow on two aspects of peace for Kosovo: "one, getting the refugees home; and two, the disarmament of the Kosovo Liberation Army."[127]

But after Belgrade indicated it was willing to pull its forces out of Kosovo, Washington decided that disarmament was not what it really meant. Indeed, after Belgrade said it would capitulate, a reporter asked State Department spokesperson Rubin if the United States would "press for a complete disarmament of the KLA." Rubin's response: "The proper word here is 'demilitarization.' I'll get you a copy of the Rambouillet accords, which describes demilitarization as envisaged in those accords. That remains the principle under which we're operating."[128]

Under the demilitarization terms reached between NATO and the KLA, the KLA agreed officially to disband but would form the core of the new Kosovo Protection Corps, which would consist of 5,000 full-time and reserve personnel. According to the agreement, the KLA would turn in an unspecified number of weapons and fully demobilize by September 20, 1999. The new KPC would then limit its activities to providing disaster relief, performing search and rescue, delivering humanitarian aid, assisting in demining the countryside, and contributing to the rebuilding of Kosovo's infrastructure. "We believe the Kosovo Protection Corps will make a useful contribution to the restoration of peace and security for all the communities of Kosovo and its progress towards democracy," said Secretary Albright in a prepared statement.[129]

After the KLA turned in roughly 10,000 guns, many of them broken or antiquated, NATO declared the demilitarization a success and claimed the KLA no longer existed.[130] "The Kosovo Liberation Army has demilitarized and has been transformed into the Kosovo Protection Corps," claimed NATO's supreme allied commander, Gen. Wesley Clark, before the U.S. Senate Armed Services Committee.[131] What Gen. Clark did not mention was that a few days before the KLA was supposed to finish demilitarizing, German KFOR soldiers stumbled on a secret cache of 10 tons of ammunition.

When UNMIK held a ceremony to swear in some of the first members of the new Kosovo Protection Corps in early 2000, the event was opened with an address by an UNMIK official. In keeping with UNMIK's claim that the KPC would be an organization of a multiethnic character, the official's remarks were being translated into both Serbian and Albanian. In the middle of the UNMIK official's speech, however, the new members of the KPC—all of whom were ethnic Albanian—disrupted the ceremony by walking out of the room in protest of the Serbian translation. KPC family members and other ethnic Albanians present at the ceremony greeted the action with applause. The KPC members returned to the ceremony only after they were assured the event would continue exclusively in Albanian. Gen. Agim Çeku, the former KLA chief turned KPC commander, later took the stage amid sustained applause. "Today you are becoming professional officers," he told the KPC members in attendance. "Just as you knew how to triumph over all the obstacles and difficulties of war . . . this time too, you will emerge victorious."[132]

Shortly after the KPC was outfitted and organized throughout Kosovo, Special Representative Kouchner invited journalists to inspect a KPC work group removing ice from the roads in Pristina. The intended message was clear—the militant KLA had been successfully reinvented as a force for public service.[133] Outside the Clinton White House, however, few people bought that message, and by March 2000, analysts at the otherwise pro-nation building International Crisis Group were reporting that, notwithstanding Washington's claim that the KLA had demilitarized, the KLA "in its various manifestations . . . remains a powerful and active element in almost every element of Kosovo life. . . . Some parts of the old KLA operate openly and essentially as before; others have been transformed; some new elements have been added; and much remains underground."[134] Just two weeks earlier, UN authorities had warned that the KLA's official successor, the KPC, was engaged in illegal activities and human rights abuses. More specifically, the UN human rights unit in Kosovo said in an internal report that several members of the KPC tortured or killed local citizens and illegally detained others, illegally attempted to conduct law enforcement activities, illegally forced local businesses to pay "liberation taxes," and threatened UN police who attempted to intervene and stop the wrongdoing.[135] UN officials also expressed concern about the fact that the KPC distributed 15,000 uniforms despite being limited to a maximum strength of 5,000 members.[136] Moreover, UN police and NATO soldiers voiced worries about seizing hundreds of forged and counterfeit KPC identity cards from people claiming to be members of the organization.[137] To date, Western taxpayers have contributed more than $10 million to the creation and maintenance of the KPC.[138]

Still, advocates of nation building refused to admit that the KLA was responsible for any of the instability in Kosovo, and instead habitually blamed Belgrade for Kosovo's postwar troubles. Writing in the *Los Angeles Times* in the summer of 2000, for example, International Crisis Group consultant Susan Blaustein did not once mention the KLA and asserted that "allied nations have tolerated a porous border with Serbia . . . enabling Yugoslav President Slobodan Milosevic to pursue his destabilizing agenda in Kosovo."[139] The harsh reality, however, was and still is that NATO and UN officials find themselves not with a peacekeeping operation in Kosovo, but with a KLA management operation. Indeed, the popular *Koha Ditore* newspaper warns that KLA elements run "illegal businesses," exploit "their position and the might of arms" for personal gain, "intrude on the privacy of certain individuals," and are directly and indirectly "implicated in political developments."[140]

Spreading Disorder

Although the Clinton administration insisted that the KLA met its requirements to demilitarize in 1999, the rebel organization nevertheless has been able to foment an insurgency across the provincial border of Kosovo in Serbia's predominantly ethnic Albanian Presevo Valley—which Albanian nationalists call "Eastern Kosovo."[141] In a disturbing replay of the strategy the KLA used from early 1998 until NATO commenced its bombing, ethnic Albanian guerrillas are attacking Serbian policemen and civilians—and ethnic Albanians loyal to Belgrade—in the hope of provoking Yugoslav authorities into a response that will incite the United States and NATO to resume their war with Yugoslavia. As a UN official in Kosovo explained, the guerrillas hope "that the Serbs will retaliate with excessive force against civilian populations and create a wave of outrage and pressure on KFOR to respond."[142]

In March 2000, the guerrillas promised U.S. diplomats that they would end their insurgency. "We're happy they did it," said one U.S. official. "We gave them a tough message, and they believed it."[143] The head of the U.S. negotiating team welcomed the promise, saying it was "an important first step."[144] The rebel group, however, took no steps to live up to its pledge and announced the next day that it "has not ceased its activities" and that it will not stop until "Eastern Kosovo is liberated."[145] The guerrillas, moreover, continued to wear KLA-like uniforms, to conduct training exercises, and to cross back and forth across the neutral zone between U.S. forces in Kosovo and Yugoslav forces in Serbia proper.[146] Though the leaders of the supposedly disbanded KLA insist they are not tied to the rebels, those killed in the Presevo Valley are buried in cemeteries reserved for KLA martyrs.[147] Moreover, the "Homeland Calling Fund," which was set up to raise money from the Albanian diaspora to fund the KLA, has been resurrected to fund the Presevo insurgents.[148]

Notwithstanding those facts, Clinton administration officials downplayed KLA involvement in the violence. In fact, Secretary Albright praised the KLA for "having met its commitment to demobilize" and she stressed that a "spirit of tolerance and inter-ethnic cooperation" will take root in Kosovo as the province's "democratic forces" come to power.[149] America's chief diplomat should have had a better grasp of Kosovo's realities. The KLA and its supporters are committed to taking power in Kosovo and expanding its dominion, not to practicing multiethnic democracy.

Not all foreign officials were as gullible as the Clinton administration's, however. Jiri Dienstbier, former Czech foreign minister turned

UN special envoy for human rights, submitted a 53-page report to the UN Human Rights Commission in March 2000 in which he sharply criticized the KLA. In particular, he accused the leaders of the organization of destabilizing the Presevo Valley with a view to creating a Greater Albania.[150] Voicing similar concerns, Gen. Reinhardt, the former commander of KFOR, warned that tensions between Serbs and ethnic Albanians in the Presevo Valley could result in a new war. Like Dienstbier, Reinhardt also expressed skepticism that the rebels were dedicated to peace. "Frankly, when we see them training with mortars . . . I do not believe them."[151] Reinhardt's concerns were underscored by same-day reports of a grenade attack on a Serbian police checkpoint on the other side of the Kosovo boundary.[152] Other attacks followed, and by July 2000 fighting between the ethnic Albanian separatists and Yugoslav security forces intensified to the point that NATO forces could hear automatic gunfire and explosions coming from over the administrative border in Serbia proper.[153] By the fall of 2000, the security situation in the Presevo Valley deteriorated even further as the number of ethnic Albanian guerrillas operating in the area reportedly tripled and the number of attacks on Serb policemen increased.[154] In December, the rebels fired upon a joint American-Russian patrol, and in January 2001, a British patrol was attacked.[155]

As troubling, ethnic Albanians from Kosovo and Albania, including KLA elements, are also involved in attempts to infiltrate and destabilize Macedonia. News reports, which began appearing as early as June 2000, highlighted the connection among organized smuggling rings, the KLA, and the political leadership in the ethnic Albanian area of western Macedonia. On June 20, 2000, two Macedonian border guards were shot near a crossing into Kosovo. The attack was attributed to ethnic Albanians who, beyond smuggling, were said to be forming the nucleus of a KLA-linked armed movement in Macedonia.[156] In a subsequent incident, four Macedonian border guards were kidnapped, allegedly to be exchanged for KLA activists who were being held in Macedonian prisons. Even though the guards were released a short time later, the Macedonian public was outraged.[157] By August 2000, NATO was relaying worrisome reports of paramilitary activity in western Macedonia, including a report that nearly 100 ethnic Albanians were conducting military exercises in the Sar Mountains, which straddle the border of Macedonia and

Kosovo.[158] On January 25, 2001, ethnic Albanian guerrillas attacked a Macedonian police station with automatic rifles and rocket launchers.[159] A month later, they attacked a Macedonian police patrol near the border with Kosovo, drawing Macedonian army units into a firefight and forcing hundreds of civilians to flee.[160] Fighting also broke out near Macedonia's second largest city, Tetevo, when rebels entered border villages from Kosovo. Should the situation get out of hand, observers fear, it could lead to more tragedy in the Balkans.

Just a "Coincidence"

Belatedly awakening to the danger posed by the KLA's cross-border activities, U.S. forces on March 16, 2000, raided arms caches and other logistical infrastructure used by the rebels to sustain its operations in the Presevo Valley.[161] In mid-April peacekeeping troops in Kosovo arrested 12 ethnic Albanians on charges of illegal possession of arms and other military materiel after the driver of a truck failed to stop when flagged down at a checkpoint. In the truck, peacekeepers found 80 anti-tank mines, 40 hand grenades, and large quantities of guns and ammunition.[162] In May, American peacekeepers seized rifles, explosives, hand grenades, and other weapons in a search operation in the eastern village of Uglijare.[163]

On June 17, 2000, NATO peacekeepers discovered the largest cache of illegal weapons in Kosovo to date. In two 30-foot by 10-foot concrete bunkers dug into a hillside in a forested area of central Kosovo, British troops found 67 tons of weapons and explosives, including 20,000 grenades, thousands of mines, and half a million bullets.[164] A KFOR spokesperson said the weapons were enough to "to eliminate the entire population of Pristina or destroy 900 to 1,000 tanks."[165] Brig. Gen. Richard Shirreff, commander of the British KFOR forces leading the operation, told reporters at the scene: "This represents a major weapons haul. It is almost certainly, entirely Albanian, all evidence we got here suggests that it is former KLA material" and the fact they did not divulge any information reflects "a degree of non-compliance" with NATO.[166]

The former military head of the KLA, Agim Çeku, denied any link between the officially disbanded organization and the massive weapons stash. "With full confidence I can say the KLA did not possess these weapons during the war," said Çeku, who now heads the Kosovo Protection Corps.[167] The statement came as NATO troops announced the discovery of more bunkers containing arms. Çeku claimed the fact that the weapons were found just a half mile from his wartime headquarters was a "coincidence."[168] The KLA has "handed in all its weapons as required of them," he added. "There is no reason for it to take responsibility for weapons that might be found."[169] NATO officials, however, announced that documents found at the sites indicated the weapons had, in fact, belonged to the KLA.[170]

In another worrisome incident, KFOR soldiers discovered a complex of bunkers and fighting positions only 12 miles from the Kosovo-Macedonia border. Without mentioning the KLA by name, a KFOR spokesperson speculated that the site was a training area "used by extremist elements," adding that fresh tire tracks and footprints suggested that it was in recent use.[171] KFOR units have since discovered several weapons stockpiles scattered throughout Kosovo.[172] One included sniper rifles, machine guns, more than 80 mines, 100 pounds of TNT, and paraphernalia to detonate bombs remotely—"clear indications of a terrorist capability," explained a prepared KFOR statement on the find.[173]

Notwithstanding such high-profile discoveries, NATO has been less than exhaustive in its efforts to root out illegal arms and end the cross-border activity. To do so would mean directly confronting the KLA and its supporters. That was something the Clinton administration was loathe to do because it would have exposed the main flaw in its Kosovo policy. Indeed, had NATO personnel started dying at the hands of the very people the administration said the United States was out to help—à la Mogadishu—then it would have been forced to admit that its de facto partners had not actually given up on their wartime objective and that the peacekeeping operation was a sham. Rather than risk that, the Clinton administration preferred to do as little as possible. Unfortunately, the KLA understood that priority as early as June 1999, and carried out its intolerant and militant activities without fear of serious resistance from the Clinton White House.

Corruption and Criminality

The legacy of the KLA has caused a multitude of problems inside Kosovo. For example, in March of 2000, Special Representative Kouchner announced that "private enterprise has restarted very well" in Kosovo.[174] Yet almost everywhere business has restarted, violence and criminality have followed. Gerard Fischer, a senior UN mission economic official, notes that "extortion is a big problem" and he suspects that former KLA members are behind it.[175] Similarly, the *Boston Globe* reports,

> Extortion is Kosovo's most robust industry. Nearly every cafe, restaurant, and shop pays tribute. Most business owners simply shrug and pay the mobsters, some of them former members of the Kosovo Liberation Army who have morphed from freedom fighters into shakedown artists. . . . "There is no law here," said John Foreman, an Englishman who runs a bar in Pristina. Foreman said he has been threatened repeatedly by former Kosovo Liberation Army members who are demanding that he pay them about $3,000 a month for the privilege of doing business. They have followed him home, telling him he is a dead man. They have stolen his generators four times. Foreman says his bar has been targeted because it is multiethnic. His staff and clientele are Albanian and Serb. . . . "This is the only multiethnic bar in Kosovo, and they can't stand the fact that we're open," he said.[176]

Former KLA members have also been implicated in efforts to collect illegal taxes and fees to fund their postwar activities. On the Kosovo-Macedonia border, for example, they reportedly forced 1,300 or so trucks passing each day to pay a "customs duty" of $20.[177] The leaders of the former KLA deny that any such taxes have been collected. But documents seized by UNMIK police show that Kosovo businessmen have been ordered to pay similar fees and that elements of the former KLA have established an elaborate sliding scale of illegal taxes for cigarettes, alcohol, juices, coffee, and gasoline.[178]

Even more disturbing, many former KLA members are reportedly involved in protection rackets, prostitution, corruption, and bribery. On January 6, 2000, UNMIK police raided the home of Gani Thaçi, a brother of former KLA political leader Hashim Thaçi. The police seized weapons and a suitcase containing $791,000 in cash. Hashim Thaçi demanded—and quickly received—an apology from UNMIK. His brother was released without charge, and his money and weapons were returned.[179] Part of the money was from a Canadian construction company working in Kosovo that had paid Gani Thaçi for what the company euphemistically called his "intermediary services" in securing lucrative reconstruction contracts after the war.[180]

In another incident, police specialists attached to KFOR's multinational peacekeeping force raided more than 10 premises in and around the town of Djeneral Jankovic on Kosovo's southern border with Macedonia, arresting 10 men and seizing cash and weapons. Among those arrested was Refki Sumen, a former KLA commander and a senior figure in the guerrilla force's civilian successor, the Kosovo Protection Corps. "The arrests were carried out as part of an ongoing investigation into an organized crime gang operating in the border area," explained a special police spokesperson. "We suspect the group to be involved in at least three homicides, extortion, and smuggling."[181]

International law enforcement authorities and drug experts also worry that former KLA members have not severed their ties with the narcotics underworld. Instead, they are now paying their patrons back with political favors and using their new profits to rebuild. "The new buildings, the better roads," explains Michel Koutouzis of the Geopolitical Drug Watch, "these have been bought by drugs."[182] There are also indications that former senior KLA figures have provided immunity for the criminal gangs or are directly involved in the postwar drug trade itself. Some analysts have warned that it could become difficult for international organizations to find former KLA members who "are not so tainted with criminality or other serious misbehavior as to be completely unacceptable." One senior UN official has even lamented that the West might be creating "a narco-mafia style society" in Kosovo.[183]

KLA Infighting

In addition to daily incidents of ethnic violence and criminality in Kosovo, many people have been left dead as a result of political rivalries between former KLA figures and their ongoing turf battles over lucrative racketeering rings and the economic spoils of war. Indeed, in the first weeks following the end of NATO's air campaign, the *New York Times* reported,

> The senior commanders of the Kosovo Liberation Army . . . carried out assassinations, arrests, and purges within their ranks to thwart potential rivals, say current and former commanders in the rebel army and some Western diplomats. The campaign, in which as many as half a dozen top rebel commanders were shot dead, was directed by Hashim Thaçi and two of his lieutenants, Azem Syla and Xhavit Haliti,

> these officials said. . . . The charges of assassinations and purges were made in interviews with about a dozen former and current Kosovo Liberation Army officials, two of whom said they had witnessed executions of Mr. Thaçi's rivals; a former senior diplomat for the Albanian Government; a former police official in the Albanian Government who worked with the rebel group, and several Western diplomats.[184]

On April 18, 2000, former KLA military leader turned KPC commander, Besim Mala, was shot in the head by a .357 Magnum and bled to death on the pavement outside a Pristina restaurant.[185] Mala was killed in an internal gangland struggle over protection rackets.[186] Three weeks later, former KLA commander Ekrem Rexha was gunned down outside his home in the southern Kosovo town of Prizren.[187] A known moderate, Rexha was a Thaçi opponent. "This could be the first of a series of political murders" as Kosovo gears up for October's municipal elections, explained one UN official, adding that Rexha would have been voted Prizren's mayor "for sure" if he ran for the office.[188] In September, Skender Gashi, a KPC district commander and former KLA officer, was found murdered with both hands cut off.[189] Gashi's death brought to 24 the number of ex-KLA killed in infighting since the war ended.[190]

Elections and Intimidation

One of the KLA's more insidious legacies has been its direct and indirect intimidation of rival politicians. Special Representative Kouchner worried early on that political violence would increase during the run up to Kosovo's October 2000 municipal elections. A prominent nongovernmental organization similarly cautioned that "one of the most serious potential areas for abuse of the elections . . . is intimidation of political parties and candidates, especially at local level."[191] The report specifically cited the area of Srbica in central Kosovo, where the moderate Democratic League of Kosovo (LDK) party encountered "a climate of intimidation and harassment."[192] In the months preceding the election, a Srbica-area LDK official was kidnapped from in front of his house and later found dead, and two aspiring LDK politicians were shot and wounded in separate attacks.[193] On September 11, 2000, journalist Shefki Popova was shot dead seven miles from Srbica. Popova was a correspondent with the Albanian-language daily newspaper *Rilindja* and a contributor to the paper's subsidiary radio station. Both media outlets are closely associated with the LDK.[194]

In the area of Prizren, former KLA commander Ramush Haradinaj was wounded in a shootout before the election. According to eyewitnesses, Haradinaj and a group of KPC members initiated the incident by attacking a home about 1:00 a.m. with automatic weapons.[195] Residents of the village said they suspected the attack was launched because many of them do not support Haradinaj's party, the Alliance for the Future of Kosovo, but support the more moderate LDK. "He wants to win the election in Kosovo by force, by killing his rivals," explained one villager.[196] The following day, UNMIK police arrested two members of the KPC, two miles south of the shootout site. In protest of the arrests, several ethnic Albanians set up roadblocks in the area. The arrested men were later released after members of the KPC surrounded the UN police station where the two were being held and KPC chief Çeku intervened to negotiate their release.[197]

British military personnel, who actually worked with Haradinaj before and during NATO's air campaign against Yugoslavia, reported that he was a highly questionable figure. One British soldier even described him as "a psychopath" and said he terrorized his own men and the local population into unquestioning loyalty to him. "Someone would pass him some information and he would disappear for two hours. The end result would be several bodies in a ditch."[198] In contrast, Clinton administration officials, who were determined to keep up the appearance that their Kosovo policy was working, portrayed Haradinaj as a burgeoning democrat. U.S. military personnel removed forensic evidence from the scene of the Haradinaj gunfight—including bullets—even though the incident took place well outside the U.S. Army's area of responsibility in Kosovo.[199] In addition, Haradinaj was flown to Germany to be treated in a U.S. Army hospital for the wounds he received from the gunfight. During that time UN investigators were denied access to him.[200]

In the end, the two political parties spawned by the KLA—Haradinaj's Alliance for the Future and Thaçi's Democratic Party of Kosovo—managed to gain only 35 percent of the vote during Kosovo's October 2000 municipal elections, compared to 58 percent received by Rugova's Democratic League of Kosovo.[201] Western officials claimed that the relative success of Rugova's party was a victory for political moderation. But the more likely explanation was that

Haradinaj's and Thaçi's parties were unorganized and suffered from a predictable backlash against their violent attacks on other ethnic Albanian politicians. Indeed, in a postelection analysis, *Koha Ditore* suggested that the two parties "paid the price of [campaign] inexperience" and for the "arrogant and violent behavior of part of their memberships."[202] The success of Rugova's party, moreover, probably had something to do with the fact that Rugova himself turned up his nationalist rhetoric during the campaign. In fact, he repeatedly affirmed his nationalist credentials by calling on the West to recognize the independence of Kosovo after the election.[203]

Competing Fears

Reinforcing Kosovo's false peace—and the destabilizing role of the KLA and its legacy—is the fact that, as in Bosnia, there is an unresolved "security dilemma" among the province's inhabitants. Indeed, even though 40,000 heavily armed peacekeepers are deployed throughout Kosovo, neither ethnic Albanians nor Serbs consider themselves secure. Kosovo's Albanians fear they may eventually be reincorporated into Yugoslavia. Kosovo's Serbs, meanwhile, fear they may eventually be left to suffer under an oppressive ethnic Albanian regime. Neither fear is unreasonable. Belgrade's new democratic government has given no indication that it has abandoned its territorial claim to the province. In fact, a senior figure in the new government says that 1,200 Yugoslav troops should soon return to Kosovo to patrol Yugoslavia's external borders with Macedonia and Albania.[204] Meanwhile, ethnic Albanians have done little to allay Serb fears about life in an independent Kosovo. Indeed, following a September 2000 political rally, Kosovo Albanians took to stoning Serb homes.[205] On February 16, 2001, Kosovo militants blew up a bus carrying Serb families on a pilgrimage to the graves of their ancestors, killing seven people, injuring 43, and leaving behind a tangle of charred metal, scraps of clothing, and scattered notebook pages covered with children's doodles.[206] Hashim Thaçi, moreover, says the ouster of Slobodan Milosevic by the democratic opposition in Belgrade does not change anything in Kosovo. "Kosovo [will] never be a part of Serbia . . . whether it [is] a dictatorial or democratic Serbia," he declares.[207]

Unfortunately, the Clinton administration's policy postponing any decision on Kosovo's final status only fed the competing fears of

Kosovo's Albanians and Serbs and perpetuated their security dilemma. Indeed, Kosovo's Albanians have spent the last two years trying to make sure their independence is a fait accompli, while Serbs inside and outside Kosovo have concentrated their efforts on making sure that it is not. The result is that nothing resembling the multiethnic democracy the Clinton administration said was necessary before U.S. troops could return home has emerged in Kosovo. In fact, ethnic Albanians, fearing Belgrade's future designs, have intentionally depopulated Kosovo of most of its non-Albanian populations and are overtly and covertly resisting the UN's effort to create a multiethnic democracy. What is more, most of Kosovo's Albanians say they are still willing to fight for the province's independence from Yugoslavia.[208] On the other hand, most of the Serbs who have fled Kosovo are not returning, and those who never left have refused to register to vote and worry that their participation in UN-organized institutions and elections will legitimize Kosovo's permanent separation from Yugoslavia. Belgrade, meanwhile, insists that Kosovo is still Serbia and that it will respond with "all possible means" if attacked by ethnic Albanian rebels.[209]

What actually exists in Kosovo, in other words, is not peace, but a NATO-enforced absence of a clear victor—two very different things that yield two very different results for the would-be nation builder. Nevertheless, many in Washington continue to insist that running Kosovo this way will eventually succeed. Believing that, the United States and several European countries have moved ahead with the so-called Balkan Stability Pact, a multilateral effort to help rebuild Kosovo specifically and the Balkans generally. The first postwar meeting to sketch a working framework for the pact was held in July 1999. European donors promised $2.1 billion for Kosovo's reconstruction, and $403 million in economic aid to Yugoslavia's neighbors Romania, Bulgaria, and Macedonia.[210] A few days later, the Clinton administration pledged $700 million to the effort.[211] Unfortunately, such well-meaning foreign charity will probably make Kosovo even more dependent on the West than it already is. At present, explains the *Wall Street Journal,*

> The locals [in Kosovo] have little independent purchasing power. Most of the cash comes from two sources: the Kosovar diaspora and the 40,000-strong international military and civilian presence, which rents the best houses and buildings, hires drivers and interpreters, and buys everything for sale.[212]

Moreover, if Bosnia is any indication of what will become of the aid package, it will simply beget corruption and requests for even more aid money down the road.

Illusory Goals

Though some analysts may claim the "Clinton administration deserves credit for having done several things right" in Kosovo, highlighting the obvious—that not everything has gone wrong—is not a compelling defense; it is a rhetorical diversion.[213] The uncomfortable truth is that Washington's nation-building effort in Kosovo rests on a false peace; the KLA has not given up its wartime agenda and Kosovo's limbo status perpetuates the competing fears of both ethnic Albanians and Serbs. There is not, in other words, a shared reason of state among Kosovo's inhabitants. That fact virtually ensures that the nation-building effort will eventually fail. Indeed, nearly a year into the effort, the U.S. General Accounting Office released a 90-page report that lamented: "The continuing hostilities and lack of political and social reconciliation between Kosovar Albanians and non-Albanians have overshadowed positive developments that have occurred since the end of NATO's bombing campaign."[214] Though full-scale military hostilities between Belgrade and KLA forces have ceased, the report added, the security situation in the Balkans is still "volatile" and "local political leaders and people of their respective ethnic groups have failed to embrace the political and social reconciliation considered necessary to build multiethnic, democratic societies and institutions."[215] In other words, like Bosnia, the conditions the Clinton administration and others said would be required for U.S. troops to one day leave Kosovo are not, in fact, being created.

As it turns out, where there is peace in Kosovo is where it is most *unlike* the Clinton administration's intended vision for the province. And those ethnic Albanians who tend to be the most content with Kosovo's current political limbo are those who are most certain that independence is just a question of time. For advocates of Clinton's policy to then characterize such people and places as evidence of "progress" or a vindication of the previous administration's efforts is intellectually dishonest.

In an extreme display of the basic incoherence of the Clinton administration's Kosovo policy, NATO Secretary-General George

Robertson warned ethnic Albanian leaders that continuing attacks against Serbs could lead the West to divide the province into separately administered sections. "Don't underestimate our determination," Robertson said. "We are going to protect a multiethnic society here and we'll do it if necessary by making sure the individual groups are protected in their homes and communities. . . . If it involves building walls round them, barbed wire round them, giving them the protection they need, then we will do it."[216] But separating pockets of non-Albanians with walls and barbed wire is not multiethnicity, it is ghettoization.

Like the situation in Bosnia, only after the contending sides have control over their political fate will their extremism lose its urgency and a reasonable politics be able to emerge. Thus, without a reworking of the Clinton administration's Kosovo policy to reflect that fact and its implications, another political and economic invalid will be created in the Balkans and NATO troops will find themselves ministering to the province indefinitely.

6. Conclusion: A Moratorium on Nation Building?

What unified the Clinton administration's nation-building efforts in Somalia, Haiti, Bosnia, and Kosovo was that they were not strict expressions of U.S. national security interests—though administration officials did often attempt to couch them in those terms. Instead, the missions were expressions of the administration's faith in the power of government, especially the U.S. government, to engineer solutions to political and social problems. That faith echoes a tradition dating back to the 18th century, when Antoine-Nicolas Condorcet argued that the physical sciences provided a model of how society could be studied and manipulated. Indeed, the phrase "social science" was coined by Condorcet, and it was he who first urged that quantification and theories of probability be used in formulating public policy.[1] In the modern incarnation of Condorcet's philosophy, solving complex political and social problems is believed to be a question of assembling the relevant facts and planning a corresponding government strategy to achieve the desired goal. Solving political and social problems, in other words, simply boils down to a matter of "technical coordination" by experts.[2]

By the end of Clinton's second term, the administration's vision of what Washington could do around the world had become extreme. Indeed, the White House had expanded its national security strategy beyond its earlier emphasis on "democratic enlargement" and "virtuous power" to what had become an almost unconstrained approach. For instance, in the final weeks of his presidency Clinton implored, "We've got to realize that there are other places in the world that we haven't fooled with enough."[3] He then presented what the White House called a "new development agenda for the 21st century," a plan for an American "response to globalization."[4] Clinton called for an "accelerated campaign against global poverty" and said technologically advanced countries have an obligation to overcome any "digital divide" that leaves the Third World lacking in wealth-creating computer technology.[5] Clinton also urged stronger steps by rich nations to combat the threat of global warming, which he characterized as "a big deal."[6]

Clinton's foreign policy, in other words, had gone far beyond the Wilsonian project of spreading democracy and good government. America's moral purpose and economic and military might, he had come to believe, should also be used to remedy political, economic, and other societal ills around the world.[7] It was indeed a clear example of what one historian has called "global meliorism," which is defined as foreign policy centered not on security issues that could endanger Americans directly, but on trying "to make the world a better place."[8] For Clinton, that meant not only continued nation building, but other efforts as well. In July 2000, for example, Clinton met with other G-8 leaders in Okinawa, Japan, to discuss the establishment of what can be described only as global welfare programs. By the end of the meeting, the assembled heads of state agreed to spend $1.3 billion to fund basic education in poor countries and to start an international school lunch program. "One of the best things we can do to get children in school is to provide them at least one nutritious meal there every day," explained Clinton.[9] The agreement came the day after the G-8 announced its Okinawa Charter on Global Information Society, an assistance program aimed at promoting worldwide computer access.

Campaign 2000

During his 2000 presidential campaign, Vice President Al Gore and his foreign policy advisers were not shy about wanting to carry on and expand Clinton's global meliorism.[10] During a September 2000 speech to the Council on Foreign Relations, Gore's top foreign policy adviser, Leon Fuerth, admitted, "I'm an exponent of an approach to foreign policy that acknowledges no substantive boundaries."[11] Besides defining overpopulation, global warming, and competition for fishing rights as national security issues, Fuerth said public nutrition and fighting the spread of malaria, tuberculosis, and other diseases were part of the vice president's "new security agenda."[12] Other senior Gore advisers, such as Bruce Jentleson, said that the "issues of poverty" and "global public health" were considered "challenges" under the Vice President's "emerging new agenda."[13]

New or not, Gore's advisers called for a strategy of "forward engagement" to "neutralize" these "challenges" before they "mature." We "view history as a kind of plastic thing," explained Fuerth, and we will "try and shape history, if we can, so that it does not have these troughs that lead us irrevocably toward war as the solution to our problems but instead gives us a chance to resolve issues, important issues in the world by other means."[14] More specifically, Jentleson called for expanding the "artificially narrow definition of what the U.S. role in the world should be" to include remedying poverty, health problems, and environmental degradation, and for "preventive peacekeeping deployments" and "early uses of force" to "coercively prevent" ethnic conflict and civil wars.[15] According to Jentleson, the United States should do all those things because advancing America's "image in the world" and seeing that the "world order is largely shaped by its values" are both national security concerns.[16] What, if anything, was then not a national security concern was left unstated.[17]

Another Gore adviser, former U.S. ambassador to NATO Robert Hunter, argued that "the quality of the world in which Americans want to live" should be a guiding principle in American national security policy.[18] Thus he proposed setting up a new Strategic Planning Office in the White House to deal with issues such as

> the rise of cross-border crime, uncontrolled migrations, pandemics like AIDS and malaria, the consequence of a digital divide both within societies and between rich and poor countries, and the challenge of societies, like much of sub-Saharan Africa, that have been left behind by the last decade's global economic advance.[19]

Addressing global health, environmental, and social issues, however, is one thing; invoking the rhetoric of national security is quite another. It risks muddying the policy waters. Indeed, if everything that harms the welfare of people is defined as a national security threat, the term loses its conceptual meaning and becomes a catch-all for things that are unpleasant.

Nation Building Debated

When it came to the flagship of Clinton's global meliorism—nation building—Gore and his allies were on board, too. Indeed, during the second presidential debate, moderator Jim Lehrer asked Gore and then Texas governor George W. Bush,

> In the last 20 years, there have been eight major actions involving the introduction of U.S. ground, air or naval forces: . . . Lebanon, Grenada, Panama, the Persian Gulf, Somalia, Bosnia, Haiti, Kosovo. If you had been president . . . would any of those interventions not have happened?[20]

Gore said he supported all the interventions except Lebanon. Bush approved of all the interventions except Haiti and Somalia after the mission was changed by the Clinton administration. "I don't think our troops ought to be used for what's called nation building," explained Bush.[21]

Gore, in turn, defended Washington's practice of nation building generally and implied that situations in places like Haiti and Bosnia could be equated with the interwar years in Western Europe. "This idea of nation-building is a kind of pejorative phrase," argued Gore,

> But think about the great conflict of the past century, World War II. During the years between World War I and World War II, a great lesson was learned by our military leaders and the people of the United States. The lesson was that in the aftermath of World War I we kind of turned our backs and left them to their own devices, and they brewed up a lot of trouble that quickly became World War II.[22]

How exactly places like Haiti or Bosnia could "brew up a lot of trouble" like an expansionistic Nazi Germany was left unsaid by Gore.

Bush's skepticism about nation building—and subsequent comments by his top aides that the Clinton administration's Balkan deployments should be phased out—provoked considerable consternation on the part of the vice president.[23] Gore claimed that Bush's idea "demonstrates a lack of judgment and a complete misunderstanding of history" because it would be a "damaging blow to NATO."[24] What was remarkable, however, was that Gore did not defend Washington's Balkan troop deployments on grounds that nation building was actually working in Bosnia or Kosovo, but rather on the grounds that it would undermine the NATO alliance if members could pick and choose their operations and how to support them.

Sadly it was Gore who seemed to suffer from a "complete misunderstanding of history," especially recent history. First of all, duties within NATO were already not being shared equally. The United States, for example, almost alone fought the Kosovo air war. It was not unreasonable, then, for Bush to suggest that the Europeans be the ones to occupy the territory of Kosovo after the war was over. Second, NATO members do already pick and choose their operations. During the U.S.-led air campaign against Yugoslavia, for example, Hungary refused to contribute any combat troops to a possible land invasion or even to divide the war's costs among the alliance when it was over.[25] Moreover, in April 1999, NATO governments, including the Clinton White House, ratified the new Combined Joint Task Force mechanism as an option that adds a needed dimension of flexibility to alliance operations. Through the CJTF mechanism, member states can decline to participate actively in a specific mission if they do not feel their vital interests are in danger, but their opting out of a mission would not stop other NATO members from participating in an intervention if they chose to do so.[26]

The Bush team's apparent skepticism about nation building also provoked indignation and gainsaying on the part of Gore's allies in the outgoing Clinton administration. Secretary of State Madeleine Albright, for example, told the *New York Times*, "I'm secretary of state until noon on January 20," and Governor Bush's position is "damaging to American foreign policy."[27] Clinton's chairman of the Joint Chiefs of Staff, Gen. Henry Shelton, publicly denied that the U.S. military was even involved in nation building in Bosnia and Kosovo. "I do draw a line between what I would call nation building and what I would call sustaining a safe and secure environment," he said. "[American] soldiers, per se, do not do [nation building]. We can provide a safe and secure environment, but we don't do the law enforcement, we don't do the court systems, we don't get commerce going again. . . . That is, in my definition, what you're doing when you get into nation building."[28] Similarly, the U.S. ambassador to the United Nations, Richard Holbrooke, claimed, "UN and U.S. troops in Bosnia and Kosovo are not nation building, they are there to create the circumstances where the people there can build their own nation."[29]

Using the U.S. military to create the "circumstances" or "environment" for an army of Washington's civilian nation builders to operate is still nation building, however. Administration officials clearly recognized it as such and even boasted about it. Just five days before the election, for example, Secretary Albright asserted,

> I think we have done more in terms of trying to deal with tragedies around the world that are of a humanitarian nature than previously. And I think one of the important questions that foreign policymakers and students of foreign policy and commentators have to think about is the value of humanitarian intervention and nation building, which is actually something that is positive, of trying to develop democracies around the world.[30]

Yet the Clinton administration's actual attempts at nation building all failed or are in the process of failing. First there was Somalia, where an attempt to capture warlord Mohammed Farah Aideed led to a destructive urban firefight that resulted in the deaths of 18 Americans and hundreds of Somali civilians. Washington gave up that misguided attempt to reconstruct a country.

Then came Haiti. In the name of democracy the administration replaced a military regime with Jean-Bertrand Aristide, who promoted violence against his political opponents. Today Haiti is a democracy in name only. After the last parliamentary election, which was marred by widespread voting irregularities, the president of the Provisional Election Council fled to America because government forces threatened his life.

Even worse is the situation in the Balkans. Washington and its allies accelerated the breakup of Yugoslavia by prematurely recognizing the breakaway republics of Croatia and Bosnia. When Serbs and Croats in Bosnia said they, too, wanted their independence, the United States said no. The Dayton Agreement then imposed the artificial state of Bosnia, which survives today only through Western military occupation.

Finally, there is Kosovo. After having allegedly fought a war in the name of a multiethnic Kosovo, Washington has watched over precisely the opposite. More than a quarter-million Serbs, Goranis, Montenegrins, Gypsies, and other non-Albanians have fled so far. The province is also riven with crime and violence. Neither ethnic Albanians nor the few remaining Serbs believe in autonomy within Serbia, the official Western goal. The result is yet another babysitting commitment that could go on for a generation or more.

That would be fine with some politicians in the Balkans. "NATO should remain in Kosovo forever," says ethnic Albanian leader Ibrahim Rugova; and in Bosnia, "We urge [NATO] forces to stay there maybe forever," too.[31] In view of those kinds of commitments—to nation-building missions that are not even working—the Bush camp made an exceedingly modest proposal during the campaign: Let the Europeans take over garrisoning the Balkans. That is the least they could do given that the Balkans are in their backyard and that Washington is looking after the Persian Gulf, the Middle East, East Asia, and the world's shipping lanes.

But more than a concern for NATO's cohesion motivated Gore's—and the Clinton administration's—hostility toward the Bush team's doubts about nation building. Questioning nation building was tantamount to questioning Gore and Clinton's meliorist assumptions that the United States knows how to help people in troubled places and that the U.S. government should dedicate the nation's credibility, as well as the lives and tax dollars of its citizens, to that purpose.

Down, but Not Out

Despite Washington's failures in Somalia, Haiti, Bosnia, and Kosovo, there has not been a shortage of nation-building advocates in the foreign policy community. In fact, just as there are "children at risk" in our domestic setting, it now seems that there are "states at risk" in the international setting, and some analysts are calling for an "early warning system" and preemptive nation-building efforts aimed at "preventing or alleviating potential humanitarian crises" before they happen.[32] Others call for an avowedly paternalistic approach. "Just as social workers attempt to educate inadequate parents to the responsibilities of parenthood," explains one scholar, "states and citizens ought to be educated about the ways in which freedom is constituted in the relations between sovereign states."[33] Still others, like *World Policy Journal* deputy editor David Rieff, call for the return of the League of Nations system for setting up protectorates; that is, a return to "[President Woodrow] Wilson's original idea, which was to take control over certain territories in order 'to build up in as short a time as possible . . . a political unit that can take charge of its own affiars.'"[34]

Though less dewy-eyed, there are still champions of nation building on the right, too. Robert Kagan and William Kristol of the *Weekly*

Standard, for example, claim that continuing nation building in Kosovo and Bosnia is essential to creating "a Europe whole and free."[35] What is remarkable, however, is that Kagan, Kristol, and other conservative nation builders do not appreciate the liberal premise of their policy recommendations; that is to say, they have a rather expansive view of the role and effectiveness of the state in promulgating government programs for people overseas, but a dim view of it domestically. Indeed, the former managing editor of *Foreign Affairs*, Fareed Zakaria, has referred to this as the "conservative confusion," and points out that

> the defining element of conservatism is realism—realism about the limits of state power, the nature of human beings and societies, the complexity of international life. Yet many conservatives who believe that the state can do nothing right at home think that it can do nothing wrong abroad. (If things go badly, why, more money, bigger bombs and ground troops will straighten it out.) Many who are scornful of social engineering at home seem sure it will work beyond our borders. They seem convinced that good intentions and a burst of state power can transform the world. How conservative is that?[36]

Moreover, conservative nation builders overlook the fact that their policy prescriptions tend to expand, rather than limit, the size and scope of the U.S. government, and tend to make the president's powers dominant at the expense of America's republican form of government, with its carefully balanced division of powers among the three branches.[37] Indeed, if the president can unilaterally launch acts of war that result in open-ended nation-building missions like the one in Kosovo, and Congress can only end those missions by directing the president to remove American forces or by cutting off funding, then Congress does not really hold the power "To declare War"; rather, it has a limited ability to veto the president's power to declare war after the fact.[38] That turns the Constitution's war declaration power on its head.[39]

The current foreign policy literature also abounds with dubious formulations that favor nation building and its standard precursor: the humanitarian intervention. Jeffrey Record, professor of international security studies at the U.S. Air War College, for example, suggests that the United States, as "the world's sole remaining superpower," should exhibit "great power behavior" and intervene in "failed states" and "small wars" that do not "involve direct threats to manifestly vital U.S. interests." Not to intervene in such situations, he claims, "emboldens enemies and puts at risk foreigners who seek America's protection."[40]

Setting aside the fact that such a prescription would encourage outmatched groups to provoke their enemies in the hopes of eliciting America's protection, Record's reasoning is also absurd in its implications.[41] He suggests, for example, that Washington is, if indirectly, responsible for "victimizing" people when it does not use or threaten to use force on their behalf. By that line of reasoning, the United States is to blame, if indirectly, for violence and misery everywhere it is not meddling.

Record also asserts that Washington should intervene in "failed states" and "small wars" because the American people are not as casualty averse as is widely presumed.[42] With "presidential leadership," a "perceived strength of interests at stake," and "visible progress," he says, Americans will tolerate body bags.[43] As proof, he cites a study that found that the public will accept casualties "in such scenarios as defending Taiwan and stopping Iraq from acquiring weapons of mass destruction."[44] What connection those two scenarios have with "failed states" like Somalia and Haiti, or "small wars" on the periphery of Europe, like Bosnia and Kosovo, he leaves unexplained. Nor does he draw a distinction between the "perceived strength of interests at stake" in denying a vengeful Saddam Hussein the ability to launch a nuclear strike on Washington, D.C., and using the U.S. military to disarm, say, a Mogadishu warlord.

Human Rights vs. Sovereignty?

Other nation builders have characterized nation building and the humanitarian intervention that typically precedes it as a stark choice between putting human rights first or putting state sovereignty first.[45] But that is a false dichotomy. State sovereignty safeguards stability and political autonomy in the international system, thereby serving to advance human rights. Indeed, are not intervention and quasi-imperialism threats to human rights, too? And is it not readily conceivable that some nations will invoke "humanitarian intervention" as a pretext for conquest? That has been the rule, not the exception, for most of modern history. In fact, according to one authority, there was perhaps one genuine humanitarian intervention in the 150 years prior to the Cold War.[46] In all the other cases, humanitarian intervention was used as a cover for other objectives. Even Adolf Hitler justified his occupation of Bohemia and Moravia in 1939 as a humanitarian intervention to protect ethnic minorities. Washington's recent actions in Kosovo and elsewhere threaten to reopen that Pandora's box.

What is more, it is not at all clear that Washington's policy of setting aside state sovereignty to intervene and nation build serves to reduce the prospect of war, which is itself a grave threat—if not the gravest threat—to human rights. Indeed, recent historical practice demonstrates that Washington's interventions have occurred solely in countries with weak militaries and no guaranteed allies. Thus, far from demonstrating that human rights are primary, Washington may actually be demonstrating the value of forming counterbalancing alliances and of acquiring weapons of mass destruction, because both moves would act as insurance policies against Washington's would-be nation builders.

Such policy reverberations are already being felt. In the aftermath of NATO's Kosovo intervention, Moscow and Beijing have accelerated their moves toward a strategic partnership aimed at countering American power and restoring a multipolar world. Russia now supplies China with advanced fighter aircraft, sophisticated anti-ship missiles, and modern guided-missile destroyers to thwart U.S. ambitions in East Asia. Moscow and Beijing also have jointly declared their opposition to the use of "pretexts such as human rights and humanitarian intervention to harm the independence of sovereign states."[47]

At the same time, NATO's Kosovo intervention has had far-reaching strategic consequences for smaller or less-developed nations. Indeed, according to one scholar, developing nations now generally fear that,

> unarmed and alone, they have little hope of resisting a resurgent Western imperialism now justifying itself on "moral" rather than strategic or even economic grounds. Increasingly, leaders of these countries are concluding that stronger militaries, even with nuclear weapons, may be needed to deter interventions by Western powers.[48]

Such reactions are not at all irrational. As legal scholar Richard Falk has correctly observed, a humanitarian intervention is an *asymmetrical* claim in international law; that is, it is a claim that can be put into practice only by strong countries against weaker ones, not the other way around. China, for example, could invoke a humanitarian rationale to intervene in Taiwan, but Taiwan could not realistically intervene in China, even to stop a replay of the Tiananmen Square massacre.[49]

Another important point to consider is that Washington's legitimization of humanitarian intervention also risks enlarging the universe of matters over which major powers can potentially disagree. That not only increases the possibility of dispute, but runs the risk of triggering unforeseen military confrontation and escalation, which are especially dangerous prospects in an era of weapons of mass destruction. Bypassing the UN Security Council to avoid a probable major power veto—as occurred during NATO's air war against Yugoslavia—does not help matters much either. Doing so only procedurally avoids the veto. In a future crisis, the objections of another major power may remain intact, and it may choose to then exercise a second kind of veto—countering the humanitarian intervention with the force of arms. It is precisely that sort of scenario that the deference to state sovereignty and the corresponding prohibition against intervention are designed to prevent, but which Washington's recent penchant for nation building makes entirely possible.[50] As such, it is a catastrophic deterioration of relations between major powers that may pose a greater threat to humanity, and thus to human rights, than intervening for humanitarian reasons somewhere less than vital to America's national interests.

Fool's Errands

Washington's nation-building diehards notwithstanding, early indications are that George W. Bush's victory over Vice President Gore in the 2000 presidential race means that Washington's eight-year fixation with how the world "ought" to be will now be replaced with a more constrained vision of how the world "is." Besides expressing a need for "humility" in foreign policy, Bush has selected Gen. Colin Powell as his secretary of state. That is relevant because Powell, while serving under the administration of Bush's father, developed a doctrine on the use of U.S. military force that came to bear his name. According to the Powell Doctrine, America's defeat in Vietnam and its victory in the Persian Gulf demonstrate that U.S. forces must be committed only when America's vital national interests are at stake and all other means of influence have been exhausted. Furthermore, the action should be overwhelming and defined, with the support of the American people and Congress.[51]

Given such parameters, the rest of Bush's team would be wise to recall the president's wariness of nation building and to remember the lessons of Washington's efforts in Somalia, Haiti, Bosnia, and Kosovo. Those lessons, as the previous chapters have sought to demonstrate, are varied, but point to the same conclusion: that there are several obstacles that can render nation building a fool's errand.

In Somalia, it was learned that a nation-building operation is unsustainable if it is entirely divorced from national self-interest but nonetheless produces casualties. Indeed, only 200 Americans were injured or killed in Somalia, but because that country was strategically irrelevant, public and congressional support evaporated, and U.S. policy was reversed. Rather than then deciding to restrict future nation building efforts to only those rare, and thus far unrepeated, times in history when it is strategically vital—such as was the case in postwar Germany and Japan—Washington took a very different approach. It decided to undertake additional nation-building missions in other nonvital places—like Haiti, Bosnia, and Kosovo—but then obsessed over "force protection"; that is, it placed the goal of its nation-building mission in a secondary position to that of making sure no Americans were killed in the process. How that hamstrung approach was expected to produce results remains a mystery.

The Haiti mission revealed that an ambitious nation-building effort cannot by itself transform a country into a self-sustaining, democratic member of the family of nations; a country must also be ripe for the effort. Not to put too fine a point on it, that means the culture and history of the place targeted for nation building matter.[52] If it is not ripe, then the finite economic assistance and military force that realistically can be mustered in Washington will ultimately prove inadequate. That fact deserves mention because the unvarnished truth is that nation building—like all other foreign policy decisions—is ultimately guided by national self-interest, and the less national self-interest at stake, the shallower the reservoir of public and congressional support will be. When there is very little national self-interest, it is therefore imperative that Washington's policies be correspondingly limited in both duration and scope, which by definition rules out open-ended nation-building missions in places that are not already ripe for the nation-building process.

After five years and counting, the Bosnia mission has shown that nation building will also flounder if it institutionalizes a "security dilemma" between formerly opposing sides in a bloody conflict. Indeed, if wartime rivals are forced to live together but still fear each other as a threat, then each side will behave accordingly and will not cooperate with the other. That noncooperation will then reinforce the outward perception that each side is still a threat to the other side, and so on, in a vicious circle. The predictable result is a chronic cycle of tension and political obstruction.

In historical contrast, the United States did not use its military might to make national borders irrelevant and to impose multiethnicity in post-World War II Europe. Instead, as one analyst has observed, Washington guaranteed the protection and economic development of the European peoples *separately* within the territorial boundaries of their own nation states.[53] Today Germany, Italy, France, and Great Britain are self-secure, democratic, prosperous, and, yes, integrating across national borders. Moreover, their populations today largely consider the events of World War II ancient history. In Bosnia, Washington took the opposite approach. It has tried to make Bosnia multiethnic *before* it has been made politically viable. The results to date have been dismal.

In neighboring Croatia, on the other hand, Washington did not try to force Croatians to live with their former wartime enemies and to reunite with Serbia. The results there have been much better. After the Croatians became secure behind their own territorial borders, the political issues that sustained the hard-liners—fear and uncertainty—evaporated. Croatia has since ousted its hard-liners, liberalized significantly, and allowed thousands of Serb refugees to return. The way this has come about may not be the most inspiring from an idealist's point of view, but it has proven more realistic than putting the proverbial cart of multiethnicity before the horse of group security.

Finally, in Kosovo it has been learned that nation building will come up short if the majority of people living where it is being attempted have not actually given up their wartime objective. Kosovo's Albanians, who were brought exceedingly close to achieving their goal of independence following NATO's bombing campaign, are still overtly and covertly pursuing that goal. Independence, however, differs sharply from the goal outlined by American officials after the bombing, and pressure for it—and Greater Albania later—has so far thwarted Washington's efforts to create a multiethnic democracy. Today, Washington is faced with a stark choice between a policy failure or a policy disaster in Kosovo. A policy failure will result if Washington's goal of creating a multiethnic society in Kosovo is undermined by ethnic Albanian nationalists. A policy disaster, however, will result if Washington decides to stand in the way of independence. "When we stop being useful to them, they will turn against us," warns a candid intelligence officer with the UN police force in Kosovo.[54] If NATO and UN personnel were to then start dying at the hands of the very people Washington said it was out to help in the first place, its entire nation-building mission could collapse as it did in Somalia.

Of course, all these lessons do not mean that nation building can never work, or that it should never be tried anywhere. What they strongly suggest, however, is that there are serious limits to when and where nation building will succeed. If the new Bush administration understands that point from the outset, the effective result will be a long overdue moratorium on the sort of ill-conceived nation-building adventures witnessed during the Clinton years.

Notes

Chapter 1

1. Quoted in Barry Schweid, "Albright Promises Refugees They Will Go Home and Run Their Own Lives," Associated Press, June 11, 1999; and Jane Perlez, "Albright in Skopje to Visit Refugees," *New York Times*, June 12, 1999, p. A8.
2. Quoted in Schweid.
3. Quoted in Michael Mandelbaum, "A Perfect Failure: NATO's War against Yugoslavia," *Foreign Affairs* 78, no. 5 (September–October 1999): 8.
4. Kim Sengupta, "Liberation of Kosovo: Clinton Visit, Kosovars Hail the Conquering Hero," *Independent* (London), June 23, 1999, p. 3.
5. Quoted in ibid.
6. Quoted in ibid.; and Jane Perlez, "Clinton Meets Refugees, and Pledges to Aid Kosovo," *New York Times*, June 23, 1999, p. A13.
7. Quoted in Mark Peceny, *Democracy at the Point of Bayonets* (University Park, Penn.: Pennsylvania State University Press, 1999), p. 1.
8. Quoted in Otto Kreisher, "The Haiti Crisis," Copley News Service, September 20, 1994.
9. See Michael E. Latham, *Modernization as Ideology: American Social Science and "Nation Building" in the Kennedy Era* (Chapel Hill, N.C.: University of North Carolina Press, 2000); Jefferson P. Marquis, "The Other Warriors: American Social Science and Nation Building in Vietnam," *Diplomatic History* 24, no. 1 (Winter 2000); and Patrick Lloyd Hatcher, *The Suicide of an Elite: American Internationalists and Vietnam* (Stanford, Calif.: Stanford University Press, 1990).
10. Carl J. Friedrich, "Nation-Building?" in *Nation Building*, ed. Karl W. Deutsch and William J. Foltz (New York: Atherton Press, 1963), pp. 27–28.
11. Ibid., p. 28.
12. Morton H. Halperin, "Guaranteeing Democracies," *Foreign Policy* 91, no. 2 (Summer 1993): 105–122.
13. Tony Smith, *America's Mission: The United States and the Worldwide Struggle for Democracy in the Twentieth Century*, (Princeton, N.J.: Princeton University Press, 1994), passim; and Stanley Hoffmann, "What Should American Foreign Policy Be?" *Dissent* (Fall 1994): 498. See also Peter Lyon, "The Rise and Fall and Possible Revival of International Trusteeship," in *Journal of Commonwealth and Commonwealth Politics* 31, no. 4 (March 1993).
14. Joshua Muravchik, *Exporting Democracy: Fulfilling America's Destiny* (Washington: American Enterprise Institute, 1991), p. 221.
15. Michael A. Ledeen, *Freedom Betrayed: How America Led a Global Democratic Revolution, Won the Cold War and Walked Away* (Washington: American Enterprise Institute, 1996), p. 7.

16. Evidently, Clinton even enlisted the first lady in his struggle to spread democracy. In 1998–1999, millions of taxpayer dollars were spent shuttling Hillary Clinton to England (for a conference on "Hearing Children's Voices"), Bulgaria, Chile, the Czech Republic, the Dominican Republic, Egypt, El Salvador, France, Guatemala, Haiti, Honduras, Ireland, Macedonia, Morocco, the Netherlands, Nicaragua, Tunisia, Switzerland (twice), and Uruguay. The first lady's spokesperson, Marsha Berry, contends that the trips were vital to the president's mission of "enlarging democracy" around the globe: "She travels at the request of the president and the secretary of state," says Berry. "These trips have been very advantageous for the country. Many of the places she visits are emerging democracies or struggling democracies or ones that have been successful, and she is rewarding their efforts." Quoted in Seth Gitell, "Jet-Setter," *New Republic*, August 9, 1999, p. 15.

17. William J. Clinton, "Confronting the Challenges of a Broader World," Address to the UN General Assembly, New York, September 27, 1993, http://www.pub.whitehouse.gov/uri-res/I2R?urn:pdi://oma.eop.gov.us/1993/9/27/4.text.1 [accessed August 15, 2000].

18. According to Albright: "Our strategy looks to the enlargement of democracy and markets abroad," and "under the President's leadership, we will be called upon to work together . . . to protect America and build a better world." See Madeleine K. Albright, "Use of Force in a Post-Cold War World," Address at the National War College, National Defense University, Fort McNair, Washington, D.C., September 23, 1993, http://dosfan.lib.uic.edu/ERC/briefing/dispatch/1993/html/Dispatchv4no39.html [accessed August 15, 2000]. Anthony Lake, "From Containment to Enlargement," Address at the School of Advanced International Studies, Johns Hopkins University, Washington, D.C., September 21, 1993.

19. Lake.

20. Ibid.

21. Quoted in Peceny, p. 158.

22. Quoted in ibid., pp. 157–158.

23. Quoted in Thomas H. Henriksen, "Clinton's Foreign Policy in Somalia, Bosnia, Haiti, and North Korea," in *Essays in Public Policy* (Stanford, Calif.: Hoover Institution, 1996), p. 5.

24. Steven A. Holmes, "Choice for National Security Advisor Has Long-Awaited Chance to Lead," *New York Times*, January 3, 1993, p. A16.

25. Quoted in Henriksen, p. 7.

26. Quoted in Benjamin Schwarz, "The World Isn't Ours to Americanize," *Los Angeles Times*, August 28, 1994, p. 5.

27. Michael R. Gordon, "Christopher, in Unusual Cable, Defends State Department," *New York Times*, June 16, 1993, p. A13.

28. Quoted in Charles Krauthammer, "Playing God in Somalia: The United States Is Not in the Business of Re-creating Nations," *Washington Post*, August 13, 1993, p. A25; and John Lancaster, "Aspin Lists U.S. Goals in Somalia," *Washington Post*, August 28, 1993, p. A1.

29. William J. Clinton, "Address to the Nation on Somalia," *Weekly Compilation of Presidential Documents* 29, no. 40 (October 11, 1993): 2022–25.

30. William J. Clinton, "Text of a Letter from the President to the Speaker of the House of Representatives and the President Pro Tempore of the Senate," March 21, 1995, http://www.pub.whitehouse.gov/uri-res/I2R?urn:pdi://oma.eop.gov.us/1995/3/22/4.text.1 [accessed August 15, 2000].

31. William J. Clinton, "Statement by the President on Bosnia," December 18, 1997, http://www.pub.whitehouse.gov/uri-res/I2R?urn:pdi://oma.eop.gov.us/1997/12/18/8.text.1 [accessed August 15, 2000].

32. See, for example, Gary Anderson, "Military Operations Other than War," *Washington Times*, June 11, 1999, p. A21; Tamar A. Mehuron, "Other than War," *Air Force*, March 1999, p. 19; and Jennifer M. Taw and Alan Vick, "From Sideshow to Center Stage: The Role of the Army and Air Force in Military Operations Other than War," in *Strategic Appraisal 1997: Strategy and Defense Planning for the 21st Century*, ed. Zalmay M. Khalilzad and David A. Ochmanek (Santa Monica, Calif.: RAND Corporation, 1997).

33. *Joint Task Force Commander's Handbook for Peace Operations*, Joint Warfighting Center, Fort Monroe, Virginia, June 16, 1997, http://www.dtic.mil/doctrine/jel/research_pubs/k516.pdf [accessed August 15, 2000].

34. Warren Christopher, "Democracy and Human Rights: Where America Stands," Speech before the World Conference on Human Rights, Vienna, Austria, June 14, 1993, http://dosfan.lib.uic.edu/ERC/briefing/dossec/1993/9306/930614 dossec.html [accessed August 15, 2000].

35. According to Wilson, it is America's "historical mission" to create a "peaceful international order based on world law." Quoted in Gordon N. Levin, *Woodrow Wilson and World Politics: America's Response to War and Revolution* (New York: Oxford University Press, 1963), p. 4.

36. David J. Scheffer, "Toward a Modern Doctrine of Humanitarian Intervention," *University of Toledo Law Review* 23 (Winter 1992): 293.

37. Quoted in David Forsythe, "Human Rights Policy: Change and Continuity," in *U.S. Foreign Policy after the Cold War*, ed. Randall Ripley and James Lindsay (Pittsburgh: University of Pittsburgh Press, 1997), p. 257.

38. Michael Kramer, "In Search of the Clinton Doctrine," *Time*, October 11, 1993, p. 41.

39. Quoted in Krauthammer.

40. Quoted in ibid.

41. Michael J. Glennon, "The New Interventionism: The Search for a Just International Law," *Foreign Affairs* 78, no. 3 (May–June 1999): 7.

42. Quoted in Michael Kelly, "A Perfectly Clintonian Doctrine," *Washington Post*, June 30, 1999, p. A31.

43. Quoted in Robert Manning, "The Clinton Doctrine: More Spin than Reality," *Los Angeles Times*, November 5, 1999, p. M2.

44. Douglas Waller, "Kosovo Crisis: Keeping the Peace; The Three Ifs of a Clinton Doctrine," *Time*, June 28, 1999, p. 35.

45. Quoted in David Rieff, "A New Age of Liberal Imperialism," *World Policy* 14, no. 2 (Summer 1999): 1.

46. Humanitarian intervention has been defined in a number of ways by lawyers and legal scholars. According to British jurist Geoffrey Robertson, humanitarian intervention is the interference "in the internal affairs of a sovereign state" in order to stop "systematic and long-extended cruelty and oppression." Dutch professor of international law Wil D. Verwey says humanitarian intervention should be understood as "coercive action taken by states . . . involving the use of armed force, for the purpose of preventing or putting a halt to serious and wide-scale violations of fundamental human rights, in particular the right to life." See Geoffrey Robertson, *Crimes against Humanity: The Struggle for Global Justice* (New York: New Press, 2000),

p. 403; and Wil D. Verwey, "Humanitarian Intervention in the 1990s and Beyond: An International Law Perspective," in *World Orders in the Making: Humanitarian Intervention and Beyond*, ed. Jan Nedervee Pieterse (New York: St. Martin's Press, 1998), p. 180.

47. Quoted in R. C. Longworth, "Bombing for Peace: Rewriting Ancient Rules of Sovereignty," *Chicago Tribune*, March 28, 1999, p. 1.

48. Ibid.

49. Jan Nedervee Pieterse, "Humanitarian Intervention and Beyond: Introduction" in *World Orders in the Making: Humanitarian Intervention and Beyond*, p. 15.

50. Fernando Tesón, *Humanitarian Intervention: An Inquiry into Law and Morality* (New York: Transnational, 1987), p. 5.

51. Press Conference of Secretary of State Madeleine K. Albright, London, United Kingdom, October 8, 1998, http://secretary.state.gov/www/statements/1998/981008a.html [accessed August 15, 2000].

52. Quoted in James Kitfield, "Not-So-Sacred Borders," *National Journal*, November 20, 1999, p. 3386.

53. Quoted in Steven Mufson, "An Uneasy Union of Morality and Pragmatism," *Washington Post*, February 6, 2000, p. B1.

54. Quoted in David R. Sands, "What's Next after Kosovo? NATO's Planners Ponder: Its First War Won, Alliance Faces Issues of New Mission, National Sovereignty," *Washington Times*, June 13, 1999, p. C1.

55. Tony Blair, "A New Moral Crusade," *Newsweek*, June 14, 1999, p. 35, and quoted in Gwynne Dyer, "Human Rights Take Centre Stage as West Rewrites World Order," *Globe and Mail* (Toronto), June 12, 1999, p. A17.

56. Lloyd Axworthy, "Canada's UN Agenda to Strengthen Human Security," *Canadian Business and Current Affairs* 19, no. 9 (January–February 1999): 15–22.

57. Roger Cohen, "Crisis in the Balkans: Germany; A Generation of German Pacifists Finds Itself at Odds Over the Kosovo Air War," *New York Times*, May 16, 1999, p. A10.

58. Robert Kagan and William Kristol, "Toward a Neo-Reaganite Foreign Policy," *Foreign Affairs* 75, no. 4 (July–August 1996), http://www.ceip.org/people/kagfaff.htm [accessed August 15, 2000].

59. Robert Kagan and William Kristol, "Win It," *Weekly Standard*, April 19, 1999, p. 9.

60. Norman Podhoretz, "Strange Bedfellows: A Guide to the New Foreign-Policy Debates," *Commentary*, December 1, 1999, p. 30.

61. Norman Naimark, "Facing Up to Kosova," *Weekly Standard*, April 24–May 1, 2000, p. 45.

62. James K. Boyce and Manuel Pastor Jr., "Macroeconomic Policy and Peace Building in El Salvador," in *Rebuilding Societies after Civil War: Critical Roles for International Assistance*, ed. Krishna Kumar (Boulder, Colo.: Lynne Rienner, 1997), p. 310.

63. Joanna Macrae, "Dilemmas of Legitimacy, Sustainability and Coherence: Rehabilitating the Health Sector," in *Rebuilding Societies after Civil War*, p. 183.

64. Kimberly A. Maynard, "Rebuilding Community: Psychological Healing, Reintegration and Reconciliation at the Grassroots Level," in *Rebuilding Societies after Civil War*, p. 225.

65. Roderick K. von Lipsey, "The Intervention Cycle," in *Breaking the Cycle: A Framework for Conflict Intervention*, ed. Roderick K. von Lipsey (New York: St. Martin's, 1997), p. 32. See also David Callahan, *Unwinnable Wars: American Power and Ethnic*

Conflict (New York: Hill & Wang, 1997); Walter Clarke and Jeffrey Herbst, eds., *Learning from Somalia: The Lessons of Armed Humanitarian Intervention* (Boulder, Colo.: Westview, 1997); and John W. DePauw and George A. Luz, *Winning the Peace: The Strategic Implications of Military Civic Action* (New York: Praeger, 1992).

66. "Post-Conflict Reconstruction: The Role of the World Bank" (Washington, World Bank, 1998), pp. 4–5.

67. See Nicole Ball and Tammy Halevy, "Making Peace Work: The Role of the International Development Community," Policy Essay no. 18, Oversees Development Council, March 1996. See also John M. Goshko and R. Jeffrey Smith, "Details of Clinton's 'Democracy' Program Slowly Begin to Emerge," *Washington Post*, May 5, 1993, p. A28.

68. "Democracy and Governance," United States Agency for International Development website, http://www.usaid.gov/democracy/index.html [accessed August 9, 2000].

69. Quoted in Judy Mann, "A Stand against Domestic Violence," *Washington Post*, April 20, 1994, p. D27.

70. "Annual Performance Plan for Fiscal Year 2001," U.S. Agency for International Development website, http://www.dec.org/partners/2001_app [accessed August 9, 2000].

71. "White House Fact Sheet on U.S. Efforts to Promote Human Rights, Democracy," U.S. Newswire, December 10, 1998.

72. "About Us," National Endowment for Democracy website, http://www.ned.org/about/about.html [accessed August 29, 2000].

73. See John M. Broder, "Dollars and Foreign Policy: Practice vs. Preaching," *International Herald Tribune*, April 1, 1997, p. 1; and Barbara Conry, "Loose Cannon: The National Endowment for Democracy," Cato Institute Foreign Policy Briefing no. 27, November 8, 1993.

74. National Endowment for Democracy, "Central and Eastern Europe Grants," *1997 Annual Report*, http://www.ned.org/pubs/97annual/cee97.html [accessed August 29, 2000].

75. See Christopher Black, "The International Criminal Tribunal for the Former Yugoslavia: Impartial?" *Mediterranean Quarterly* 11, no. 2 (Spring 2000): 35.

76. See, for example, Steven M. Riskin, ed., "Three Dimensions of Peacebuilding in Bosnia: Findings from USIP-Sponsored Research and Field Projects," United States Institute of Peace *Peaceworks* no. 32, December 1999; Howard Olsen and John Davis, "Training U.S. Army Officers for Peace Operations: Lessons from Bosnia," United States Institute of Peace *Special Report*, October 1999; "Bosnia Report Card: Pass, Fail, or Incomplete?" United States Institute of Peace *Special Report*, January 1999; John Paul Lederach, *Building Peace: Sustainable Reconciliation in Divided Societies* (Washington: United States Institute of Peace, 1997); and "Restoring Hope: Real Lessons of Somalia for the Future of Intervention," United States Institute of Peace *Special Report*, July 1994.

77. See Ruzica Rosandic, "Grappling with Peace Education in Serbia," United States Institute of Peace *Peaceworks* No. 33, April 2000; and "Three Dimensions of Peacebuilding in Bosnia: Findings from USIP-Sponsored Research and Field Projects."

78. Strobe Talbott, "U.S. Leadership and the Balkan Challenge," Remarks at the National Press Club, Washington D.C., November 9, 1995, http://www.state.gov/www/regions/eur/bosnia/bostal2.html [accessed August 15, 2000].

79. William J. Clinton, "Remarks by the President to the AFSCME Biannual Convention," Washington D.C., March 23, 1999, http://www.pub.whitehouse.gov/uri-res/I2R?urn:pdi://oma.eop.gov.us/1999/3/23/2.text.1 [accessed August 15, 2000].

80. William J. Clinton, "The Perils of Indifference: Lessons Learned from a Violent Century," Remarks at Millennium Evening, Washington, D.C., April 12, 1999, http://www.pub.whitehouse.gov/uri-res/I2R?urn:pdi://oma.eop.gov.us/1999/4/13/4.text.1 [accessed August 15, 2000].

81. William J. Clinton, "Remarks by the President to Illinois Air National Guard Personnel," Chicago, Ill., June 12, 1999, http://www.pub.whitehouse.gov/uri-res/I2R?urn:pdi://oma.eop.gov.us/1999/6/15/6.text.1 [accessed August 15, 2000].

82. "Text of Remarks Delivered by Vice President Albert Gore Regarding the 50th Anniversary of NATO," Federal Document Clearing House, April 21, 1999.

83. Quoted in George Melloan, "From 'Mother Teresa' Diplomacy to Where?" *Wall Street Journal*, February 12, 1996, p. A15.

84. Robert Manning and Patrick Clawson, "The Clinton Doctrine," *Asian Wall Street Journal*, December 31, 1997, p. 6.

85. International Crisis Group, "Is Dayton Failing?: Bosnia Four Years after the Peace Agreement," October 28, 1999, http://www.crisisweb.org [accessed August 15, 2000].

86. Ibid. The International Crisis Group also recommends turning Bosnia into an outright protectorate, claiming, "A protectorate could implement rapid refugee returns, remove obstructionist officials, institute the rule of law, restructure communist-era economic and political structures." Quoted in "Bosnia Remains Far from Unified: Dayton Pact Largely a Fiction, Report Says," *Chicago Tribune*, November 3, 1999, p. 22.

87. David Rieff, "Bosnia's Refugees Hold Lesson for NATO," *USA Today*, May 26, 1999, p. A25.

88. Quoted in Ron Nordland and Zoran Cirjakovic, "Dictatorial Democrats," *Newsweek*, October 5, 1998, p. 28.

89. Ibid.

90. Quoted in Thomas Wagner, "Somali Peace Unlikely, UN Military Chief Says Advice Next Time: More Troops, No Pullout," *Times-Picayune* (New Orleans), January 19, 1994, p. A10.

91. Richard N. Haass, *Intervention: The Use of American Military Force in the Post-Cold War World*, rev. ed. (Washington: Brookings Institution, 1999), pp. 112–13.

92. Hugh Byrne and Rachel Neild, "Success in Haiti Is Possible, but Not 'Overnight,'" *Christian Science Monitor*, November 28, 1997, p. 18.

93. Georgie Anne Geyer, "Kosovo Checkmate," *Washington Times*, March 26, 2000, p. B3.

94. Georgie Anne Geyer, "Two Men Strive for Order in Chaotic Kosovo; German General, Kouchner Call It 'Impossible Task,'" *Washington Times*, March 19, 2000, p. C11.

95. Larry Diamond, Juan Linz, and Seymour Lipset, *Democracy in Developing Countries*, 3 vols. (Boulder, Colo.: Lynne Rienner, 1989); and Guillermo O'Donnell, Philippe Schmitter, and Laurence Whitehead, *Transitions from Authoritarian Rule: Prospects for Democracy*, 4 vols. (Baltimore: Johns Hopkins University Press, 1986).

96. Paul F. Diehl, Jennifer Reifschneider, and Paul R. Hensel, "United Nations Intervention and Recurring Conflict," *International Organization* 50, no. 4 (Autumn 1996).

97. Between 1955 and 1961, the United States pumped more than $1 billion in economic and military aid into Vietnam. The U.S. government built roads, bridges, railroads, and schools. American development experts worked on agricultural projects, and Vietnamese teachers, civil servants, and police were trained in the "American way." See George C. Herring, *America's Longest War: The United States and Vietnam, 1950–1975*, 2d ed. (New York: Alfred A. Knopf, 1986), pp. 56–61. See also John Prados, *The Hidden History of the Vietnam War* (Chicago: Ivan R. Dee, 1995), p. 21.

98. "A Quagmire," *MacNeil/Lehrer NewsHour*, September 16, 1993.

99. Joshua Muravchik, "Beyond Self-Defense; Dangers of American Military Involvement in Somalia; When, Where and How to Use Force," *Commentary*, December 1993.

100. "No Exit," *New Republic*, April 22, 1996, p. 6.

101. Krishna Kumar, "The Nature and Focus of International Assistance for Rebuilding War-Torn Societies," in *Rebuilding Societies after Civil War*, p. 1.

102. According to the U.S. State Department, the U.S. goal in postwar Germany was to prevent "Germany from ever again becoming a threat to the peace of the world." See "Documents on Germany 1944–1985," U.S. Department of State, Office of the Historian, Bureau of Public Affairs, (Washington, D.C., 1985), as cited in Richard L. Merritt, *Democracy Imposed: U.S. Occupation Policy and the German Public, 1945–1949* (New Haven, Conn.: Yale University Press, 1995), p. 370. With respect to the U.S. economic and security interest in postwar Europe generally, it has been written that it "rested squarely on an American conviction that European economic recovery was essential to the long-term interests of the United States. . . . Policymakers in the Truman administration were convinced that a 'dynamic economy' at home required American trade and investment abroad, which in turn required the reconstruction of major trading partners in Europe and their reintegration into a multilateral system of world trade. . . . The defeat of Germany and the exhaustion of Britain and France had left a power vacuum in Central and Western Europe into which the Soviet Union might expand unless the United States assembled the components of a viable balance of power. This meant filling the vacuum by rebuilding economic and political systems strong enough to forestall aggression and defeat communist parties, whose rise to power seemed the most likely way for the Soviets to extend their influence." See Michael J. Hogan, *The Marshall Plan: America, Britain, and the Reconstruction of Western Europe, 1947–1952* (Cambridge: Cambridge University Press, 1987), pp. 26–27. See also Melvyn P. Leffler, "The American Conception of National Security and the Beginnings of the Cold War, 1945–1948," *American Historical Review* 89 (April 1984): 346–81.

103. Merritt, p. 392.

104. Ibid., p. 394.

105. John W. Dower, *Embracing Defeat: Japan in the Wake of World War II* (New York: Norton, 1999), pp. 23–24, 84.

106. See Ludwig Erhard, *Germany's Comeback in the World Market* (Westport, Conn.: Greenwood, 1976); Gustav Stolper, Karl Hauser, and Kurt Borchardt, *The German Economy: 1870 to the Present* (New York: Brace and World, 1967); Egon Sohman, "Competition and Growth: The Lesson of West Germany," *American Economic Review* 49, no. 1 (1959); and Henry Wallich, *Mainsprings of the German Revival* (New Haven, Conn.: Yale University Press, 1955).

107. See Ruth Benedict, *The Chrysanthemum and the Sword: Patterns of Japanese Culture* (New York: Houghton Mifflin, 1989).

108. For an in-depth treatment of this phenomenon, see Barbara Walter and Jack Snyder, eds., *Civil Wars, Insecurity and Intervention* (New York: Columbia University Press, 1999).

109. Hans Morgenthau, *Politics among Nations: The Struggle for Power and Peace* (New York: Knopf, 1948).

110. For a discussion of how U.S. foreign policy may influence the rational power-balancing calculations of other countries, see Samuel P. Huntington, "The Lonely Superpower," *Foreign Affairs* 78, no. 2 (March–April 1999). For a discussion of the various incentives for acquiring nuclear weapons, see Zachary S. Davis, "The Realist Nuclear Regime," pp. 79–99; and Richard K. Betts, "Paranoids, Pygmies, Pariahs, and Nonproliferation Revisited," pp. 100–124, both in *The Proliferation Puzzle: Why Nuclear Weapons Spread and What Results*, ed. Zachary S. Davis and Benjamin Frankel (London: Frank Cass, 1993).

111. There is increasing evidence that this is already the case. See, for example, Edwin Dorn et al., *American Military Culture in the Twenty-First Century* (Washington: Center for Strategic and International Studies, 1999); Steven Lee Myers, "Good Times Mean Hard Sell for the Military," *New York Times*, November 3, 1998, p. A16; "Nation Update: Air Force Faces Pilot Shortage," *San Diego Union-Tribune*, October 1, 1998, p. A12; Brian Mitchell, "Air Force Heads for Bumpy Flight," *Investor's Business Daily*, September 25, 1998, p. 1; Bradley Graham and Eric Pianin, "Military Readiness, Morale Show Strain," *Washington Post*, August 13, 1998, p. A1; Bradley Graham, "Army to Shift Bosnia Duties," *Washington Post*, April 17, 1998, p. A28; Dave Moniz, "More Youths Tell Uncle Sam: 'I Don't Want You,'" *Christian Science Monitor*, March 24, 1997, p. 1; United States Department of Defense, *Youth Attitudes toward Military Service in the Post-Cold War Era*, Defense Manpower Data Center, report no. 97–001 (San Antonio, Tex., 1966); and Clyde Haberman, "Recruiting in Shadow of Bosnia," *New York Times*, December 6, 1995, p. B1.

Chapter 2

1. Quoted in Walter Clarke, "Failed Visions and Uncertain Mandates," in *Learning from Somalia: The Lessons of Armed Humanitarian Intervention*, ed. Walter Clarke and Jeffrey Herbst (Boulder, Colo.: Westview, 1997), p. 18.

2. For the full text of the resolution, see United Nations Security Council Resolution 814, United Nations, New York, March 26, 1993, http://www.un.org/Docs/scres/1993/814e.pdf [accessed September 8, 2000].

3. Quoted in Karin von Hippel, *Democracy by Force: U.S. Military Intervention in the Post-Cold War World* (Cambridge: Cambridge University Press, 2000), p. 64.

4. William J. Clinton, "Address to the Nation on Somalia," *Weekly Compilation of Presidential Documents*, 29, no. 40 (October 11, 1993): 2022–2025.

5. "Letter to the Congress of the United States," White House Office of the Press Secretary, (Washington: the White House, October 13, 1993), http://www.pub.whitehouse.gov/uri-res/I2R?urn:pdi://oma.eop.gov.us/1993/10/13/3.text.1 [accessed September 14, 2000].

6. Douglas Farah, "To Clinton, Mission Accomplished," *Washington Post*, March 30, 1995, p. A1. For various incidents of when American soldiers were injured or killed, see von Hippel, p. 55; Kenneth Allard, *Somalia Operations: Lessons Learned* (Washington: National Defense University Press, 1995), p. 20; James Burk, "Public Support for Peacekeeping in Lebanon and Somalia: Assessing the Casualties Hypothesis," in *The New American Interventionism: Lessons from Successes and Failures*, ed.

Demetrios James Caraley (New York: Columbia University Press, 1999), p. 73; and Allison Mitchell, "First Marines Leave Somalia, a Signal to the UN," *New York Times*, January 20, 1993, p. A3.

7. Martin Ganzglass, "The Restoration of the Somali Justice System," in *Learning from Somalia*, pp. 87–92.

8. Allard, p. 9.

9. Lennox Samuels, "Somaliland Struggles for a Place among Nations; Separatist Region Forsakes Dream of National Unity," *Dallas Morning News*, February 16, 1993, p. A1.

10. I. M. Lewis and James Mayall, "Somalia," in *The New Interventionism 1991–1994: United Nations Experience in Cambodia, Former Yugoslavia and Somalia*, ed. James Mayall (Cambridge: Cambridge University Press, 1996), p. 103.

11. von Hippel, p. 58.

12. George B. N. Ayittey, "The Somali Crisis: Time for an African Solution," Cato Institute Policy Analysis no. 205, March 28, 1994, http://www.cato.org//pubs/pas/pa-205.html [accessed September 10, 2000].

13. Ibid.

14. Imperial College Publications, *New African Yearbook 1991–92* (London: Imperial College Publications, 1991), p. 303.

15. Donatella Lorch, "In Another Part of Somalia, Resentment of the UN," *New York Times*, September 30, 1993, p. A3.

16. Said Samatar, *Somalia: A Nation in Turmoil* (London: Minority Rights Group, 1991), p. 26.

17. Quoted in Didrike Schanche, "Red Cross Appeals for Civilians' Safety, Fighting Continues," Associated Press, November 29, 1991.

18. Quoted in Dudley Althaus, "Somalia: A Nation at the Abyss," *Houston Chronicle*, November 15, 1992, p. 6.

19. Lewis and Mayall, p. 107.

20. See, for example, "Don't Forsake Somalia," editorial, *New York Times*, November 4, 1992, p. A30; "The Hell Called Somalia," editorial, *New York Times*, July 23, 1992, p. A22; and Harry Johnston and Ted Dagne, "Congress and the Somali Crisis," in *Learning from Somalia*, pp. 192–195.

21. Excerpts from Smith Hempstone's cable were printed as "Think Three Times before You Embrace the Somali Tarbaby," *U.S. News & World Report*, December 14, 1992, p. 30. See also Smith Hempstone, *Rogue Ambassador: An African Memoir* (Sewanee, Tenn.: University of the South Press, 1997), pp. 214–231.

22. For the full text of the resolution, see United Nations Security Council Resolution 794, United Nations, New York, December 3, 1992, http://www.un.org/documents/sc/res/s92r794e.pdf [accessed September 25, 2000].

23. Clarke, p. 9.

24. Lewis and Mayall, p. 112.

25. William Hyland, *Clinton's World: Remaking American Foreign Policy* (Westport, Conn.: Praeger, 1999), p. 55.

26. Madeleine K. Albright, "Building a Collective Security System," Statement before the Subcommittees on Europe and the Middle East and on International Security, International Organizations, and Human Rights of the House Foreign Affairs Committee, Washington, D.C., May 3, 1993, U.S. Department of State, *Dispatch* 4, no. 19, May 10, 1993, http://dosfan.lib.uic.edu/ERC/briefing/dispatch/1993/html/Dispatchv4no19.html [accessed September 28, 2000].

27. Robert Houdek, "Update on Progress in Somalia," Statement before the Subcommittee on Africa of the House Foreign Affairs Committee, Washington, D.C., February 17, 1993, U.S. Department of State, *Dispatch* 4, no. 8, February 22, 1993, http://dosfan.lib.uic.edu/ERC/briefing/dispatch/1993/html/Dispatchv4no08.html [accessed September 28, 2000].

28. "Rebuilding a Nation in Ruins; Wish List: Get Somalia Working; $253 Million Plan Envisions Peace," *Atlanta Journal and Constitution*, February 22, 1993, p. A2.

29. Stuart Auerbach, "'It Just Seems Our Job Is Done'; Tired Marines, Eager to Return Home, Await UN Takeover in Somalia," *Washington Post*, March 1, 1993, p. A11.

30. Ganzglass, pp. 26–27.

31. Madeline K. Albright, Statement before the Subcommittee on Foreign Operations, Export Financing, and Related Programs of the House Appropriations Committee, Washington, D.C., March 12, 1993.

32. Walter Clarke and Jeffrey Herbst, "Somalia and the Future of Humanitarian Intervention," in *Learning from Somalia*, p. 241. See also Associated Press, "UN Approves Large Force for Somalia," *Los Angeles Times*, March 27, 1993, p. A10.

33. United Nations Security Council Resolution 814.

34. Quoted in Daniel Williams, "U.S. Troops to Remain in Somalia; Force Assisting UN in 'Re-creating' Nation," *Washington Post*, August 11, 1993, p. A1.

35. Lewis and Mayall, p. 116.

36. James Bone, "Pressure Grows for U.S. to Stop Calling Shots in Somalia," *Times* (London), July 14, 1993; and Keith Richburg, "UN Takes Command of Troops in Somalia," *Washington Post*, May 5, 1993, p. A23.

37. Quoted in Mark Fineman, "Now It's Their Turn; When the UN Takes Control of Somalia Today, It Begins a $1.5 Billion Experiment," *Los Angeles Times*, May 4, 1993, WR1.

38. Richburg, "UN Takes Command of Troops in Somalia."

39. Keith Richburg, "UN Force Reasserts Clout in Somalia," *Washington Post*, July 7, 1993, p. A27.

40. Quoted in Bone.

41. Quoted in ibid.

42. Quoted in Richburg, "UN Takes Command of Troops in Somalia."

43. Quoted in ibid.

44. Quoted in Donatella Lorch, "As UN Prepares for Somalia Command, Rebuilding Is Most Urgent Task," *New York Times*, May 2, 1993, p. A16.

45. Quoted in ibid.

46. See, for example, Jim Abrams, "Clinton Welcomes Home Troops as House Debates Authority to Send Them," Associated Press, May 5, 1993.

47. Steven Holmes, "The Man Who Makes Somalia Worse," *New York Times*, August 15, 1993, p. WR4.

48. Keith Richburg, "It Makes a Warlord Smile," *Washington Post*, June 24, 1993, p. A32.

49. John L. Hirsch and Robert B. Oakley, *Somalia and Operation Restore Hope: Reflections on Peacemaking and Peacekeeping* (Washington: United States Institute of Peace, 1995), pp. 115–16.

50. Quoted in Gérard Prunier, "Somalia: Civil War, Intervention and Withdrawal 1990–1995," United Nations High Commissioner for Refugees, Writenet Issue Paper

(July 1995), http://www.unhcr.ch/refworld/country/writenet/wrisom.htm [accessed October 21, 2000].

51. Hirsch and Oakley, p. 117.

52. For Howe's take on the lessons of Somalia, see Jonathan T. Howe, "The United States and United Nations in Somalia: The Limits of Involvement," *Washington Quarterly* 18, no. 3 (Summer 1995): 49–62.

53. Keith Richburg, "U.S. Planes Hit Mogadishu Again," *Washington Post*, June 13, 1993, p. A1; and Keith Richburg, "U.S. Planes Launch UN Attack on Somali Warlord," *Washington Post*, June 12, 1993, p. A1.

54. See, for example, Keith Richburg, "UN Unit Kills 14 Somali Civilians," *Washington Post*, June 14, 1993, p. A1.

55. Quoted in ibid.

56. Ibid.

57. Quoted in ibid.

58. Quoted in Keith Richburg, "Somali Warlord's Tactics Confound UN," *Washington Post*, June 16, 1993, p. A1.

59. Keith Richburg, "UN Troops Battle Somalis," *Washington Post*, June 18, 1993, p. A1.

60. Quoted in ibid.

61. Quoted in Keith Richburg, "It Makes a Warlord Smile."

62. Jennifer Parmelee, "Waltzing with Warlords; Will the West Make Martyrs of Thugs in Somalia?" *Washington Post*, June 20, 1993, p. C1.

63. Richburg, "It Makes a Warlord Smile"; Michael Maren, "The Mogadishu Paradox," *Village Voice*, November 16, 1993, p. 18; and Aryeh Neier, "Watching Rights," *Nation*, November 15, 1993, p. 562.

64. Madeline K. Albright, "Myths of Peace Keeping," Statement before the Subcommittee on International Security, International Organizations, and Human Rights of the House Committee on Foreign Affairs, Washington, D.C., June 24, 1993, U.S. Department of State, *Dispatch* 4, no. 26 (June 24, 1993): 464.

65. Peter Tarnoff, "U.S. Policy on Somalia," Statement before the Senate Foreign Relations Committee, Washington, D.C., July 29, 1993, U.S. Department of State, *Dispatch* 4, no. 32 (August 9, 1993): 23–24.

66. Charles Krauthammer, "Playing God in Somalia," *Washington Post*, August 13, 1993, p. A25.

67. Henry Kissinger, "Cooking Up a Recipe for a New World Chaos," *Houston Chronicle*, September 5, 1993, p. O1.

68. Quoted in Charles Doe, "U.S. Bolsters Force with Rangers," United Press International, August 24, 1993.

69. Quoted in Richburg, "UN Force Reasserts Clout in Somalia."

70. Quoted in Robin Wright, "Raids Redefine Rules for UN Peacekeeping," *Los Angeles Times*, June 13, 1993, p. A1.

71. Keith Richburg, "Somali Mob Kills Three Journalists," *Washington Post*, July 13, 1993, p. A1.

72. Ibid.

73. Ibid.

74. Associated Press, "UN Raids Somali Clan's Base," *New York Times*, July 13, 1993, p. A1.

75. Quoted in Richburg, "Somali Mob Kills Three Journalists."

76. Quoted in ibid.

77. Quoted in Keith Richburg, "UN Helicopter Assault in Somalia Targeted Aideed's Top Commanders," *Washington Post*, July 16, 1993, p. A1.

78. Ibid.

79. Richburg, "Somali Mob Kills Three Journalists."

80. Quoted in Keith Richburg, "Criticism Mounts over Somali Raid; 'Pack up and Go Home,' U.S. Troops Urged," *Washington Post*, July 15, 1993, p. A21.

81. Quoted in ibid.

82. Quoted in ibid.

83. Alexander Cockburn, "Somalia Slips from Hope to Quagmire," *Los Angeles Times*, July 13, 1993, p. B7.

84. Quoted in "Somali Warlord Urges Uprising Against UN," *Washington Post*, July 19, 1993, p. A10.

85. "Americans Wounded in Somali Blast," Press Association Newsfile, August 4, 1993; and "Somalian Fighting," *USA Today*, August 4, 1993, p. A5.

86. "Two Americans Are Wounded by a Mine Blast in Somalia," *New York Times*, August 5, 1993, p. A9.

87. Keith Richburg, "4 U.S. Soldiers Killed in Somalia," *Washington Post*, August 9, 1993, p. A1.

88. Quoted in ibid.

89. Keith B. Richburg, "U.S. Patrol Clashes with Somalis at Rally," *Washington Post*, August 13, 1993, p. A27.

90. Quoted in ibid.

91. Burk, p. 73.

92. John Lancaster, "U.S. Raid Was Based on Tip; Troops Miss Warlord, Detain UN Workers," *Washington Post*, August 31, 1993, p. A1.

93. Keith Richburg, "Somali Guerrillas Shell Peacekeepers," *Washington Post*, September 11, 1993, p. A1.

94. Michael Gordon and John Cushman Jr., "After Supporting Hunt for Aidid, U.S. Is Blaming UN for Losses," *New York Times*, October 18, 1993, p. A1.

95. Quoted in "Senator McCain Wants End to U.S. Mission in Somalia," *CBS Evening News*, September 10, 1993.

96. Johnston and Dagne, p. 202.

97. For a detailed account of the October events in Mogadishu see Mark Bowden, *Black Hawk Down: A Story of Modern War* (New York: Penguin Books, 2000).

98. Quoted in John Cushman Jr., "5 GIs Are Killed as Somalis Down 2 U.S. Helicopters," *New York Times*, October 4, 1993, p. A1.

99. Quoted in R. W. Apple, "Clinton Sending Reinforcements after Heavy Losses in Somalia," *New York Times*, October 5, 1993, p. A1.

100. "2 Killed in Somalia Are to Get Medal of Honor," *New York Times*, May 15, 1994, p. A29.

101. Quoted in Gordon and Cushman.

102. Quoted in Paul Bedard, "Clinton Refuses to 'Run' from Somalia," *Washington Times*, October 8, 1993, p. A1.

103. von Hippel, p. 77.

104. Gordon and Cushman.

105. Ibid.

106. Ibid.

107. Madeleine K. Albright, "Yes, There Is a Reason to Be in Somalia," *New York Times*, August 10, 1993, p. A19.

108. John Lancaster, "Aspin Lists U.S. Goals In Somalia," *Washington Post*, August 28, 1993, p. A1.

109. Clinton.

110. Richard Haass, *Intervention: The Use of American Military Force in the Post-Cold War World*, 2d ed. (Washington: Brookings Institution, 1999), p. 112.

111. Burk, p. 78.

112. Ibid.

113. Ibid., p. 79.

114. Ibid., pp. 76, 79.

115. Quoted in Keith Richburg, "Stuck in Somalia? American Mission Is Unclear, Open-Ended," *Washington Post*, September 21, 1993, p. A1.

116. Ibid.

117. Burk, p. 77. Emphasis added.

118. Walter Pincus, "Senate Authorizes Troops to Somalia," *Washington Post*, February 5, 1993, p. A10.

119. Burk, p. 86.

120. Johnston and Dagne, p. 199–200.

121. Quoted in "Senator McCain Wants End to U.S. Mission in Somalia."

122. Johnston and Dagne, p. 197.

123. Burk, p. 86.

124. Quoted in Thomas Ricks, "Defense Secretary Aspin Draws Heaviest Fire as Criticism Mounts over U.S. Role in Somalia," *Wall Street Journal*, October 8, 1993, p. A16.

125. Keith Richburg, "Somali Markets Shaken Up by Influx of Food," *Washington Post*, December 30, 1992, p. A15.

126. Diane Jean Schemo, "As Hunger Ebbs, Somalia Faces Need to Rebuild," *New York Times*, February 7, 1993, p. A3.

127. Diana Jean Schemo, "Sweep for Weapons in Somali Port Brings Relief Operations to a Halt," *New York Times*, March 2, 1993, p. A2; and Diana Jean Schemo, "Worry in Gunless Somalia Aid Offices," *New York Times*, March 1, 1993, p. A6.

128. Jonathan Stevenson, "Hope Restored in Somalia?" *Foreign Policy* 91, no. 2 (Summer 1993): 139.

129. Ibid.

130. Rakiya Omaar and Alex de Waal, "Somalia's Uninvited Saviors," *Washington Post*, December 13, 1992, p. C1.

131. Jane Perlez, "Witnesses Report a Somali Massacre before U.S. Arrival," *New York Times*, December 29, 1992, p. A1.

132. Allison Mitchell, "Fifth Horseman of Somalia: Stealing," *New York Times*, January 23, 1993, p. A1.

133. von Hippel, p. 85.

134. Ibid.

135. Clarke and Herbst, p. 242.

136. Prunier.

137. Ibid.

138. Ibid.

139. Donatella Lorch, "Army Team's 'Marketing' Job Is Selling U.S. Role," *New York Times*, December 27, 1992, p. A10.

140. Quoted in Wright.

141. David Laitin, "Somalia: Civil War and International Intervention," in *Civil Wars, Insecurity, and Intervention*, ed. Barbara F. Walter and Jack Snyder (New York: Columbia University Press, 1999), pp. 159–160.

142. Quoted in Thomas W. Lippman, "U.S., UN Aides Defend Somalia 'Police Action,'" *Washington Post*, July 30, 1993, p. A15.

143. Quoted in Richburg, "UN Helicopter Assault in Somalia Targeted Aideed's Top Commanders."

144. Quoted in Lippman.

145. Douglas Jehl, "Fear of New Factional Strife Worries UN in Mogadishu," *New York Times*, October 24, 1993, p. I10; Associated Press, "Planned Protest Raises Tensions in Somalia," *Newark Star Ledger*, 25 October 25, 1993, p. 8; Associated Press, "10 Somalis Killed and 45 Wounded in Battles along Aideed's Stronghold," *Newark Star Ledger*, October 26, 1993, p. 6; and as cited in Stephen Shalom, "Gravy Train: Feeding the Pentagon by Feeding Somalia," *Z Magazine*, February 1993.

146. Ken Menkhaus, "International Peacebuilding and the Dynamics of Local and National Reconciliation in Somalia," in *Learning from Somalia*, p. 43.

147. Quoted in ibid., p. 58.

148. Ibid., p. 58; emphasis added.

149. Christopher Wren, "Mismanagement and Waste Erode UN's Best Intentions," *New York Times*, June 23, 1995, p. A1.

150. "UN Reports 16 Million Dollars in Waste and Fraud," Deutsche Presse-Agentur, October 24, 1995.

151. Quoted in ibid.

152. Quoted in ibid.

153. "Clinton's Words on Somalia: 'The Responsibilities of American Leadership,'" *New York Times*, October 8, 1993, p. A15.

154. von Hippel, p. 61.

155. Shalom; and Alex de Waal and Rakiya Omaar, "The Failings of Operation Restore Hope," *Peace and Democracy News*, Summer 1993, p. 33.

156. Perlez.

157. Tom Bethell, "Exporting Famine," *American Spectator*, December 1993.

158. Quoted in Eric A. Nordlinger, *Isolationism Reconfigured: American Foreign Policy for a New Century* (Princeton, N.J.: Princeton University Press, 1995), p. 25.

159. Richard K. Betts, "The Delusion of Impartial Intervention," *Foreign Affairs* 73, no. 6 (November–December 1994).

160. Ibid.

161. Ibid.

162. Michael Maren, "Nongovernmental Organizations and International Development Bureaucracies," in *Delusions of Grandeur: The United Nations and Global Intervention*, ed. Ted Galen Carpenter (Washington: Cato Institute, 1997), pp. 229–230.

163. Hendrik Groth, "Fears as Well as Hopes as Somalia Elects a President," Deutsche Presse-Agentur, August 26, 2000.

164. George Mwangi, "A 'City of Death' Symbolizes the Hopes of War-Weary Somalia," Associated Press, October 2, 2000.

165. Groth; and Stephen Buckley, "Mogadishu Mourns Death of Faction Leader," *Washington Post*, August 3, 1996, p. A18.

166. Mwangi.

167. Groth.

Chapter 3

1. For a highly readable and comprehensive survey of Haiti's turbulent history see Robert Debs Heinl Jr. and Nancy Gordon Heinl, *Written in Blood: The Story of the Haitian People, 1492–1995*, 2d ed. (New York: New York University Press, 1996). As a U.S. Marine colonel, Robert Heinl led the U.S. Navy military mission to Haiti in the early 1960s. The Marines were sent to modernize the Haitian armed forces in the early Duvalier years. Their inability to do so despite the utter professionalism of the mission itself is discussed at length in Charles T. Williamson, *The U.S. Naval Mission to Haiti, 1959–1963* (Annapolis, Md.: Naval Institute Press, 1999).

2. For the full text of the resolution, see UN Security Council Resolution 940, United Nations, New York, July 31, 1994, http://srch1.un.org:80/plwebcgi/fastweb?state_id=972308425&view [accessed October 23, 2000].

3. Tom Squitieri, "Congress Acts to Get Troops Out of Haiti," *USA Today*, September 2, 1999, p. A12. Consider only the first $329 million spent on the civilian side of Operation Uphold Democracy. Most of that money was spent on items such as payment of debt arrears ($25 million), budget support ($45 million), short-term make work ($19 million), or feeding programs ($90 million) and basic public health ($50 million). Of the $62 million designated for institution-building purposes, $43 million was for the police and $13 million was for elections. Virtually nothing was spent on developmental aid. Also see Carla Anne Robbins, "Social Insecurity: Haiti Tastes Freedom, But Efforts to Rebuild Run into Roadblocks," *Wall Street Journal*, October 30, 1996, p. A1.

4. William G. Hyland, *Clinton's World: Remaking American Foreign Policy* (Westport, Conn.: Praeger, 1999), p. 60.

5. Quoted in Mark Peceny, *Democracy at the Point of Bayonets* (University Park, Penn.: Pennsylvania State University Press, 1999), p. 163.

6. Quoted in ibid.

7. Quoted in Hyland, p. 61.

8. Karin von Hippel, *Democracy by Force: U.S. Military Intervention in the Post–Cold War World* (Cambridge: Cambridge University Press, 2000), p. 100.

9. Quoted in Hyland, p. 61.

10. Quoted in ibid., p. 63.

11. George Will, "And Then What?" *Washington Post*, September 18, 1994, p. C9; and Charles Krauthammer, "Clinton's Little War," *Washington Post*, September 16, 1994, p. A27.

12. Douglas Farah, "To Clinton, Mission Accomplished," *Washington Post*, March 30, 1995, p. A1.

13. UN Security Council Resolution 940.

14. Farah.

15. Ibid.

16. von Hippel, p. 105.

17. Ibid.

18. For the full text of the resolution, see UN Security Council Resolution 1063, United Nations, New York June 28, 1996, http://srch1.un.org:80/plweb-cgi/fastweb?state_id=972933631&view [accessed October 30, 2000].

19. Quoted in Peceny, p. 168.

20. Ibid.

21. Quoted in ibid., p. 169.

22. Steven Holmes, "U.S. General Recommends Pullout from Haiti," *New York Times*, March 14, 1999, p. A17.

23. Quoted in Douglas Farah, "General Calls for Pullout from Haiti," *Washington Post*, March 13, 1999, p. A13.

24. Mark Mueller, "Remaining U.S. Troops Face Hostility," *Boston Herald*, June 13, 1999, p. 14.

25. Ibid.

26. Reuters, "5 Years after Invasion, Haiti's Problems Remain," *Baltimore Sun*, September 19, 1999, p. A25.

27. Quoted in ibid.

28. See, for example, Jennifer L. McCoy, "Introduction: Dismantling the Predatory State—The Conference Report," pp. 1–26; Antony V. Vatanese, "Priorities in the Economic Reconstruction of Rural Haiti," pp. 189–198; and Marc E. Prou, "Haitian Education under Siege: Democratization, National Development, and Social Construction," pp. 215–228, in Robert I. Rotberg, ed. *Haiti Renewed: Political and Economic Prospects* (Washington: Brookings Institution, 1997).

29. Mats Lundahl, "The Haitian Dilemma Reexamined: Lessons from the Past in the Light of Some New Economic Theory," in *Haiti Renewed*, pp. 61–64. Haiti's early wealth was appreciated by Adam Smith, who described Saint-Domingue's wealth as the equal of the entire British possessions in the Caribbean combined. Smith also attributed the superiority of Saint-Domingue (Saint Domingo to Smith) "to the good conduct of the colonists, . . . and this superiority has been remarked in nothing so much as in the good management of their slaves." See Adam Smith, *An Inquiry into the Nature and Causes of the Wealth of Nations* (Chicago: University of Chicago Press, 1976), vol. 2, p. 101.

30. Heinl and Heinl, pp. 95–116.

31. For an account of one of the latter, the rule of President Fabre Geffrard, see ibid., pp. 206–224. Despite some good works, Geffrard, too, proclaimed himself president-for-life and was promptly overthrown in 1867. He ruled 8 years following the disastrous twelve-year reign of President Faustin Soulouque, who early on proclaimed himself Emperor Faustin I. Despite his conspicuous lack of accomplishment, however, Soulouque ruled longer than anyone else in 19th-century Haiti.

32. Donald E. Shultz, "Political Culture, Political Change and the Etiology of Violence," in *Haiti Renewed*, pp. 93–117. Shultz's essay is nothing if not honest in its assessment of the governing political culture in Haiti throughout most of its history. He says, for example, in catalogue fashion: "[Haiti's] self-destructive political behavior [is] marked by authoritarianism, paternalism, personalism, patronage, nepotism, demagogy, corruption, cynicism, opportunism, racism, incompetence, parasitism, rigidity, intolerance, violence, distrust, insecurity, vengeance, intrigue, superstition, volatility, violence, paranoia, xenophobia, exploitation, class hatred, institutional illegitimacy, and mass apathy, aversion, and submission." Ibid., p. 95. For a rare case of a predatory state inflicting harm on the elites in 15th-century Florence, see Niccolo Machiavelli, *History of Florence and the Affairs of State* (New York: Harper and Row, 1960), pp. 165–166. It took another four centuries for the Italy of Machiavelli's time to emerge as a nation-state. Observers of modern Italy wonder if that process is yet to be completed.

33. Michel-Rolph Trouillot, "A Social Contract for Whom? Haitian History and Haiti's Future," in *Haiti Renewed*, pp. 47–59.

34. For a sample of the theory of Haiti's nonexceptionalism, see ibid., pp. 49–50.

35. Thomas Hobbes, *The Leviathan or the Matter, Forme and Power of a Commonwealth Ecclesiastical and Civil* (New York: Collier Books, 1962), p. 100. Consider the per capita income, for example, of Jesus of Nazareth. By profession a carpenter, by avocation a teacher, Jesus' per capita income particularly during his three years of preaching would be difficult to estimate. It likely would be hardly better than that of the average Haitian peasant of today, or even less, depending largely on the kindness of strangers. If the biblical text is correct, Jesus' only piece of property was the cloak for which the Roman soldiers drew lots. See John 19:23–24.

36. Robert I. Rotberg, "Preface: Haiti's Last Best Chance," in *Haiti Renewed*, p. xi.

37. Like Haiti, South Korea and Taiwan were also poor in natural resources with a population density that had reached Malthusian proportions, but the latter two turned adversity into good fortune through hard work and good policy (as well as a judicious amount of foreign aid) and thus have long lost their status as hopelessly impoverished.

38. McCoy, p. 6. The sanctions may have shredded the Haitian economy—for example, its most dynamic sector, the industrial assembly factories in Port-au-Prince, collapsed and have yet to revive fully—but the junta remained in power until threatened with a massive U.S. military invasion. For an account of that episode, see Bob Shacochis, *The Immaculate Invasion* (New York: Viking Penguin, 1999). For the full Inter-American Development Bank report, see *Basic Socio-Economic Data for 16 October 2000*, Statistics and Quantitative Analysis Unit, Integration and Regional Programs Department, http://www.iadb.org/int/sta/ENGLISH/brptnet/english/htibrpt.htm [accessed October 13, 2000].

39. McCoy, p. 2. The remaining forested area of Haiti was halved between the 1970s and early 1990s. As of now, Haiti has less than 35,000 acres of forest. Rotberg, p. viii. In 1995, the entire mining sector in Haiti constituted a minuscule 0.1 percent of GDP. Charles P. Trumbull, ed., *2000 Britannica Book of the Year* (Chicago: Encyclopedia Britannica, 2000), p. 616.

40. Lundahl, p. 63. Haiti's population density approaches Javanese levels, it is said, and, at 2,605 inhabitants per square kilometer, Haiti ranks ahead of Jamaica (at 2,259) and is virtually equal to El Salvador. But El Salvador, despite a decade of civil war, has a far more productive economy that is rapidly industrializing. These figures are given in Rotberg, p. viii. Regarding Malthus, Lawrence E. Harrison makes the same point in his *Underdevelopment Is a State of Mind* (Lanham, Md.: Madison Books, 1985), p. 60. Haiti's agricultural impoverishment was virtually guaranteed from the first days of the republic. The south under Alexander Pétion divided the once flourishing estates into small holdings for peasants who were then left to their own devices. In the north under Henry Christophe, the plantations were maintained under new management and remained productive. But these too were dissolved after Christophe's suicide in 1820. Ibid., pp. 76–77.

41. Lundahl, p. 85. That estimate was made in 1988 by economist Uli Locher, but there is little reason to believe it is off by much. Uli Locker, "Land Distribution, Land Tenure and Land Erosion in Haiti," in *Haiti Renewed*, pp. 15–16.

42. Rotberg, p. x. See also Clive Gray, "Alternate Models for Haiti's Economic Reconstruction," in *Haiti Renewed*, pp. 185–86. The assembly plants did not stop at supporting those who earned a paycheck, mostly women in any case. Those paychecks, it has been estimated, supported six dependents. Moreover, the sector also provided jobs in the informal sector supporting it. All in all, some one million Haitians were affected, forming 15 percent of the entire population. See Elizabeth D. Gibbons,

Sanctions in Haiti: Human Rights and Democracy under Assault (Westport, Conn.: Praeger and the Center for Strategic and International Studies, 1999), pp. 10–11.

43. McCoy, pp. 9–10. Also Anthony V. Catanese, "Priorities in the Economic Reconstruction of Rural Haiti," in *Haiti Renewed*, pp. 194–195.

44. The refusal to act on this question triggered the resignation of Prime Minister Smarck Michel in October 1995. See Robert I. Rotberg, "Introduction: Dismantling the Predatory State—The Conference Report," in *Haiti Renewed*, pp. 9–10. See also Robert Pastor, "A Popular Democratic Revolution in a Predemocratic Society: The Case of Haiti," in *Haiti Renewed*, pp. 125–126.

45. Canute James, "Aristide Plots Return from the Wilderness to Haitian Presidency," *Financial Times*, September 16, 1999, p. 8.

46. Shelley Eming, "Billions of U.S. Dollars Later, Haiti No Better Off," *Washington Times*, March 23, 1999, p. A6.

47. *Plus ça change*. When the author was in Haiti as a journalist awaiting the red-eye departure of the Duvaliers, he interviewed a UN official who had been in charge of a housing project for more than a decade. Asked how many houses had been built under the program at that time, he answered "none."

48. For pioneer works on the influence of what is now called political culture on economic development and political stability, see David C. McClelland, *The Achieving Society* (Princeton, N.J.: Van Nostrand, 1961); and Edward C. Banfield, *The Moral Basis of a Backward Society* (New York: Free Press, 1958). Banfield's study of southern Italy found the roots of its impoverishment were in such "values" as "amoral familism"—the belief there is no right or wrong outside the nuclear family and its advancement—can certainly be found in Haiti from top to bottom. But Haiti's elite demonstrates Banfield's hypothesis best of all. See Banfield, pp. 83–101.

49. Harrison, pp. 120–123. The one-generation leap into a political culture that supports rather than undercuts economic development is extremely rare. On another point, the roots of failure are not racial either. Barbados, for example, is largely black with the bulk of the population coming from the same region of West Africa as in Haiti. Like Haiti, Barbados has a slave past that was often brutal. But present-day Barbados is democratic, stable, and on per capita terms, better off than Argentina in the early 1990s. See Harrison, pp. 97–99, and in Lawrence E. Harrison, *The Pan-American Dream* (Boulder, Colo.: Westview, 1997), p. 41.

50. Some observers argue that Haiti does not even have a society as such—that is, one nation based on *shared* values and beliefs. That observation is important and requires further elaboration. See also Trouillot, pp. 47–59. For the Harrison quote, see Lawrence E. Harrison, *Who Prospers? How Cultural Values Shape Economic and Political Success* (New York: Basic Books, 1992), p. 3.

51. Heinl and Heinl, pp. 33–34. Their exact numbers in 1789 were 40,000 whites (all classes), 28,000 free mulattos, and 452,000 slaves. Harrison, *Underdevelopment Is a State of Mind*, p. 63.

52. Black rulers like Dessalines, Christophe, Soulouque, and the Duvaliers were as repressive toward Haiti's blacks as any mulatto ruler, sometimes worse. The only Haitian leader who actually attempted to alleviate the misery of the black masses was Pétion, who was himself an aristocratic mulatto.

53. Harrison, *Underdevelopment Is a State of Mind*, p. 81. *Noblesse oblige*, of course, is a French expression.

54. This thumbnail sketch of Haiti's political culture can be found in Harrison, *Underdevelopment Is a State of Mind*, pp. 80–87. Harrison's work is based on that of

many students of Haiti whose work spans the last century. They include James Leyburn, Rayford Logan, and Melville Herskovitz.

55. For a full-length history and critique of the American occupation, see Hans Schmidt, *The United States Occupation of Haiti, 1915–1934* (New Brunswick, N.J.: Rutgers University Press, 1971).

56. New Frontier hubris was matched only by Nikita Khrushchev's. He would boast about the same time that the Soviet Union would catch up economically with the United States in the same year—1970. Thirty years later Russia enjoys a GDP the size of the Netherlands. For a critical account of the Alliance as an exercise in modernization and nation building, see Michael E. Latham, *Modernization as Ideology: American Social Science and "Nation-Building" in the Kennedy Era* (Chapel Hill, N.C.: The University of North Carolina Press, 2000), pp. 69–108.

57. Quoted in Williamson, p. 18. Captain Williamson served on the mission in Haiti for nearly its entirety and drew the conclusions that are found below. Just why Duvalier wanted a mission in the first place is explained by Williamson. Papa Doc wanted to acquire arms, ammunition, and equipment he needed to remain in power. Ibid., p. 50. Duvalier also wanted a visible symbol of U.S. support, useful in cowing his numerous enemies, both foreign and domestic. In fact, the United States during World War II did send an Army training mission to Haiti, but it proved spectacularly inept. Its one achievement: changing the name of Haiti's military to the more grand sounding *Forces Armées d'Haïti*. Ibid., pp. 355–356.

58. Quoted in ibid., p. 18. For government, of course, read the ever-suspicious François Duvalier, who saw enemies everywhere and, like Joseph Stalin, was often right in his suspicions.

59. Ibid., pp. 36–37. As for the competence of the enlisted men, one sample from Williamson's memoir should suffice: "Practical application rarely if ever followed up on classroom lectures. Soldiers lacked the necessary infantry skills that could only be learned in the field. They did not know the difference between cover and concealment and would not know how to take advantage of either, since they had never heard of terrain appreciation. They had never seen a map or compass." Ibid., p. 48. As for the basics in logistics, Williamson remembers: "Such spare parts or supplies as existed were stored and forgotten in cluttered storerooms and storage depots. The Fad'H lacked inventory controls, so no one had any idea what was on hand, least of all commanding officers and supply officers." Ibid., p. 50.

60. Ibid., p. 345. These accomplishments, too, would prove temporary, but the effects were real enough and some lasted longer than others; all lasted longer than any other reforms in Haiti's long history.

61. One cannot successfully argue that a good beginning at least had been made and that only Duvalier's peculiarities prevented success. Blaming one individual for Haiti's failings has been a perennial trap for journalists and policymakers. For an entertaining firsthand account of that invasion and its aftermath see Shacochis, passim. As for the successes, the Marines were able to train a rifle team for competitive shooting matches that the Haitian team succeeded in winning on occasion. Marine advisers were also successful in getting some units to clean their weapons—at least for a while. The army never did learn how to march. Williamson, pp. 131–132, 144–145, and 255.

62. Quoted in Hyland, pp. 24–25, 62.

63. Quoted in Peceny, pp. 167–168.

64. The unopposed landing was not without its comic touches. The lack of casualties was because of former President Jimmy Carter's unasked for, last-minute diplomacy in which the Georgian convinced the Haitian military junta to step down. Carter's involvement displeased the White House and confused the United Nations, whose special advisor on Haiti, Dante Caputo, a former Argentine foreign minister, was left unconsulted and then subsequently resigned. Although the United States supplied the bulk of the forces, 26 other nations, including faraway Nepal and Bangladesh, contributed some 2,000 troops. von Hippel, pp. 103–104. Another casualty of the UN Mission in Haiti was the Organization of American States, which played no role in Haiti although the island was supposedly in the OAS's purview, thereby demonstrating its utter lack of purpose. The total disregard of the organizations will have added consequences for the future.

65. For an unusually detailed description of the effects of the sanctions on Haiti, see Gibbons, pp. 9–46. Gibbons notes that even the exceptions to the sanctions in the form of humanitarian aid added to the distortions already imposed on Haitian society.

66. In the complicated world of UN and domestic U.S. politics, nothing is ever straightforward. The Haitian intervention proved to be no exception. After Somalia and Bosnia, UN members were reluctant to use the United Nations to bail out an essentially American embarrassment. Consequently, although the international organization took on the assignment, it did so with some conditions. First, the multinational (although largely American) military force was specifically not assigned nation-building duties. In the shadow of the Somalia venture, even basic security functions were not performed. For example, U.S. troops were specifically forbidden to intervene in private disputes that were often political in nature. The collection of weapons was largely for show purposes; thousands of arms were left in private hands. Meanwhile, nation-building tasks would be carried out, in succession, by the UN Mission in Haiti, the UN Support Mission in Haiti, the UN Transition Mission in Haiti, and finally, the UN Civilian Police Mission to Haiti. von Hippel, pp. 104–07.

67. Ibid, p. 116.

68. "Remarks by President William Clinton, United Nations Secretary-General Boutros Boutros-Ghali, and President Jean Bertrand Aristide," United Nations Transition Ceremony, The National Palace, Port-au-Prince, Haiti, March 31, 1995.

69. von Hippel, pp. 108–12.

70. Ibid., pp. 109–10.

71. Jess T. Ford, associate director of the International Relations and Trade Issues section of the National Security and International Affairs division of the U.S. General Accounting Office, "Lack of Haitian Commitment Limited Success of U.S. Aid to Justice System," Statement before the House Committee on International Relations, Washington, D.C., September 19, 2000, pp. 4–5. On the question of discipline, the GAO notes: "During our visits to several police units, we saw that many lower ranking police officers did not show much respect for high-ranking officers and were milling around police facilities, reading newspapers, or watching soccer games on television." Ibid., p. 4.

72. Ibid., p. 6. As it no doubt was designed to do by Haiti's new rulers. It is no coincidence that in the approximate time since the disappearance of an effective Inspector General, the share of cocaine imports into the United States routed through Haiti has risen from 10 to 14 percent. Aggravating that problem is that Haiti's narcotics unit lacks a commander and its authorized complement of 75 officers consists of only 28 officers. Ibid., pp. 5–6.

73. William G. O'Neill, "No Longer a Pipe Dream? Justice in Haiti," in *Haiti Renewed*, p. 200.

74. Ibid., p. 201.

75. Richard Chacón, "In Crisis, Haiti Feels U.S. Chill," *Boston Globe*, October 2, 2000, p. A1.

76. Statement of Jess T. Ford, p. 7.

77. For the whole sorry record, see Heinl and Heinl, passim.

78. Pastor, p. 119–120.

79. Peter F. Romero, Assistant Secretary of State for Western Hemisphere Affairs, Statement before the House International Relations Committee, Washington, D.C., April 5, 2000.

80. "Haiti: Counted Out," *Economist*, June 24, 2000, pp. 40–42; "Haiti: A Vote for Misrule," *Economist*, July 22, 2000, pp. 36–7; David Gonzalez, "Few Haitians Turn Out for Runoff Election," *New York Times*, July 10, 2000, p. A8; and "Haitian Runoff Election Draws Few Voters," *Washington Post*, July 11, 2000, p. A18. This particular fiasco should have been apparent long before the election. The Provisional Electoral Council itself was subject to a grenade attack shortly before the May 21 election, opposition politicians were harassed, and in at least one case, an opposition journalist shot to death. A year earlier the independent International Republican Institute that for 10 years had been attempting to develop viable political institutions was forced to leave Haiti by the government and its Lavalas supporters. See "Hapless in Haiti," editorial, *Washington Post*, August 30, 1999, p. A18.

81. Barry Schweid, "Albright, Ministers Meet about Haiti," The Associated Press, September, 13, 2000. http://www.newsday.com/ap/washington/ap315.htm [accessed October 24, 2000].

82. David Gonzalez, "Haiti Cast Ballots, Preparing the Way for Aristide Encore," *New York Times*, November 27, 2000, p. A1; and Michelle Faul, "Fear, Apathy Keep Voters from Polls," *Washington Times*, November 27, 2000, p. A15.

83. Ibid.

84. Quoted in Nora Boustany, "Diplomatic Dispatches: American Seeks New Deal with OAS Neighbors," *Washington Post*, September 8, 2000, p. A29.

85. Quoted in Ben Barber, "U.S. Officials See Failed Haiti Policy," *Washington Times*, November 29, 2000, p. A13.

86. See Samuel R. Berger, "A Foreign Policy for the Global Age," *Foreign Affairs* 79, no. 6 (November–December 2000): 35; and Al Gore's comments in Election 2000 Presidential Debate Transcript, October 11, 2000, http://www.cnn.com/ELECTION/2000/debates/transcripts/u221011.html [accessed October 24, 2000].

87. Quoted in Barber.

Chapter 4

1. An estimated 150,000–200,000 Muslims, Serbs, and Croats perished during the war. See Steven L. Burg and Paul S. Shoup, *The War in Bosnia-Herzegovina: Ethnic Conflict and International Intervention* (New York: M. E. Sharpe, 1999), pp. 169–170.

2. Paul Hockenos, "Former Communists Gain in Bosnia's Municipal Elections," *Christian Science Monitor*, April 26, 2000, p. 5; and Paul Watson, "Elections: Moderates Gain among Muslim Voters, but Serbs and Croats Stay with Hard-Line Candidates," *Los Angeles Times*, April 10, 2000, p. A10.

3. John J. Mearsheimer, "The Only Exit from Bosnia," *New York Times*, October 7, 1997, p. A31.

4. It should be noted, however, that the division of armaments applies only to the quantity, not the quality, of weapons, and the Muslim-Croat Federation has superior and more up-to-date weapons than the Republika Srpska.

5. "Advanced Text of Remarks to Be Delivered by Secretary of State Madeleine K. Albright to Ministerial Meeting of the North Atlantic Council," Florence, Italy, Federal News Service, May 24, 2000.

6. Misha Glenny, *The Fall of Yugoslavia: The Third Balkan War* (New York: Penguin, 1996), p. 163.

7. William J. Clinton, "President's Statement on Bosnian Peacekeeping Mission," The White House, Washington, D.C., November 27, 1997, http://www.pub.whitehouse.gov/urires/I2R?urn:pdi://oma.eop.gov.us/1995/11/28/1.text.1 [accessed August 15, 2000].

8. Quoted in Robert Burns, "U.S. Extends Bosnia Troop Deployment," *Boston Globe*, November 16, 1996, p. A2.

9. Strobe Talbott, "Job Can Be Done in Bosnia and Risks Can Be Managed," Remarks delivered to the Pittsburgh World Affairs Council, December 14, 1995.

10. Associated Press, "Local Vote Delayed Again in Bosnia Move Won't Affect NATO Troops' Exit," *Arizona Republic*, October 23, 1996, p. A15.

11. William J. Clinton, Remarks by the President, The White House, November 15, 1996, http://www.pub.whitehouse.gov/uri-res/I2R?urn:pdi://oma.eop.gov.us/1996/11/15/6.text.1 [accessed August 15, 2000].

12. Quoted in James Bennet, "Clinton Calls for Keeping Troops in Bosnia with No New Exit Date," *New York Times*, December 19, 1997, p. A1.

13. Quoted in Harry Summers, "Nation-Building Reality Check," *Washington Times*, April 2, 1998, p. A14.

14. Quoted in R. Jeffrey Smith, "How Far Off Is 'Self-Sustaining' Bosnian Peace?" *Washington Post*, December 28, 1997, p. A24.

15. Tom Carter, "House Rejects Troop-Deployment Curbs," *Washington Times*, March 19, 1998, p. A11.

16. Richard Holbrooke, *To End a War* (New York: Random House, 1998), p. 362.

17. See Carl Bildt, "There Is No Alternative to Dayton," *Survival* 39, no. 4 (Winter 1997–98): 19–21; Pauline Neville-Jones, "Washington Has a Responsibility Too," *Survival* 39, no. 4 (Winter 1997–98): 21–24; John Lampe, "Policy Forum: Bosnia—After the Troops Leave," *Washington Quarterly* 19, no. 3 (Summer 1996): 73–77.

18. Charles Lane, "Policy Forum: Bosnia—After the Troops Leave," *Washington Quarterly* 19, no. 3 (Summer 1996): 81.

19. Jane M. O. Sharp, "Dayton Report Card," *International Security* 22, no. 3 (Winter 1997–98): 101–137.

20. See Ivo Daalder, "Bosnia after SFOR: Options for Continued US Engagement," *Survival* 39, no. 4 (Winter 1997–98): 5–18; Mearsheimer; Henry Kissinger, "Limits to What the U.S. Can Do in Bosnia," *Washington Post*, September 22, 1997, p. A19; Kay Bailey Hutchison, "The Bosnia Puzzle Needs a New Solution," *New York Times*, September 11, 1997; and Michael O'Hanlon, "Bosnia: Better Left Partitioned," *Washington Post*, April 10, 1997, p. A25. For competing views on the stabilizing effects of partition, see Chaim D. Kaufmann, "When All Else Fails: Ethnic Population Transfers and Partitions in the Twentieth Century," *International Security* 23, no. 2 (Fall 1998): 120–156; and Radha Kumar, *Divide and Fall? Bosnia in the Annals of Partition* (New York: Verso, 1997).

21. Robert Pape, "Partition: An Exit Strategy for Bosnia," *Survival* 39, no. 4 (Winter 1997–98): 25.

22. United States General Accounting Office, *Balkans Security: Current and Projected Factors Affecting Regional Stability* (Washington, D.C., April 2000), p. 24.

23. "Carlos Westendorp; Bosnia's Euro-Spanish Viceroy," *Economist*, September 5, 1998, p. 52.

24. Smith.

25. Quoted in Peter Baker, "Clinton Sees Hope in Bosnia Trip," *Washington Post*, December 23, 1997, p. A1.

26. As one veteran of the European Community Monitoring Mission in Bosnia observed: "Something as basic as playing interethnic football remains totally beyond the scope of most people's toleration. . . . There are now three separate football leagues—one for Muslims, one for Croats, and one for Serbs—and in many places, former clubs can no longer use their old stadia because they are now located on the wrong side of an artificial monstrosity called the 'Interentity Boundary Line.' Two Serb football referees sitting at a bar outside Sarajevo summed up the whole situation rather well: 'When you spend four years seeing someone through gun sights you cannot [then] play sport with them. Maybe our grandchildren will, but not us.'" Brendan O'Shea, *Crisis at Bihac: Bosnia's Bloody Battlefield* (Phoenix Mill, U.K.: Sutton, 1998), p. 233.

27. See Charles Boyd, "Making Bosnia Work," *Foreign Affairs* 77, no. 1 (January–February 1998): 43.

28. Quoted in Lenard J. Cohen, "Whose Bosnia? The Politics of Nation Building," *Current History* 97, no. 617 (March 1998): 112.

29. Quoted in ibid; emphasis added.

30. Jeffrey Smith, "Bosnians to Decide on Path Toward Future," *Washington Post*, September 12, 1998, p. A21.

31. See, for example, "Bosnian Muslim Returnee Killed, Two Injured in Explosion," Agence France Presse, March 31, 2000; "Policeman Hurt in Car Bomb Explosion in Central Bosnia," BBC Summary of World Broadcasts, January 12, 2000; "Muslim Attacks Serb Returnee in Southern Bosnia," BBC Summary of World Broadcasts, September 14, 1999; "Muslim Returnee's House Set on Fire in Stolac," BBC Summary of World Broadcasts, March 23, 1999; "Croat Police Officer Seriously Hurt in Car Explosion," Agence France Presse, February 10, 1999; "Bosnia: Explosive Device Goes Off Outside Croat Shop in Mostar," BBC Worldwide Monitoring, November 19, 1998; "Bomb Explodes in Front of Croat Policeman's Home in Central Bosnia," BBC Summary of World Broadcasts, September 23, 1998; "Policeman Killed in Blast in Central Bosnia Town," BBC Worldwide Monitoring, August 11, 1998; "Bosnia: Explosion Rocks Independent Magazine's Premises in Sarajevo," BBC Worldwide Monitoring, August 10, 1998; "Bosnian Croat Leader Threatens 'Return of Para-Organizations' Over Killings," BBC Worldwide Monitoring, July 31, 1998; "Explosions Rattle Three Towns in Bosnia," *New York Times*, July 30, 1998, p. A10; "Bosnia: Blast Damages Muslim Shop in Brcko," BBC Worldwide Monitoring, July 2, 1998; "Bomb Killing Policeman 'Act of Political Terrorism' Against Bosnian Croats," BBC Worldwide Monitoring, June 13, 1998; "Bosnian Serb Police Confirm Muslim Grenade Attack on Serb Village," BBC Worldwide Monitoring, April 28, 1998; and "Serbs, Muslims Square Off After Violence," *Washington Post*, April 28, 1998, p. A14; Colin Soloway, "International: Mayor Injured in Croat Revenge Riot," *Daily Telegraph* (London), April 25, 1998, p. 13; Srecko Latal, "Serbs' Attack on Croatian Cardinal Fuels Payback Riot

at UN Post," *Washington Times*, April 25, 1998, p. A8; "UN Officials Flee Bosnian Town," *Washington Post*, April 25, 1998, p. A12; "World Update: Rifle Grenade Scars Bosnian Monastery," *San Diego Union-Tribune*, April 7, 1998, p. A10; "Bosnia: Explosions Demolish Muslim, Croat Houses," BBC Worldwide Monitoring, March 27, 1998; "Bosnia: Hand Grenade Thrown at Sarajevo Building," BBC Worldwide Monitoring, December 26, 1997; "Bosnia: Explosion Reported in 'Former Separation Zone' near Brcko," BBC Worldwide Monitoring, December 19, 1997; "Bosnia: Sarajevo Policeman Shot by Gunman Inside Serb Entity," BBC Worldwide Monitoring, December 18, 1997; "Blast Damages Serb Transmitter," *Washington Post*, October 21, 1997, p. A15; "Explosion at Serb Orthodox Church in Bosnia," Associated Press, October 27, 1997; "Bosnia, Opposition Paper's Offices Destroyed," *Los Angeles Times*, September 29, 1997, p. A4; Reuters, "Bomb Kills 1, Injures 2 near Bosnian Serb Leader's Office," *Rocky Mountain News* (Denver), August 30, 1997, p. A52; and "Two Killed as Gunmen Ambush Bosnian Muslims," *Independent* (London), August 16, 1997, p. 10.

32. See, for example, "Bosnia: Explosion Shakes Mostar," BBC Worldwide Monitoring, January 2, 1998; "Sarajevo Radio Reports Upsurge in Attacks on Muslims in Bosnia," BBC Worldwide Monitoring, January 31, 1998; and "Bosnia: Powerful Explosion Rocks Muslim-Controlled Mostar," BBC Worldwide Monitoring, February 24, 1998; "Bosnia: Three Explosions Reported in Mostar," BBC Worldwide Monitoring, February 9, 1998; and "Bosnia: Two Explosions in Mostar; No One Injured," BBC Worldwide Monitoring, February 7, 1998.

33. Kevin Done, "Unification a Slow Process," *Financial Times*, October 21, 1998, p. II.

34. Quoted in ibid.

35. See David Bosco, "Reintegrating Bosnia: A Progress Report," *Washington Quarterly* 21, no. 2 (Spring 1998): 67–70; "Special Anti-Terrorist Police Unit Will Investigate Recent Bombings," AP Worldstream, October 4, 1998; "Explosions Rattle Three Towns in Bosnia," *New York Times*, July 30, 1998, p. A10; "Shots Reported, Tension Said to Be Mounting in Southern Bosnian Canton," BBC Worldwide Monitoring, November 29, 1998; "Bosnian Croat Villagers Block Road Following Reported Arrest by NATO Forces," BBC Worldwide Monitoring, November 29, 1998; and "NATO Tightens Security in Bosnia after Attacks," *Washington Times*, November 27, 1998, p. A25.

36. Done.

37. United States General Accounting Office.

38. "Minority Returns 2000," United Nations High Commissioner for Refugees, Sarajevo, Bosnia, http://www.unhcr.ba/Operations/Statistical%20package/t7-min10.pdf [accessed December 13, 2000]; and Peter Ford, "Bosnia Four Years Later: Few Gains," *Christian Science Monitor*, February 28, 2000, p. 1.

39. David Buchan, "Trappings of Fragile Statehood," *Financial Times*, October 21, 1998, p. I.

40. International Crisis Group, "Is Dayton Failing? Four Years After the Peace Agreement," (Washington: October 28, 1999), p. 33.

41. See Charles Boyd, "Policy Weakness May Doom Bosnia Mission," *San Diego Union-Tribune*, December 12, 1997, p. G1.

42. Buchan.

43. Quoted in John Pomfret, "Rivalries Stall Reconstruction of Bosnia," *Washington Post*, October 10, 1996, p. A1.

44. Stephen M. Walt, "Two Cheers for Clinton's Foreign Policy," *Foreign Affairs* 79, no. 2 (March–April 2000): 76.

45. "The Bubbling Balkans," *Economist*, May 27–June 2, 2000, p. 50.

46. Douglas A. Macgregor, "The Balkan Limits to Power and Principle," *Orbis* 45, no. 1 (Winter 2001): 96.

47. "Keeping the Peace," *NewsHour with Jim Lehrer*, May 18, 2000.

48. Quoted in Neil King Jr., "Life Support: In Latter-Day Bosnia, Foreigners Try to Piece It All Back Together," *Wall Street Journal*, August 26, 1998, p. A1.

49. Senior Deputy High Representative Hanns Schumacher quoted in David Chandler, "Bosnia: Prototype of a NATO Protectorate," in *Masters of the Universe? NATO's Balkan Crusade*, ed. Tariq Ali (New York: Verso, 2000), p. 275.

50. National Public Radio, *All Things Considered*, "Foreigners Still Involved in Bosnia," September 18, 1998.

51. Ibid.

52. Ibid.

53. Interview with High Representative Carlos Westendorp, "Carlos Westendorp Reveals His Opinion about Bosnian Politicians," *Slobodna Bosna* (Sarajevo), November 30, 1997, http://www.ohr.int/press/i971130a.htm [accessed October 1, 1998].

54. Interview with the High Representative Carlos Westendorp, *Nasa Borba* (Belgrade), December 12, 1997, http://www.ohr.int/press/i971212a.htm [accessed October 1, 1998].

55. Neely Tucker, "*E Pluribus Unum* Not Catching On," *Gazette* (Montreal), July 28, 1999, p. B1; Chris Hedges, "With West's Help, Bosnian Serb President May Form Cabinet," *New York Times*, January 13, 1998, p. A3; and R. Jeffrey Smith, "UN Official in Bosnia Ends Currency Debate," *Washington Post*, January 20, 1998, p. A15.

56. David Buchan, "A Peaceful Army Working for Reconstruction," *Financial Times*, October 21, 1998, p. III.

57. "Westendorp Sacks Moslem Mayor of Bosnian Town," Agence France Presse, July 20, 1999; "Sacked Bosnian Croat Official Continues to Work Regardless," BBC Worldwide Monitoring, March 7, 1999.

58. Tucker.

59. "Europe: The Protectorate," *Economist*, February 14, 1998, p. 50.

60. Ibid.

61. Michael Kelly, "A Chance to Change History," *Washington Post*, January 21, 1998, p A21.

62. Carlos Westendorp, Speech of the High Representative Carlos Westendorp at the Stability Pact Dinner, Sarajevo, Bosnia, July 29, 1999, http://www.ohr.int/speeches/s990729a.htm [accessed August 15, 2000].

63. Quoted in Darla Sito-Sucic, "Bosnia Officials Sacked for Obstructing Peace," Reuters, November 29, 1999.

64. Quoted in Aida Cerkez-Robinson, "22 Bosnian Politicians Fired," Associated Press, November 29, 1999.

65. Quoted in Peter Ford, "Bosnia Four Years Later: Few Gains," *Christian Science Monitor*, February 28, 2000, p. 1.

66. Joint Office of the High Representative/Organization for Security and Cooperation in Europe Press Release, "Fifteen Public Officials Removed for Obstructing Property Law Implementation" (Sarajevo, Bosnia, September 8, 2000), http://www.ohr.int/press/p20000908a.htm [accessed September 13, 2000].

67. Frank Dahl, "West Slams Bosnia Assembly over Draft Election Law," Reuters, January 20, 2000.

68. Quoted in Mike O'Connor, "On Local Level, at Least, Bosnians Try to Get Along," *New York Times*, May 4, 1998, p. A6.

69. "Carlos Westendorp, Bosnia's Euro-Spanish Viceroy."

70. Quoted in "Europe: The Protectorate."

71. O'Connor.

72. David Chandler, *Bosnia: Faking Democracy after Dayton* (London: Pluto, 1999), p. 88.

73. Ibid.

74. Edward Cody, "Serb Military Gives Boost to President," *Washington Post*, August 1997, p. A21; Chris Hedges, "Bosnia's Latest Power Struggle Pits Serb against Serb," *New York Times*, August 27, 1997, p. A3; and Raymond Bonner, "Belgrade and Moscow Stall Bosnia Vote Desired by U.S.," *New York Times*, October 16, 1997, p. A5.

75. State Department Daily Briefing, Federal News Service, August 15, 1997.

76. R. Jeffrey Smith, "U.S. Likely to Send Aid to Serbs Despite Criticism on War Criminals," *Washington Post*, December 16, 1997, p. A17.

77. Quoted in ibid.

78. Philip Smucker, "Left Hand Hinders Right on Bosnia," *Washington Times*, December 6, 1998, p. A1.

79. R. Jeffrey Smith, "Dollar Diplomacy in Bosnia," *Washington Post*, August 3, 1998, p. A18.

80. Quoted in ibid.

81. Quoted in Peter Finn, "Serb Hard Liners Take Strong Lead in Bosnian Voting," *Washington Post*, September 17, 1998, p. A23.

82. Guy Dinmore, "Serbs Throw Doubt on Poll," *Financial Times*, September 17, 1998, p. 3.

83. Jack Kelley, "Hard-line Serb Still Apparent Election Winner," *USA Today*, September 22, 1998, p. A11.

84. Tom Walker, "Triumph for Radicals Imperils Bosnia Peace," *Times* (London) September 17, 1998, http://www.the-times. co.uk/cgi-bin/BackIssue?3002148 [accessed October 1, 1998].

85. Ibid.

86. Quoted in Guy Dinmore, "West Clings to Bosnia Hopes," *Financial Times*, September 25, 1998, p. 2.

87. "Envoy Sacks Hardline Bosnian Serb President," Reuters, March 5, 1999.

88. Quoted in Smith, "Dollar Diplomacy in Bosnia."

89. Interviewed on the *NewsHour with Jim Lehrer*, "Bosnia on the Brink?," September 25, 1998, http://www.pbs.org/newshour/bb/bosnia/july-dec98/bosnia_9-25.html [accessed October 1, 1998].

90. Guy Dinmore, "Hopes to Rebuild Bosnia Face Test," *Financial Times*, September 11, 1998, p. 2.

91. Joint Office of the High Representative/Organization for Security and Cooperation in Europe, "SRS Must Refile Application for Party Registration" (Sarajevo, Bosnia, October 5, 1999).

92. OSCE Mission to Bosnia and Herzegovina Press Release, "PEC Denies Certification for Serb Radical Party and SRSS Parties for the Municipal Elections 2000," Sarajevo, October 25, 1999.

93. Chandler, p. 90.

94. Hockenos.

95. Quoted in "Bosnians Turning Away from Wartime Political Agendas: Petritsch," Agence France Presse, April 21, 2000.

96. Philippa Fletcher, "Bosnian Nationalists' Poll Showing Hits Moderates," Reuters, November 14, 2000.

97. Philippa Fletcher, "Bosnian Nationalists Strike Election Blow to West," Reuters, November 13, 2000.

98. Daria Sito-Sucic, "Croat HDZ Declares Joint Bosnian Federation Dead," Reuters, February 28, 2001.

99. Daria Sito-Sucic, "Peace Envoy Sacks Bosnian Croat Leader," Reuters, March 7, 2001.

100. NPR Radio.

101. Nermina Durmic-Kahrovic, "Bosnian Education Struggle: Five Years after the Bosnian War, Ethnic Divisions and Rivalries Are Now Being Reinforced in the Republic's Classrooms," Institute for War and Peace Reporting, *Balkan Crisis Report* no. 159, July 25, 2000, http://www.iwpr.net/ index.pl5?archive/bcr/bcr_20000725_8_eng.txt [accessed July 28, 2000].

102. See Tina Rosenberg, "Trying to Break the Cycle of Revenge in Bosnia," *New York Times*, November 22, 1998, p. WK16.

103. Ermin Cengic, "The Historical Divide," *Transitions*, January 1999, pp. 69–70.

104. *Report of the High Representative for Implementation of the Peace Agreement to the Secretary-General of the United Nations*, Office of the High Representative (Sarajevo, Bosnia, October 14, 1998), www.ohr.int/reports/r981014a.htm [accessed October 22, 1998].

105. Kevin Sullivan, "Education-Bosnia: Western School Textbook Inspectors Trigger Row," Inter Press Service, November 8, 1998.

106. Quoted in ibid.

107. Office of the High Representative Spokesperson James Furgusson, "NATO Joint Press Conference" (Sarajevo, Bosnia, August 25, 1999).

108. Paul Watson, "Postwar Bosnia Still Battling Ethnic Hatreds," *Los Angeles Times*, November 19, 2000, p. A1.

109. "Analysis: Bosnia's Independent Media Commission Get to Work," BBC Worldwide Monitoring, August 6, 1998; and Philip Shenon, "Allies Creating Press-Control Agency in Bosnia," *New York Times*, April 24, 1998, p. A8.

110. Shenon.

111. Ibid.

112. Aida Cerkez-Robinson, "Bosnian Serb TV Station Banned," Associated Press, April 15, 1999; and "Media Monitoring Commission Shuts Down Kanal S TV," Beta News Service, April 14, 1999.

113. Quoted in R. Jeffrey Smith, "Serbs Get One Side of News," *Washington Post*, April 5, 1999, p. A14.

114. "Bosnia: IMC Says Five Broadcasters Violated Election Rules," BBC Worldwide Monitoring, April 27, 2000.

115. Janez Kovac, "Pre-Election Mischief in Bosnia," Institute for War and Peace Reporting, *Balkan Crisis Report* no. 161 (August 1, 2000), http://www.iwpr.net/index.pl5?balkans_index.html [accessed August 7, 2000].

116. Quoted in ibid.

117. Quoted in John Omicinski, "World Bank Seeks $5 Billion for Bosnia Reconstruction," Gannett News Service, December 15, 1995.

118. United States General Accounting Office, *Bosnia Peace Operation: Mission, Structure, and Transition Strategy of NATO's Stabilization Force* (Washington, D.C., October 1998), p. 30.

119. Quoted in Mike O'Conner, "Political Parties Opposed to Bosnia Peace Get Millions in Rent from NATO," *New York Times*, October 13, 1998, p. A10.

120. Robert Wright and Irena Guzelova, "Inward Investment Needed," *Financial Times*, December 18, 2000, p. II.

121. Robert Wright, "Vouchers Buy Little Confidence in Bosnia Sell-Off Scheme," *Financial Times*, May 10, 2000, p. 3; Buchan, "Trappings of Fragile Statehood"; and Office of the High Representative, Press Release, "Decisions by the High Representative on Property Laws" (Sarajevo, Bosnia, November 6, 1998), http://www.ohr.int/press/p981106a.htm [accessed January 1, 1999].

122. Quoted in Carol Giacomo, "U.S. and Allies May Turn Off Bosnia Aid Tap," Reuters, November 9, 1998.

123. Quoted in Jeffrey Smith, "Outside Efforts Do Little to Mend Fractured Bosnia," *Washington Post*, January 23, 2000, p. A25.

124. Wright, "Vouchers Buy Little Confidence in Bosnia Sell-Off Scheme."

125. See, for example, Mike O'Connor, "Bosnia Economy Still at Mercy of Political Leaders," *New York Times*, November 22, 1998, p. A3.

126. Quoted in Mark Nelson, "Messed-Up Market: Two Bosnians Selling Gasoline Shed Light on Nation's Economy," *Wall Street Journal*, August 19, 1996, p. A1.

127. Tracy Wilkinson, "Bureaucracy, Corruption Plague Foreign Investment in Bosnia," *Los Angeles Times*, March 29, 1998, p. D1.

128. Quoted in ibid.

129. Ibid.

130. "The Balkans—Pick a Plan: Western Reconstruction Efforts Overlook the Obvious, Fixing the Economy," *Wall Street Journal Europe*, June 28, 1999, p. 8.

131. Nedim Dervisbegovic, "Bosnia Payment Bureau Undermines Economy—U.S. Report," Reuters, February 17, 1999.

132. Ibid.

133. "The Balkans—Pick a Plan: Western Reconstruction Efforts Overlook the Obvious, Fixing the Economy."

134. Peter Bennett, "The Danube Blues: Kosovo Conflict Exacts a High Toll on Region's Businesses," *Wall Street Journal Europe*, May 31, 1999, p. 12.

135. Quoted in Richard Mertens, "Private Enterprise Moves Slowly to Reshape Battered Bosnia," *Christian Science Monitor*, November 7, 1997, p. 6.

136. Associated Press, "Ethnic Loyalties at Stake in Bosnian Election," *New York Times*, April 8, 2000, p. A4.

137. Ibid.

138. Quoted in Smith, "How Far Off Is 'Self-Sustaining' Bosnian Peace?"

139. Gerald P. O'Driscoll Jr., Kim R. Holmes, and Melanie Kirkpatrick, *2001 Index of Economic Freedom* (Washington: Heritage Foundation and Wall Street Journal, 2001), pp. 18–22.

140. International Crisis Group, *Brcko: What Bosnia Could Be* (Washington, D.C., February 10, 1998), http://www.intl-crisis-group.org/projects/bosnia/reports/bh31main.htm; and Jane Perlez, "Balkan Economies Stagnate in Grip of Political Leaders," *New York Times*, August 20, 1996, p. A1.

141. O'Connor, "Political Parties Opposed to Bosnia Peace Get Millions in Rent from NATO."

142. Quoted in ibid.

143. Quoted in ibid.

144. All examples cited in ibid.

145. "Seselj's Campaign Financed with OSCE's Money," *Oslobodjenje* (Sarajevo), Jan 31, 1999, http://www/vu.nl/frankti/tno/9902/01/c.html; and "Seselj Robbed OSCE," *Vjesnik* (Zagreb), February 4, 1999, http://www/vu.nl/frankti/tno/9902/05/c.html.

146. Melissa Eddy, "Bosnia Facing Economic Crash as Corruption, Inefficiency Stymie Progress," Associated Press, January 1, 2000.

147. World Bank, Press Release, "World Bank Announces Strategy for Bosnia and Herzegovina," (Washington, D.C., May 19, 2000), http://www.worldbank.org.ba/news/2000/pr-may0-03.htm [accessed August 15, 2000].

148. Nevertheless, in late 1997 High Representative Carlos Westendorp and others denied that any reconstruction aid had been used inappropriately by the Bosnian or entity governments. But the U.S. General Accounting Office has warned, "We did not conduct an investigation to obtain information to support or refute [Westendorp's] claims." United States General Accounting Office, *Bosnia Peace Operation: Pace of Implementing Dayton Accelerated as International Involvement Increased* (Washington, D.C., June 1998), p. 137.

149. Tom Hundley, "As Aid Flows, Bosnians Divert Goods, 'Tax' Allies Army, Take Food Meant for Refugees," *Chicago Tribune*, February 2, 1996, p. 3.

150. Ibid.

151. Pomfret.

152. Jon Swain, "Bosnia Aid Millions Go Missing," *Sunday Times* (London), July 27, 1997, p. 15.

153. Quoted in ibid.

154. Quoted in Michael Binyon, "Cook Warns Bosnia Aid May Be Cut Off," *Times* (London), July 30, 1997, p. 11.

155. Quoted in Michael Binyon, "Pounds 360m of Bosnian Aid 'Stolen by Fraudsters,'" *Times* (London), March 6, 1998, p. 17.

156. Quoted in ibid.

157. Luke Allnut, "The Bleak Winter of Yugoslavia's Discontent," *Prague Post*, October 27, 1999.

158. Chris Hedges, "Leaders in Bosnia Are Said to Steal up to $1 Billion," *New York Times*, August 17, 1999, A1.

159. Ibid.

160. All examples cited in Jeffrey Smith, "Outside Efforts Do Little to Mend Fractured Bosnia," *Washington Post*, January 23, 2000, p. A25.

161. Hedges, "Leaders in Bosnia Are Said to Steal up to $1 Billion."

162. "International Panel Rejects Action against NY Times for Bosnia Report," Associated Press, February 28, 2000,

163. Ibid.

164. Jeffrey Smith, "Fund Misuse Tied To a Top Bosnian," *Washington Post*, November 9, 2000, p. A20.

165. Quoted in "Bosnia Appeals for Help to House Refugees," Reuters, June 30, 2000.

166. Quoted in Steven Komarow, "Bosnia Peace Uneasy Despite NATO Rule: Opposing Factions Could Ignite, Some Fear," *USA Today*, February 16, 1999, p. A11.

167. Quoted in "UN Envoy Wants $1.2 Million for Bosnian T-Shirts," Reuters, October 27, 1999.

168. Quoted in R. Jeffrey Smith, "Bosnian Mart Becomes Den of Criminal Enterprise; Thieves, Tax Cheats Thrive in U.S.-Sponsored Venture," *Washington Post*, December 26, 1999, p. A33.

169. Ibid.

170. Hedges, "Leaders in Bosnia Are Said to Steal up to $1 Billion."

171. Melissa Eddy, "Bosnia Still Littered with Land Mines, Corruption Slows Cleanup Process," *Washington Times*, June 5, 2000, p. A12.

172. Quoted in Barry Schweid, "Albright: No Further Bosnia Partition," *Washington Times*, September 1, 1998, p. A13.

173. Susan L. Woodward, "Bosnia and Herzegovina: How Not to End a Civil War," in *Civil Wars, Insecurity, and Intervention*, ed. Barbara F. Walter and Jack Snyder (New York: Columbia University Press, 1999), pp. 98–99.

174. Michael O'Hanlon, "What to Do in Bosnia?" *Washington Post*, letters, October 13, 1997.

175. Quoted in "Petritsch Will Not Ask for Changes to Dayton," *Glas Srpski* (Banja Luka), April 7, 2000, http://teletubbie.het.net.je/sjaak/domovina/domovina/tno/0004/08/i.html [accessed August 15, 2000].

176. Chandler, p. 150.

177. Richard Holbrooke, "In Bosnia, Patience," *Washington Post*, September 28, 1997, p. C7.

178. For example, voter turnout for Bosnia's September 1997 municipal elections was 90 percent; the turnout for Bosnia's April 2000 municipal elections was 66 percent. See "Nationalists Won Most Seats in Bosnia's Local Elections: OSCE," Agence France Presse, April 20, 2000; Colin Woodard, "In Still-Angry Bosnia, Democracy Shows Its Face," *Christian Science Monitor*, September 16, 1997, p. 5; and "Electoral Commission Says Ruling Party Won: Final Unofficial Results," BBC Summary of World Broadcasts, September 19, 1997.

179. Stephen Schwartz, "As Dayton Peace Pact Breaks Apart, Dealmaker Holbrooke Gets Blamed," *Investor's Business Daily*, February 24, 2000, p. A24.

180. Quoted in King.

181. Quoted in "Croatia, Bosnia to Sign 25 Agreements, Bosnian Foreign Minister," BBC Worldwide Monitoring, January 13, 2000.

182. Quoted in "They Do Not Want a Protectorate," *Vecernje Novosti* (Belgrade), April 10, 2000, http://teletubbie.het.net.je/sjaak/domovina/domovina/tno/0004/11/i.html [accessed August 15, 2000].

183. Quoted in Aida Cerkez, "Bosnia Leader Criticizes U.S. Envoy," Associated Press, May 8, 1998.

184. Tucker.

185. Smith, "Outside Efforts Do Little to Mend Fractured Bosnia."

186. Quoted in P. H. Liotta, "If It's Not One Thing, It's Another: Bosnia and the Economics of War and Peace," *Mediterranean Quarterly* 11, no. 3 (Summer 2000): 100; emphasis in original.

187. Smith, "Bosnian Mart Becomes Den of Criminal Enterprise; Thieves, Tax Cheats Thrive in U.S.-Sponsored Venture."

Chapter 5

1. For the full text of the resolution, see United Nations Security Council Resolution 1244, United Nations, New York, June 10, 1999, http://www.un.org/Docs/scres/1999/99sc1244.htm [accessed July 6, 2000].

2. Secretary of State Madeleine K. Albright, Press Conference at International Press Center, Cologne, Germany, June 10, 1999, http://secretary.state.gov/www/statements/1999/990610b.html [accessed July 6, 2000]. Albright reiterated this view when she traveled to Kosovo in July 1999.

3. See Jeffrey Fleishman, "One Year after Bombings, Kosovo Remains Marred by Ethnic Bloodshed," *Philadelphia Inquirer*, March 24, 2000.

4. Christian Jennings, "Democracy in Kosovo Needs Time, Warns UN," *Independent* (London), June 13, 2000, p. 16.

5. General Accounting Office, *Balkans Security: Current and Projected Factors Affecting Regional Stability*, (Washington, D.C., April 2000), p. 24, and note on p. 39; and Samuel R. Berger, "Rebuilding Kosovo," *Washington Post*, June 10, 2000, p. A23.

6. Chris Stephen, "U.S. Investigates Kosovo Aid Fraud," *Scotsman* (Edinbourgh), December 2, 1999, p. 12.

7. Quoted in Christopher Lord, "Kosovo Needs UN to Govern," *Prague Post*, April 19, 2000.

8. United Nations Interim Administration Mission in Kosovo, "What is UNMIK?" Online Background Information, Pristina, http://www.un.org/peace/kosovo/pages/unmik12.html [accessed July 6, 2000].

9. Margaret Coker, "Kosovo Peace Is Fragile One Year after War," *Times-Picayune* (New Orleans), June 11, 2000, p. A3; Betsy Pisik, "UN Overwhelmed by Pledge to Help Kosovo Rebuild," *Washington Times*, May 2, 2000, p. A1; and Steven Erlanger, "After Slow Start, UN Asserts Role in Running Kosovo," *New York Times*, August 11, 1999, p. A1.

10. Quoted in Kevin Cullen, "A Year after Kosovo War, UN Is Facing a Quagmire," *Boston Globe*, March 19, 2000, p. A1.

11. Tyler Marshall, "U.S. in Kosovo for the Long Haul," *Los Angeles Times*, June 10, 2000, p. A1.

12. Madeleine K. Albright, "Our Stake in Kosovo," *New York Times*, April 28, 2000, p. A23.

13. Berger.

14. Quoted in Marshall.

15. Quoted in ibid.

16. United States Department of Defense, *Worldwide Manpower Distribution by Geographical Area* (Washington: United States Department of Defense, March 31, 1997), p. 16.

17. For views on why Belgrade ultimately capitulated, see Ivo H. Daalder and Michael E. O'Hanlon, *Winning Ugly: NATO's War to Save Kosovo* (Washington: Brookings Institution, 2000); Barry R. Posen, "The War for Kosovo: Serbia's Political-Military Strategy," *International Security* 24, no. 4 (Spring 2000): 39–84; and Zbigniew Brzezinski, "NATO Must Stop Russia's Power Play," *Wall Street Journal Europe*, June 15, 1999, p. 12.

18. Secretary of State Madeleine K. Albright, Interview by Bryant Gumbel, CBS *Early Show*, Camp Bondsteel, Kosovo, November 23, 1999, http://secretary.state.gov/www/statements/1999/991123.html [accessed July 18, 2000].

19. David Chandler, "Bosnia: Prototype of a NATO Protectorate," in *Masters of the Universe? NATO's Balkan Crusade*, ed. Tariq Ali (New York: Verso, 2000), p. 281.
20. Niko Price, "Judges Get to Work in Kosovo," Associated Press, July 3, 1999.
21. Jonathan Steele, "UN Forces Fight to Make Old Foes Work Together," *Guardian* (London), July 16, 1999, p. 18.
22. "KFOR Shuts Down Albanian Newspaper, Arrests Publisher," Kosovapress, August 9, 1999.
23. Quoted in Garentina Kraja, "Kosovo Board Planned to Oversee Media," *Washington Times*, October 18, 1999, p. A15; and "Kosovo's Incipient Media Ministry," editorial, *New York Times*, August 30, 1999, p. A22.
24. Krister Thelin, "Journalism in Kosovo," letter, *New York Times*, September 6, 1999, p. A16.
25. International Crisis Group, "Elections in Kosovo: Moving Toward Democracy?" *Balkans Report*, no. 97, (Pristina/Washington/Brussels, July 7, 2000), p. 17.
26. "Media Commissioner Mulling Action against Kosovo Newspaper," Agence France Presse, June 30, 2000.
27. Richard Mertens, "UN Censorship: Kosovo Press Names Names, Vigilantes Act," *Christian Science Monitor*, August 4, 2000.
28. Quoted in ibid.
29. Quoted in ibid.
30. "Serb Radio in Kosovo Defies UN Shutdown Order," Reuters, August 14, 2000.
31. Carlos Westendorp, "Lessons Bosnia Taught Us," *Wall Street Journal Europe*, May 19, 1999, p. 10.
32. Quoted in Chandler, p. 280.
33. "On the Authority of the Interim Administration in Kosovo," Regulation no. 1999/1, Issued by the United Nations, July 25, 1999, http://www.un.org/peace/kosovo/pages/regulations/reg1.html [accessed July 10, 2000].
34. Quoted in Steven Erlanger, "UN Envoy Pushes for Kosovo Democracy," *New York Times*, August 30, 1999, p. A6
35. Quoted in Steven Erlanger, "Aide Takes Stock of UN in Kosovo," *New York Times*, July 17, 2000, p. A4.
36. Cullen.
37. Gramoz Pashko, "Kosovo: Facing Dramatic Economic Crisis," in *Kosovo: Avoiding Another Balkan War*, ed. Thanos Veremis and Evangelos Kofos (Athens: Hellenic Foundation for European and Foreign Policy, 1998), p. 339.
38. Ibid, p. 348.
39. Miranda Vickers, *Between Serb and Albanian: A History of Kosovo* (New York: Columbia University Press, 1998), p. 276.
40. Stefan Wagstyl, "Small-Scale Private Enterprise Starts to Lift Kosovo's Economy from the Ruins of War," *Financial Times*, March 31, 2000, p. 8.
41. Irena Guzelova, "Kosovo Town Looks to the Future in Mines of Trepca," *Financial Times*, July 11, 2000, p. 3.
42. KFOR Spokesperson Lt. Col. Henning Phillip, "UNMIK-KFOR Press Briefing," Pristina, April 12, 2000, http://www.un.org/peace/kosovo/briefing/pressbrief12apr.html [accessed July 7, 2000].
43. Ibid.
44. Alison Mutler, "Peacekeepers Launch Symbolic Kosovo Cleanup, as Disease Spread by Rats Grows," Associated Press, April 15, 2000.
45. Quoted in ibid.

46. Carl Fredrik Rygh Bø, "KFOR on Social Patrols," *KFOR Online* (Pristina, May 28, 2000), http://kforonline.com/news/reports/nr_28may00.htm [accessed July 10, 2000].

47. Ibid.

48. Yngve Lie and Torgrim H. Halvari, "Stoves for Macedonian Schools," *KFOR Online* (Pristina, June 20, 2000), http://kforonline.com/news/reports/nr_21jun00_2.htm [accessed July 10, 2000].

49. Quoted in ibid.

50. Quoted in ibid.

51. United States Agency for International Development, *Kosovo Crisis Fact Sheet* no. 144 (Washington, D.C., April 7, 2000), http://www.info.usaid.gov/ofda/kosofs144.html [accessed July 7, 2000].

52. United States Agency for International Development, *Kosovo Field Report: May 19–June 2, 2000.*

53. Bernard Kouchner, "The European Union Support to Peace and Reconstruction in Kosovo: A Successful Partnership with UNMIK," Letter to the European Parliament (Pristina, June 22, 2000), p. 21.

54. Stefan Racin, "Kouchner Signs Kosovo Municipal Elections Law," United Press International, July 11, 2000.

55. United Nations Interim Administration Mission in Kosovo, "UNMIK Conference on Women in Elections and the Peace Process in Kosovo," *UNMIK News Report* (Pristina, May 30, 2000), http://www.un.org/peace/kosovo/news/99/may00_5.htm [accessed July 7, 2000].

56. Ibid.

57. KFOR Press Update, *KFOR Online* (Pristina, May 27, 2000), http://kforonline.com/news/updates/nu_27may00.pdf [accessed July 10, 2000].

58. Quoted in "Kosovo Serbs Kept Away from Anti-Violence Rally by Threat of Violence," Agence France Presse, September 10, 2000.

59. Quoted in "Kosovars Rally against Violence," Agence France Presse, September 9, 2000.

60. Ibid.

61. Quoted in Jim Hoagland, "Kosovos to Come," *Washington Post*, June 27, 1999, p. B7.

62. Albright, "Our Stake in Kosovo."

63. Quoted in Gary Dempsey, "Theater of the Absurd Now Playing in Kosovo," *Anchorage Daily News*, August 28, 1999, p. E11.

64. "Now Kosovo Albanians Want K-FOR Out," BBC News, June 28, 2000, http://news.bbc.co.uk/hi/english/world/europe/newsid_810000/810550.stm [accessed July 6, 2000].

65. Quoted in Paul Watson, "Rapper in Kosovo Vents Anger at UN," *Los Angeles Times*, August 6, 2000, p. A1.

66. Quoted in Gary Dempsey, "Kosovo Anniversary without Celebration," *Washington Times*, March 24, 2000, p. A18.

67. Fisnik Abrashi, "Albanian Leader Bolts UN Council," Associated Press, July 4, 2000; and "Kosovo Party Freezes Relations with UN," Reuters, July 4, 2000.

68. Ljiljana Staletovic, "Why Did Thaçi Withdraw from the PAVK? Agreement Is an Excuse," *Glas Javnosti* (Belgrade), July 5, 2000.

69. United Nations High Commissioner for Refugees and Organization for Security and Cooperation in Europe, *UNHCR/OSCE Overview of the Situation of Ethnic Minorities*

in Kosovo (Vienna, November 3, 1999), http://www.osce.org/kosovo/publications/ethnic_minorities/minorities3.htm [accessed July 6, 2000].

70. See Human Rights Watch, *Federal Republic of Yugoslavia: Abuses against Serbs and Roma in the New Kosovo* (New York, N.Y., August 9, 1999), http://www.hrw.org/reports/1999/kosov2 [accessed July 6, 2000].

71. Albright, "Our Stake in Kosovo."

72. Berger.

73. Lulzim Cota, "Serbs Ask EU Support for Refugees Return in Kosovo," United Press International, March 31, 2000; and Claire Snegaroff, "Multi-Ethnic Kosovo Still a Distant Dream One Year after War," Agence France Presse, March 21, 2000.

74. Robert Fisk, "Serbs Murdered by the Hundred Since 'Liberation,'" *Independent* (London), November 24, 1999, p. 15.

75. United Nations High Commissioner for Refugees and Organization for Security and Cooperation in Europe, *UNHCR/OSCE Update on the Situation of Ethnic Minorities in Kosovo: Period Covering February Through May 2000* (Vienna, May 31, 2000), http://www.osce.org/kosovo/publications/ethnic_minorities/minorities5.PDF [accessed July 6, 2000].

76. United Nations High Commissioner for Refugees and Organization for Security and Cooperation in Europe, *UNHCR/OSCE Overview of the Situation of Ethnic Minorities in Kosovo* (Vienna, November 3,1999), http://www.osceprag.cz/kosovo/reports/minorities_1103.htm [accessed November 4, 1999]; and Raska-Prizren Diocese of Serbian Orthodox Church, *The List of Serbs Kidnapped in Kosovo and Metohia (13 June–31 August 1999)*, Gracanica, Yugoslavia, http://www.kosovo.com/destinies/lk_kidnapped.html [accessed December 15, 1999].

77. Quoted in Christian Jennings, "UN 'Has Failed Kosovo Minorities,'" *Independent* (London), August 17, 2000, p. 11.

78. Quoted in "Belgian Doctors Leave Kosovo," Associated Press, August 7, 2000.

79. Christian Jennings, "City Life: Pristina—The Only Thing That's Organised Here Is the Crime," *Independent* (London), June 27, 2000, p. 18.

80. Tony Karon, "There's More to Life than Democracy, Madeleine," Time.com, June 2000, http://www.time.com/time/daily/special/look/0%2C2633%2C48979%2C00.html [accessed August 15, 2000].

81. Tim Judah, *Kosovo: War and Revenge* (New Haven, Conn.: Yale University Press, 2000), p. 115.

82. "Liberation Army of Kosovo Gives Itself a Bad Profile," *Jane's Intelligence Review*, October 1, 1996, p. 436.

83. Chris Hedges, "Kosovo's Next Masters?" *Foreign Affairs* 78, no. 3 (May–June 1999): 27–8. See also Chris Hedges, "Fog of War—Coping with the Truth about Friend and Foe, Victims Not Quite Innocent," *New York Times*, March 28, 1999, p. WK1.

84. See Kusovac; Donald Forbes, "Kosovo Could Be the New Threat to Balkan Stability," *Prague Post*, December 23, 1997; Julius Strauss, "Funeral Gunmen Demand Home Rule for Kosovo," *Daily Telegraph* (London), December 1, 1997, p. 10; "Albanian Terrorist Group Claims Kosovo Attacks," Deutsche Presse-Agentur, September 17, 1997; "Yugoslavia—Kosovo Underground Group Takes Responsibility for More Violence" Associated Press, March 29, 1997; Philip Smucker, "Serbs Wield Terror to Keep Ethnic Region in Line; Kosovo's Albanian Majority Live in a Serb 'Holy Land,'" *Washington Times*, February 2, 1997, p. A6.

85. Chris Smith, "Light Weapons Proliferation: A Global Survey," *Jane's Intelligence Review*, July 1, 1999.

86. Briseida Mema, "Trading Firepower for a Better Future," *Washington Times*, January 31, 1999, p. A8.

87. Ibid; Chris Smith; and Judah, pp. 128–9.

88. See Peter Klebnikov, "Heroin Heroes: The United States Propped up the KLA in the Kosovo Conflict," *Mother Jones*, January 1, 2000, p. 64; Alex Roslin, "The Kosovo Connection: The Shooting Has Stopped, But the Kosovo Liberation Army Isn't Resting. It Is Still a Major Player in the International Heroin Trade," *Gazette* (Montreal), November 27, 1999, p. B1; Roger Boyes and Eske Wright, "Drugs Money Linked to the Kosovo Rebels," *Times* (London), March 24, 1999; Tim Ripley, "Life in the Balkan 'Tinderbox' Remains as Dangerous as Ever," *Jane's Intelligence Review*, March 1, 1999, p. 10; Neil Mackay, "Police Alert as KLA Heroin Floods Britain," *Sunday Herald* (Glasgow), June 27, 1999, p. 1; Jerry Seper, "KLA Buys Arms with Illicit Funds," *Washington Times*, June 4, 1999, p. A1; Frank Viviano, "KLA Linked to Enormous Heroin Trade; Police Suspect Drugs Helped Finance Revolt," *San Francisco Chronicle*, May 5, 1999, p. A1; "The Kosovo Liberation Army: Does Clinton Policy Support Group with Terror, Drug Ties?" United States Republican Policy Committee, March 31, 1999, http://www.senate.gov/rpc/releases/1999/fr033199.htm; Roberto Ruscica, "Albanian Mafia, This Is How It Helps the Kosovo Guerrilla Fighters," *Corriere della Sera* (Milan), October 15, 1998; "Major Italian Drug Bust Breaks Kosovo Arms Trafficking," Agence France Presse, June 9, 1998; "Speculation Plentiful, Facts Few about Kosovo Separatist Group," *Baltimore Sun*, March 6, 1998, p. 20A; Zoran Kusovac, "Another Balkans Bloodbath?" *Jane's Intelligence Review*, February 1, 1998, p. 13; Marko Milivojevic, "The 'Balkan Medellin,'" *Jane's Intelligence Review*, February 1, 1995, p. 68; and Frank Viviano "Drugs Paying for Conflict in Europe: Separatists Supporting Themselves with Traffic in Narcotics," *San Francisco Chronicle*, June 10, 1994, p. A14.

89. Viviano, "Drugs Paying for Conflict in Europe."

90. Ibid.

91. Quoted in ibid.

92. Ibid.

93. Boyes and Wright.

94. Ibid.

95. Klebnikov.

96. Ibid.

97. Boyes and Wright.

98. Quoted in Seper.

99. "Terrorist Group Claims Responsibility for Attacks in Neighboring Macedonia," Associated Press, January 07, 1998. See also Tom Walker, "Rebuke by U.S. Adds to Woes of Milosevic," *Times* (London), January 16, 1998.

100. "Kosovo Militants Claim Three Murders," Agence France Presse, February 28, 1998; "Ethnic Albanian Killed in Armed Attack in Kosovo," Agence France Presse, February 20, 1998; "Ethnic Albanian Killed in Kosovo," Agence France Presse, February 13, 1998; "Serb Found Shot Dead in Troubled Kosovo Province," Agence France Presse, January 23, 1998; "Kosovo Serbs in Belgrade for Talks with Yugoslav President on Recent Killings," BBC Worldwide Monitoring, January 13, 1998; "Gunmen Kill One in Serbia's Kosovo Province," Agence France Presse, January 12, 1998; and "Serb Killed in Tense Serbian Province," Associated Press, January 10, 1998.

101. "Kosovo Serbs in Belgrade for Talks with Yugoslav President on Recent Killings."

102. Quoted in "Washington Ready to Reward Belgrade for 'Good Will,' Envoy," Agence France Presse, February 23, 1998.

103. "Two Serbian Police, Five Ethnic Albanians Killed in Kosovo," Agence France Presse, February 28, 1998.

104. Ibrahim Osmani, "In Serbia's Kosovo, Police Clampdown Leaves at Least 20 Dead," Agence France Presse, March 01, 1998.

105. Quoted in Philip Shenon, "U.S. Says It Might Consider Attacking Serbs," *New York Times*, March 13, 1998, p. A10.

106. Chris Hedges, "Serbs Renew Crackdown on Albanian Villages in Kosovo," *New York Times*, March 25, 1998, p. A1.

107. Jonathan Landay, "Inside the Kosovo Peace Talks," *Christian Science Monitor*, February 10, 1999, p. 5; and Jane Perlez, "Kosovo Albanians, in Reversal, Say They Will Sign Peace Pact," *New York Times*, February 24, 1999, p. A1.

108. Deputy State Department Spokesperson James Foley, U.S. State Department Daily Briefing, U.S. State Department, Washington, D.C., March 18, 1999.

109. Quoted in Linda Wheeler, "Marchers Strut Support for Independence for Kosovo," *Washington Post*, April 28, 1999, p. B3.

110. Steven Erlanger, "After Slow Start, UN Asserts Role in Running Kosovo," *Financial Times* (London), August 4, 1999.

111. See Paul Watson, "Reports Detail Cycle of Violence in Kosovo," *Los Angeles Times*, December 7, 1999, p. 9; R. Jeffrey Smith, "Kosovo Rebels Make Own Laws; UN Accuses Group of Illegal Evictions, Tax Collections," *Washington Post*, November 24, 1999, p. A1; and "Hatred Flares As Serb Homes Are Torched," *Los Angeles Times*, August 10, 1999, p. 10.

112. See Human Rights Watch, *Federal Republic of Yugoslavia: Abuses against Serbs and Roma in the New Kosovo* (New York, N.Y., August 9, 1999), http://www.hrw.org/reports/1999/kosov2 [accessed July 6, 2000].

113. Judah, p. 290.

114. Organization for Security and Cooperation in Europe, "Kosovo/Kosova: As Seen, As Told, Part II, June to October 1999" (Vienna, December 6, 1999), http://www.osce.org/indexe-se.htm [accessed July 6, 2000].

115. "Moderate Kosovo Albanian Politician Killed," *Glas Javnosti* (Belgrade), June 16, 2000; Paul Watson, "Extremist Albanians Target Moderates in Kosovo Strife," *Los Angeles Times*, November 20, 1999, p. A1.

116. David Rohde, "Kosovo Seething," *Foreign Affairs* 79, no. 3 (May–June 2000): 72–73.

117. Veton Surroi, "Kosovo Fascism, Albanian's Shame," *Koha Ditore* (Pristina), August 25, 1999; English translation at http://www.iwpr.net/index.pl5?archive/bcr/bcr_19990825_1_eng.txt [accessed July 6, 2000].

118. Quoted in Judah, p. 294.

119. Quoted in Watson, "Extremist Albanians Target Moderates in Kosovo Strife."

120. International Crisis Group, "What Happened to the KLA?" (Pristina/Washington/Brussels, March 3, 2000), pp. 1–2, http://www.crisisweb.org/projects/showreport.cfm?reportid=24 [accessed August 1, 2000].

121. Quoted in ibid.

122. Julius Strauss, "Legacy of War: The Terror Is over But Peace Brings Its Own Problems," *Telegraph* (London), February 10, 2000, p. 20.

123. "Masked Gunmen Kill Moderate Albanian Politician," Associated Press, June 16, 2000.

124. Quoted in ibid.

125. Secretary of State Madeleine K. Albright, Interview by Larry King, CNN *Larry King Live*, Washington, D.C., April 7, 1999.

126. Secretary of State Madeleine K. Albright, "U.S. and NATO Policy Towards the Crisis in Kosovo," Statement before the House International Relations Committee, Washington, D.C., April 21, 1999.

127. State Department Spokesperson James Rubin, U.S. Department of State Daily Press Briefing, U.S. State Department, Washington, D.C., May 7, 1999, http://secretary.state.gov/www/briefings/9905/990507db.html [accessed July 6, 2000].

128. State Department Spokesperson James Rubin, U.S. Department of State Daily Press Briefing, U.S. Department of State Daily Press Briefing, U.S. State Department, Washington, D.C., June 3, 1999, http://secretary.state.gov/www/briefings/9906/990603db.html [accessed July 6, 2000].

129. Secretary of State Madeleine K. Albright and Foreign Ministers of Germany, France, Italy, and the United Kingdom Statement on the Kosovo Protection Corps, New York, September 21, 1999, http://secretary.state.gov/www/statements/1999/990921.html [accessed July 14, 2000].

130. According to one UN official, "The KLA was supposed to disarm after the war. They turned in 10,000 weapons, but they were mostly junk. There are still a lot of weapons out there." Quoted in Jeffrey Fleishman, "Once the Oppressors, Serbs Now the Victims; NATO, UN Unable to Keep the Peace," Knight Ridder News Service, November 18, 1999. See also "An Agonized 'Peace,'" *Los Angeles Times*, August 9, 1999, p. B4.

131. "Prepared Statement of General Wesley K. Clark before the Senate Committee on Armed Services," Federal News Service, February 2, 2000.

132. Quoted in Jeremy Scahill, "Washington's Men in Kosovo: A Year after the NATO Occupation, Terror Reigns," Common Dreams News Center, July 19, 2000, http://www.commondreams.org/views/071900-107.htm [accessed July 20, 2000]. Scahill is a reporter for Pacifica Radio's Democracy Now! He reported daily from Yugoslavia during and after the 78-day NATO bombing, and was on the ground in Kosovo during the first months of NATO's occupation.

133. Strauss.

134. International Crisis Group, "What Happened to the KLA?" pp. 1–2.

135. R. Jeffrey Smith, "Kosovo Albanian Unit Is Accused of Abuses; UN Report Says Former KLA Rebels Threatened, Tortured, Killed Civilians," *Washington Post*, March 15, 2000, p. A24; and John Sweeney and Jens Holsoe, "Revealed: UN Corps' Reign of Terror in Kosovo; 'Disaster Response Service' Stands Accused of Murder and Torture," *Observer* (London), March 12, 2000, p. 23.

136. Tom Walker, "Serbian Doctor Dies in Albanian 'Cleansing,'" *Times* (London), March 5, 2000.

137. R. Jeffrey Smith, "Kosovo Rebels Make Own Laws."

138. "Top UN Official in Kosovo Pleads for More Funds," *Los Angeles Times*, December 17, 1999, p. A4.

139. Susan Blaustein, "Independence May Be Only Way to Save the Mission," *Los Angeles Times*, August 6, 2000, p. M2.

140. "Kosovo Protection Corps and Its Involvement in Incidents in Kosovo," *Koha Ditore* (Pristina), July 11, 2000, p. 3.

141. International Crisis Group, "What Happened to the KLA?"

142. Quoted in Steven Erlanger, "Kosovo Rebels Regrouping Nearby in Serbia," *New York Times,* March 2, 2000, p A1. Lt. Col. James Shufelt, who commands the U.S. Army outpost on the border between Kosovo and Serbia in the affected region, reached the same conclusion: "The concern here isn't that the Serbian police will come across, but that Albanian attacks on Serb police and army will inspire a response great enough to cause public clamor for a KFOR response." Quoted in ibid. See also R. Jeffrey Smith, "Kosovo Rebels' Serbian Designs Concern NATO," *Washington Post,* February 28, 2000, p. A9.

143. Quoted in Peter Finn, "Kosovo Rebel Group Issues Peace Pledge," *Washington Post,* March 24, 2000, p. A20.

144. Quoted in ibid.

145. John Shindler, "Presevo: The Next Kosovo?" *Jane's Intelligence Review,* June 1, 2000.

146. Peter Finn, "Kosovo Militia Fails to Honor Vow to Disarm; Group of Ethnic Albanians May Press Attacks in Serbia," *Washington Post,* March 28, 2000, p. A16.

147. Shindler.

148. Ibid. See also Steven Erlanger, "Multiplying Albanian Insurgents in Yugoslavia Threaten Belgrade's New Democracy," *New York Times,* January 21, 2001, p. 10.

149. Madeleine K. Albright, "Building a Europe Whole and Free," Remarks at event sponsored by the Bohemia Foundation, Prague, Czech Republic, March 7, 2000, http://secretary.state.gov/www/statements/2000/000307.html [accessed July 6, 2000].

150. See "Dienstbier Criticizing NATO Raids, Missions in Kosovo Again," Czech News Agency, March 29, 2000.

151. Quoted in Allison Mutler, "Kosovo Instability Warned," Associated Press, April 17, 2000.

152. Ibid.

153. Fredrik Dahl, "KFOR Steps up Security along Serbia Boundary," Reuters, July 30, 2000; "Increased Fighting between Rebels and Yugoslavian Forces: KFOR," Agence France Presse, July 28, 2000; "Mortars Fired at Serb Police Checkpoint near Kosovo," Reuters, July 11, 2000; "Bomb Blasts Rock Southern Serbia near Kosovo," Reuters, June 21, 2000; "Bomb Injures Five Serbian Police Officers near Kosovo Border," Agence France Presse, June 9, 2000; and "Police Checkpoint Attacked," *Danas* (Belgrade), May 25, 2000.

154. Aleksander Vasovic, "Yugoslav Army, Serb Police Shot At," Associated Press, December 5, 2000; Aleksander Vasovic, "Mortars Fired at Serb Police," Associated Press, December 4, 2000; "NATO Troops Seize Kosovo Arms Headed for Rebels in Serbia," Agence France Presse, November 30, 2000; "Yugo Army Says Kosovo Boundary Situation Worsening," Reuters, November 15, 2000; "Serbian Policeman Killed in Mine Blast near Kosovo," Agence France Presse, November 10, 2000; Nick Wood, "Champagne of Revolution Quick to Go Flat in Valley of Fear," *Guardian* (London), October 21, 2000, p. 18; "Two Yugoslav Police Officers Killed in Blast," Agence France Presse, October 13, 2000; Christian Jennings, "Clashes Increasing in Kosovo," *Scotsman* (Edinbourgh), October 9, 2000, p. 9; and "Three Ethnic Albanian Rebels Killed in Serbia," Agence France Presse, September 20, 2000.

155. Fisnik Abrashi, "Albanian Rebels Shoot at NATO Peacekeepers," *Washington Times,* December 18, 2000, p. A15; and Nicholas Wood, "British K-For Troops under Fire," BBC News, January 25, 2001, http://news.bbc.co.uk/hi/english/world/europe/newsid_1137000/1137189.stm [accessed January 26, 2001].

156. Louis Economopoulos, "Macedonia Destabilization Threat Causes Concern," CNS News, June 21, 2000; and Mirka Velinovska, "New Paramilitary Army Is Ready in Macedonia!" *Start* (Skopje), June 2, 2000.

157. "Constitution Watch," *East European Constitutional Review* 9, no. 3 (Summer 2000): 25.

158. KFOR Press Update, *KFOR Online* (Pristina, August 1, 2000), http://kforonline.com/news/updates/nu_01aug00.htm [accessed August 2, 2000].

159. "Ethnic Albanian Kosovo Rebels Claim Macedonia Attack," Agence France Presse, January 25, 2001.

160. Konstantin Testorides, "Insurgents, Macedonian Police Clash," *Associated Press*, February 26, 2001.

161. Philip Shenon, "U.S. Troops Seize Weapons from Albanians in Kosovo," *New York Times*, March 16, 2000, p. A1; and Robert Suro, "GIs Raid Militias in Kosovo," *Washington Post*, March 16, 2000, p. A1.

162. See Stefan Racin, "KFOR Arrest 12 Albanians on Different Charges," United Press International, April 15, 2000.

163. "U.S. Soldiers Seize Weapons in Kosovo," *New York Times*, May 20, 2000, p. A8.

164. "Kosovo Arsenal Triggers New Hunt," *Times* (London), June 20, 2000; George Jahn, "Commander of Former KLA Denies Links to Huge Weapons Find," Associated Press, June 18, 2000; and Shaban Buza, "Kosovo NATO Force Makes Biggest Illegal Arms Seizure," Reuters, June 17, 2000.

165. Quoted in "Kosovo Arsenal Triggers New Hunt."

166. Quoted in Buza.

167. Quoted in "Ex-KLA Head Denies Kosovo Arms Link as Peacekeepers Find More Bunkers," Agence France Presse, June 19, 2000.

168. Quoted in ibid.

169. Quoted in ibid.

170. George Jahn, "NATO Links Weapons Cache to KLA," Associated Press, June 23, 2000.

171. "Kosovo Peacekeepers Discover, Destroy Bunker Network," Reuters, July 21, 2000.

172. KFOR Press Update, *KFOR Online* (Pristina, November 8, 2000), http://kforonline.com/news/updates/nu_08nov00.htm [accessed, November 8, 2000]; and KFOR Press Update, *KFOR Online* (Pristina, July 31, 2000), http://kforonline.com/news/updates/nu_31jul00.htm [accessed August 2, 2000].

173. Quoted in KFOR Press Update, July 31, 2000.

174. Quoted in Wagstyl.

175. Quoted in ibid.

176. Kevin Cullen, "A Year after Kosovo War, UN Is Facing a Quagmire," *Boston Globe*, March 19, 2000, p. A1.

177. R. Jeffrey Smith, "Kosovo Rebels Make Own Laws."

178. Ibid.

179. Paul Watson, "A Serb, and Ethnic Albanian. Torn apart by Kosovo's War, They Manage to Remain Best Friends," *Los Angeles Times*, March 17, 2000, p. A1.

180. Lutz Kleveman, "The Patriots of Kosovo Fight over the Spoils in Pristina," *Daily Telegraph* (London), June 12, 2000, p. 10.

181. Quoted in "Kosovo Guerrilla Chief Arrested in Mafia Probe," *Agence France Presse*, August 24, 2000.

182. Klebnikov.

183. International Crisis Group, "What Happened to the KLA?" pp. 1–2.

184. Chris Hedges, "Leaders of Kosovo Rebels Tied to Deadly Power Play," *New York Times*, June 25, 1999, p. A1. See also "KLA Secret Service Persecuted Albanian Politicians," *Bota Sot* (Pristina), July 11, 2000.

185. Christian Jennings, "Kosovo's Local Heroes on UN's Wanted List," *Scotland on Sunday* (Edinburgh) June 11, 2000, p. 22; Paul Harris, "Kosovo Suffers Law and Disorder," *Jane's Intelligence Review*, June 1, 2000.

186. Jennings, "Kosovo's Local Heroes on UN's Wanted List."

187. Carlotta Gall, "Kosovo Towns Mourn a Slain Guerrilla Army Commander," *New York Times*, May 12, 2000, p. A4.

188. "Slain Former Kosovo Rebel Leader Buried near Town He Fought For," Agence France Presse, May 11, 2000.

189. "Kosovo Protection Force Commander Murdered," Reuters, September, 21, 2000.

190. Gall and ibid.

191. "Kosovo Politician Kidnapped," Agence France Presse, July 27, 2000.

192. Quoted in ibid.

193. Ibid; "Missing Kosovo Politician Found Dead," Agence France Presse, August 7, 2000; Shaban Buza, "Kosovo Albanian Officials Wounded in Shooting," Reuters, August 3, 2000; and KFOR Press Update, *KFOR Online* (Pristina, August, 3 2000), http://kforonline.com/news/updates/nu_03aug00.htm [accessed August 3, 2000].

194. "Kosovo Journalist Gunned Down," BBC News, September 11, 2000, http://news.bbc.co.uk/hi/english/world/europe/newsid_920000/920046.stm [accessed September 12, 2000].

195. See "Musaj Family: We Were Attacked," *Zëri* (Pristina), July 11, 2000.

196. Robert H. Reid, "UN Police Investigating Shootout Involving Prominent Ethnic Albanian," Associated Press, July 8, 2000.

197. "Ex-Guerrilla Chief Attacked Us: Kosovo Albanians," Agence France Presse, July 9, 2000.

198. Quoted in Nick Wood, "U.S. 'Covered Up' for Kosovo Ally," *Observer* (London), September 10, 2000.

199. Ibid.

200. Ibid.

201. "Rugova's LDK Wins Historic Kosovo Poll, Thaçi Cries Foul," Agence France Presse, October 31, 2000.

202. Merita Dhimgjoka, "Violence Cost KLA Kosovo Election," *Washington Times*, October 31, 2000, p. A13.

203. See, for example, "Rugova's LDK Wins Historic Kosovo Poll, Thaçi Cries Foul"; see also Anatoly Verbin, "Rugova Wants Quick Independence after Poll," Reuters, October 29, 2000.

204. "Yugoslav Troops Will Return to Kosovo by Year's End: Djindjic," Agence France Presse, October 11, 2000.

205. "Thaçi Supporters Stone Serb Homes," Agence France Presse," September 22, 2000.

206. Merita Dhimgjoka, "Kosovo Bus Blast Kills 7 Serbs," Associated Press, February 16, 2001.

207. Quoted in "Albanian Leader Says Kosovo Will Not Be Part of Serbia," United Press International, September 20, 2000; and David R. Sands, "Kosovo Mission End Not in Sight; UN Official: U.S. Exit 'Years' Away," *Washington Times*, September 30,

2000, p. A1. Elsewhere Thaçi stated: "The changes in Belgrade can certainly have a positive reflection on democratic developments in the region. [But] Kosovo's fate does not depend on Kostunica. Kosovo's fate depends on the Kosovars and the international community." See "Interview: Ex-KLA Chief Wants Proof Kostunica Is Democrat," Reuters, October 10, 2000.

208. USAID poll cited in *Balkans Security: Current and Projected Factors Affecting Regional Stability*, p. 25.

209. Serbian Deputy Prime Minister Nebojsa Covic quoted in "Kostunica Gives up on KFOR, Seeks New Solution to Border Violence," Agence France Presse, December 20, 2000.

210. Peter James Spielmann, "Donors Pledge $2B to Help Kosovo," Associated Press, July 28, 1999; and Ann Compton, "Rebuilding the Balkans," ABC News, July 30, 1999.

211. Arshad Mohammed, "Clinton Offers $700m Package to Help Balkans," Reuters, July 30, 1999.

212. Therese Raphael, "Where's the End of the Road in Kosovo?" *Wall Street Journal*, July 6, 2000, p. A26.

213. Brzezinski. See also George Robertson, "What's Going Right in Kosovo," *Washington Post*, December 7, 1999, p. A31.

214. *Balkans Security: Current and Projected Factors Affecting Regional Stability*, p. 27.

215. Ibid., p. 4.

216. Quoted in "NATO's Robertson Warns of Ethnic Cantons in Kosovo," Reuters, July 19, 2000; and "NATO Warning over Kosovo Violence," BBC News, July 18, 2000, http://news.bbc.co.uk/hi/english/world/europe/newsid_840000/840308.stm [accessed July 18, 2000].

Chapter 6

1. See Thomas Sowell, *A Conflict of Visions: Ideological Origins of Political Struggles* (New York: William Morrow, 1987), p. 74.

2. Ibid.

3. William J. Clinton, "A Foreign Policy for the Global Age," Speech Delivered at the University of Nebraska, Kearney, Nebraska, December 8, 2000, http://www.pub.whitehouse.gov/uri-res/I2R?urn:pdi://oma.eop.gov.us/2000/12/8/8.text.2 [accessed December 11, 2000].

4. Quoted in T. R. Reid, "Clinton Urges U.S., Other Rich Nations to Help Poor," *Washington Post*, December 15, 2000, p. A33.

5. Quoted in ibid.

6. Quoted in ibid.

7. Not even the Pentagon was immune from the Clinton administration's distinctive approach to foreign policy. For example, DefenseLINK, billed as "the official Website for the Department of Defense and the starting point for finding U.S. military information online," links to more than 38,000 documents, but few of them actually explain what the current and potential military threats are to the U.S. homeland. Instead, DefenseLINK posts "special reports" on Earth Day, National Domestic Violence month, American Indian Heritage, and baby formula and diapers. There are even 16 documents on neutering cats. As one reporter observed, interested Americans logging on to DefenseLINK, "can find Pentagon recipes for cooking zesty Tex-Mex food from fajitas and chili to gorditas and puffy tacos. But they can't find anything

about China's CSS-N-3 Giant Wave 1 submarine-launched ballistic missile. . . . Thousands of DefenseLINK documents—3,517 at last count—refer to the environment. . . . But there's nothing on the [Chinese] SU-30 multirole fighter-bomber; . . . [and] nothing on Russia's supersonic TU-160 strategic bomber." J. Michael Waller, "The Embarrassing Pentagon Website," *Insight,* December 11, 2000, http://www.Insightmag.com [accessed February 13, 2001].

8. Walter A. McDougall, *Promised Land, Crusader State: America's Encounters with the World Since 1776* (New York: Houghton Mifflin, 1997) pp. 172, 173, and 198.

9. Quoted in Patrice Hill, "G-8 to Spend $1.3 Billion to Educate Poor Nations," *Washington Times,* July 23, 2000, p. A1.

10. Gore truly shared Clinton's faith in the power of the U.S. government to solve complex social problems overseas. In 1994, Gore asked the Central Intelligence Agency to analyze the correlates of state collapse. The CIA found that "new democracies tend to fall most often when they have a high infant-mortality rate." Gore then proposed developing foreign-aid programs to promote healthy babies and quality parental care around the globe, on the theory that the result would be enhanced world peace. Karen Tumulty, "The Secret Passion of Al Gore," *Time,* May 24, 1999, p. 44.

11. Leon Fuerth, "Engaging Abroad: Vice President Gore and U.S. Foreign Policy," Speech Delivered at the General Meeting of the Council on Foreign Relations, Washington, D.C., September 20, 2000, http://www.cfr.org/p/pubs/Fuerth_9-20-00_Transcript.html [accessed December 2, 2000].

12. Ibid.

13. Remarks by Bruce Jentelson, senior foreign policy adviser to Gore/Lieberman 2000, "Campaign 2000: Gore/Lieberman Foreign Policy," Foreign Press Center, Washington, D.C., October 24, 2000.

14. Fuerth.

15. Remarks by Bruce Jentelson; and Bruce Jentelson, "Coercive Prevention: Normative, Political, and Policy Dilemmas," United States Institute of Peace, *Peaceworks* no. 35 (October 2000), pp. 31–35.

16. Bruce Jentelson, "Coercive Prevention: Normative, Political, and Policy Dilemmas," p. 12.

17. For more, and sometimes differing, views on Gore's foreign policy and its influences, see Jacob Heilbrunn, "President Gore's Foreign Policy," *World Policy Journal* 17, no 2 (Summer 2000): 48–55; Sam O'Neill, "Leon Fuerth: Tutoring 'Prince Albert,'" *World Policy Journal* 16, no. 4, (Winter 1999–2000): 55–62.

18. Robert Hunter, "Revive Strategic Thought," *Defense News,* December 11, 2000, p. 15.

19. Ibid.

20. Election 2000 Presidential Debate Transcript, October 11, 2000, http://www.cnn.com/ELECTION/2000/debates/transcripts/u221011.html [accessed October 24, 2000].

21. Ibid.

22. Ibid.

23. Bush foreign policy aide Condoleezza Rice, for example, stated: "We are not withdrawing the kind of support we can provide, like air power. But when it comes to nation building or civilian administration or indefinite peacekeeping, we do need for the Europeans to step up to their responsibilities. We are not going to do anything precipitous, but unless we set this a firm goal, we will never get it done." Quoted

in Michael Gordon, "Bush Would Stop U.S. Peacekeeping in Balkan Fights," *New York Times*, October 21, 2000, p. A1.

24. Quoted in Bill Sammon, "Bush's Balkans Idea Hit; Gore Claims Pullout Plan Shows 'Lack of Judgment,'" *Washington Times*, October 22, 2000, p. C3.

25. "Hungarian Minister Rules Out Involvement in Land Action in Yugoslavia," BBC Worldwide Monitoring, April 18, 1999; and "Hungarian Minister Rejects German Idea of All NATO States Sharing War Costs," BBC Worldwide Monitoring, June 1, 1999.

26. See John Hulsman, "Kosovo: The Way Out of the Quagmire," Heritage Foundation Backgrounder, no. 1349, February 25, 2000.

27. Quoted in Brian Knowlton, "Bush under Fire over Balkans Plan," *International Herald Tribune*, October 23, 2000, p. 1.

28. Quoted in Associated Press, "Shelton: Peacekeeping Missions Unavoidable," *Washington Post*, November 17, 2000, p. A2.

29. Quoted in Dale Dempsey, "Holbrooke Praises Dayton Accords," *Dayton Daily News*, November 16, 2000, p. A1.

30. Madeleine K. Albright, "Secretary of State Delivers Remarks on Visit to North Korea," Federal Document Clearing House, November 2, 2000.

31. Quoted in Robert Reid, "Prospects of Balkan Pullout Alarms Bosnians, Kosovars," Associated Press, November 8, 2000; and James Hannah, "NATO Peacekeepers Grab Attention," Associated Press, November 18, 2000.

32. John Davies and Ted Gurr, "Preventive Measures: An Overview," in *Preventive Measures: Building Risk Assessment and Crisis Early Warning Systems*, ed. John Davies and Ted Gurr (Lanham, Md.: Rowman & Littlefield, 1998), p. 1–14; and Donald Krumm, "Early Warning: An Action Agenda," in ibid., p. 248–254.

33. Mervyn Frost, "What Ought to Be Done about the Condition of States?" in *The Condition of States*, ed. Cornelia Navari (Philadelphia: Open University Press, 1991), p. 195.

34. David Rieff, "A New Age of Liberal Imperialism?" *World Policy Journal* 14, no. 2 (Summer 1999): 9.

35. Robert Kagan and William Kristol, "Europe Whole and Free," *Weekly Standard*, October 16, 2000, p. 11. See also Adam Wolfson, "How to Think about Humanitarian War," *Commentary* 108, no. 7 (July–August 2000).

36. Fareed Zakaria, "Conservative Confusion on Kosovo," *Wall Street Journal*, April 14, 1999, p. A26.

37. For historical examples of this phenomenon, see Robert Higgs, *Crisis and Leviathan: Critical Episodes in the Growth of American Government* (Oxford: Oxford University Press, 1987); and Arthur Schlesinger Jr., *The Imperial Presidency* (Boston: Houghton Mifflin, 1973).

38. U.S. Constitution, art. 1, sec. 8.

39. This critique is found in Gene Healy, "Arrogance of Power Reborn: The Imperial Presidency and Foreign Policy in the Clinton Years," Cato Institute Policy Analysis no. 389, December 13, 2000.

40. Jeffrey Record, "Failed States and Casualty Phobia: Implications for Force Structure and Technology Choices," Center for Strategy and Technology, Occasional Paper no. 18, Air War College, October 2000, pp. 5–6, 9.

41. Ethnic Albanian rebels are attempting precisely such provocation in Serbia's Presevo Valley. They have launched hit-and-run attacks on Serb police and military

personnel, eliciting a predictable backlash. The rebels are now demanding the withdrawal of Serb police and troops from the Presevo Valley and the deployment of a force modeled on KFOR, the NATO-led peacekeeping force in Kosovo. See "Rebels Fix Demands as First Results of Talks Seen in Serbia Conflict," Agence France Presse, January 5, 2000.

42. Ibid. p. 12.

43. Ibid.

44. Ibid. p. 13.

45. See, for example, essays in Peter Wallensteen, ed., *International Intervention: New Norms in the Post-Cold War Era?* (Uppsala, Sweden: Uppsala University Press, 1997); Gene M. Lyons and Michael Mastanduno, eds., *Beyond Westphalia? State Sovereignty and International Intervention* (Baltimore, Md: Johns Hopkins University Press, 1995); Marianne Heiberg, ed., *Subduing Sovereignty: Sovereignty and the Right to Intervene* (London: Pinter, 1994); and Laura W. Reed and Carl Kaysen eds., *Emerging Norms of Justified Intervention* (Cambridge, Mass.: American Academy of Arts and Sciences, 1993).

46. Ian Brownlie, *International Law and the Use of Force by States* (London: Oxford University Press, 1963), p. 340. Cited in Stephen Rosskamm Shalom, *Imperial Alibis: Rationalizing U.S. Intervention after the Cold War* (Boston: South End, 1993), pp. 111–112.

47. Quoted in Henry Chu and Richard C. Paddock, "Russia Looks to China as an Ally Amid West's Ire," *Los Angeles Times*, December 8, 1999, p. A1. See also Charles Glover, "Yeltsin and Jiang Attack U.S. Hegemony," *Financial Times*, August 26, 1999; John Thornhill and James Kynge, "China and Russia Pull Together," *Financial Times*, June 10, 1999; Tyler Marshall, "Chinese Raise the Arms Stakes with $500-Million Destroyer," *Los Angeles Times*, February 12, 2000; and John Pomfret, "China Plans for a Stronger Air Force," *Washington Post*, November 9, 1999, p. A17.

48. William E. Ratliff, "'Madeleine's War' and the Costs of Intervention," *Harvard International Review* 22, no. 4 (Winter 2001): 70–76.

49. Cited in Shalom, p. 112.

50. Article 2.1 of the UN Charter states that the "Organization is based on the principle of the sovereign equality of all its Members." The legal prohibition against the use or threat of force is codified in Article 2.4, which states: "All Members [of the UN] shall refrain in their international relations from the threat or use of force against the territorial integrity or political independence of any state," except in cases of "self-defense" (Article 51), UN-approved "countermeasures" against "threats to international peace" (Chapter VII), and the (now obsolete) provisions for actions against the "Enemy States" of World War II (Articles 106 and 107). In sharp contrast to the Clinton administration's position, when the UN Charter was being negotiated in San Francisco in 1945, the U.S. delegate at the conference stated that the ban on the use of force was an "absolute all-inclusive prohibition." See Antonio Cassese, *International Law in a Divided World* (Oxford: Clarendon, 1986), p. 137; and Caroline Thomas, *New States, Sovereignty, and Intervention* (New York: St. Martin's, 1985), p. 40.

51. Quoted in James Kitfield, "Lessons from Kosovo," *National Journal*, December 23, 2000, p. 3937–3938. See also Colin L. Powell, "U.S. Forces: Challenges Ahead," in Richard N. Haass, *Intervention: The Use of American Military Force in the Post-Cold War World*, rev. ed. (Washington: Brookings Institution, 1999), pp. 215–221.

52. Several recent books that emphasize the importance of culture and history in the unassisted economic and political development of countries include: *Culture Matters: How Values Shape Human Progress*, ed. Lawrence E. Harrison and Samuel P.

Huntington (New York: Basic Books, 2000); *Reputation: Studies in the Voluntary Elicitation of Good Conduct*, ed. Daniel B. Klein (Ann Arbor, Mich.: University of Michigan Press, 1997); and Francis Fukuyama, *Trust: The Social Virtues and the Creation of Prosperity* (London: Hamish Hamilton, 1995).

53. Douglas A. Macgregor, "The Balkan Limits to Power and Principle," *Orbis* 45, no. 1 (Winter 2001): 105.

54. Author's conversation with an UNMIK intelligence officer in Kosovo on October 31, 1999. Quoted in Gary Dempsey, "A View from Inside Kosovo," *Washington Times*, November 23, 1999, p. A15.

Index